Nonlinearity, Complexity and Randomness in Economics

Nonlinearity, Complexity and Randomness in Economics

Towards Algorithmic Foundations for Economics

Edited by Stefano Zambelli and Donald A.R. George

WILEY-BLACKWELL

A John Wiley & Sons, Ltd., Publication

This edition first published 2012
Chapters © 2012 The Authors
Book compilation © 2012 Blackwell Publishing Ltd
Originally published as a special issue of the *Journal of Economic Surveys* (Volume 25, Issue 3)

Blackwell Publishing was acquired by John Wiley & Sons in February 2007. Blackwell's publishing program has been merged with Wiley's global Scientific, Technical, and Medical business to form Wiley-Blackwell.

Registered Office
John Wiley & Sons Ltd, The Atrium, Southern Gate, Chichester, West Sussex, PO19 8SQ, United Kingdom

Editorial Offices
350 Main Street, Malden, MA 02148-5020, USA
9600 Garsington Road, Oxford, OX4 2DQ, UK
The Atrium, Southern Gate, Chichester, West Sussex, PO19 8SQ, UK

For details of our global editorial offices, for customer services, and for information about how to apply for permission to reuse the copyright material in this book please see our website at www.wiley.com/wiley-blackwell.

The right of Stefano Zambelli and Donald A.R. George to be identified as the authors of the editorial material in this work has been asserted in accordance with the UK Copyright, Designs and Patents Act 1988.

Wiley also publishes its books in a variety of electronic formats. Some content that appears in print may not be available in electronic books.

Designations used by companies to distinguish their products are often claimed as trademarks. All brand names and product names used in this book are trade names, service marks, trademarks or registered trademarks of their respective owners. The publisher is not associated with any product or vendor mentioned in this book. This publication is designed to provide accurate and authoritative information in regard to the subject matter covered. It is sold on the understanding that the publisher is not engaged in rendering professional services. If professional advice or other expert assistance is required, the services of a competent professional should be sought.

Library of Congress Cataloging-in-Publication Data

Nonlinearity, complexity and randomness in economics : towards algorithmic foundations for economics / edited by Stefano Zambelli and Donald A.R. George.
    p. cm.
  Includes index.
  ISBN 978-1-4443-5031-9 (pbk.)
1. Economics, Mathematical. 2. Econometrics. I. Zambelli, Stefano. II. George, Donald A.R., 1953–
  HB135.N662 2012
  330.01′519–dc23

                                                                                2011038342

A catalogue record for this book is available from the British Library.

Typeset in 10/12pt Times by Aptara Inc., New Delhi, India
Printed in Malaysia by Ho Printing (M) Sdn Bhd

1   2012

CONTENTS

Notes on Contributors

Stefano Zambelli	University of Trento
K. Vela Velupillai	University of Trento
Hector Zenil	IHPST, Université de Paris (Panthéon-Sorbonne) Dept. of Computer Science, University of Sheffield
Jean-Paul Delahaye	Laboratoire d'Informatique Fondamentale de Lille (USTL)
Sundar Sarukkai	Manipal Centre for Philosophy and Humanities, Manipal University
Sami Al-Suwailem	Islamic Development Bank Group
Cassey Lee	School of Economics, University of Wollongong
Shu-Heng Chen	National Chengchi University
Shu G. Wang	National Chengchi University
Toichiro Asada	Chuo University
Carl Chiarella	University of Technology, Sydney
Peter Flaschel	Bielefeld University
Tarik Mouakil	University of Cambridge
Christian Proaño	New School University
Willi Semmler	New School University
Joseph L. McCauley	University of Houston
Donald A.R. George	University of Edinburgh

1

INTRODUCTION

Stefano Zambelli

1. Background, Motivation and Initiatives

Almost exactly two years ago,[1] Vela Velupillai wrote to the Editor of the *Journal of Economic Surveys*, Professor Donald George, with a tentative query, in the form of a proposal for a Special Issue on the broad themes of *Complexity, Nonlinearity and Randomness*. Donald George responded quite immediately – on the very next day, in fact – in characteristically generous and open-minded mode as follows:

> 'Special Issue topics for 2009 and 2010 are already decided, and 2011 is the Journal's 25th year so we are intending some form of "special Special Issue" to mark that. However I'll forward your email to the other editors and see what they think. Your proposed topic is certainly of interest to me (as you know!)'

By the time the Conference was officially announced, in the summer of 2009, the official title had metamorphosed into *Nonlinearity, Complexity and Randomness*, but without any specific intention to emphasise, by the reordering, any one of the triptych of themes more than any other.[2] On the other hand, somehow, the dominant, even unifying, theme of the collection of papers viewed as a whole turned out to be one or another notion of complexity, with Nonlinearity and Randomness remaining important, but implicit, underpinning themes.[3]

There were, however, two unfortunate absences in the final list of contributors at the Conference. Professor Tönu Puu's participation was made impossible by administrative and bureaucratic obduracy.[4] Professor Joe McCauley's actual presence at the Conference was eventually made impossible due to unfortunate logistical details of conflicting commitments. However, Professor McCauley was able to present the paper, which is now appearing in this Special Issue at a seminar in Trento in Spring, 2010.

Nonlinearity, *Complexity* and *Randomness* are themes which have characterised Velupillai's own research and teaching for almost 40 years, with the latter two topics originated from his deep interest in, and commitment to, what he has come to refer to

Nonlinearity, Complexity and Randomness in Economics, First Edition.
Stefano Zambelli and Donald A.R. George.

as *Computable Economics*. This refers to his pioneering attempt to re-found the basis of economic theory in the mathematics of classical computability theory,[5] a research programme he initiated more than a quarter of a century ago.

That there are many varieties of theories of complexity is, by now, almost a cliché. One can, without too much effort, easily list at least *seven varieties of theories of complexity*[6]: computational complexity, Kolmogorov complexity/algorithmic information theory, stochastic complexity, descriptive complexity theory, information-based theory of complexity, Diophantine complexity and plain, old-fashioned, (nonlinear) dynamic complexity. Correspondingly, there are also many *varieties of theories of randomness* (*cf.*, for example, Downey and Hirschfeldt, 2010; Nies, 2009). Surely, there are also varieties of nonlinear dynamics, beginning with the obvious dichotomy between continuous and discrete dynamical systems, but also at least, in addition, in terms of symbolic dynamics, random dynamical systems and ergodic theory (*cf.*, Bedford *et al.*, 1991; Nillson, 2010) and, once again, plain, simple, stochastic dynamics (*cf.* Lichtenberg and Lieberman, 1983).

It was Velupillai's early insight (already explicitly expressed in Velupillai, 2000 and elaborated further in Velupillai, 2010a) that *all three of these concepts* should – and could – be underpinned in a theory of computability. It is this insight that led him to develop the idea of *computationally universal dynamical systems*, within a computable economics context, even before he delivered the *Arne Ryde Lectures* of 1994.[7] This early insight continues to be vindicated by frontier research in complexity theory, algorithmic randomness and in dynamical systems theory.

The triptych of themes for the conference, the outcome of which are the contents of this Special Issue, crystallized out of further developments of this early insight. However, to these were added work Velupillai was doing, in what he has come to call *Classical Behavioural Economics*,[8] which encapsulated bounded rationality, satisficing and adaptive behaviour within the more general[9] framework of Diophantine decision problems. He was able to use the concept of computationally universal dynamical systems to formalise bounded rationality, satisficing and adaptive behaviour, and link Diophantine decision problems with dynamical systems theory underpinned by the notion of universal computation in the sense of Turing computability (*cf.*, Velupillai, 2010b). Some of the contributions in this Special Issue – for example, those by Cassey Lee, Sami al Suwailem and Sundar Sarukkai – reflect aspects of these latter developments.

2. Summary and Outline of the Contributions

The 10 contributions to this Special Issue could, perhaps, be grouped in four sub-classes as follows: *Towards and Algorithmic Revolution in Economic Theory* by Velupillai, the lead article, and Sundar Sarukkai's contributions could be considered as unifying, methodological essays on the main three themes of the Conference. The contributions by Asada *et al.* and Zambelli to nonlinear macrodynamics; The papers by Cassey Lee, Shu-Heng Chen (jointly with Geroge Wang) and Sami al Suwailem are best viewed as contributions to behavioural and emergent complexity investigations in agent-based models. Hector Zenil's and Velupillai's (second contribution) could be viewed as contributions to aspects of dynamical systems theory, algorithmic complexity theory, touching also on the notion of algorithmic randomness. Joe MCauley's stimulating paper is, surely, not only a contribution to a fresh vision of finance theory but also to the imaginative use to which the classic recurrence theorem of Poincaré can be put in such theories, when formulated dynamically in an interesting way.

Velupillai, in the closely reasoned, meticulously documented, lead article, delineates a possible path towards an algorithmic revolution in economic theory, based on foundational debates in mathematics. He shows, by exposing the non-computational content of classical mathematics, and its foundations, that both *set theory* and the *tertium non datur* can be dispensed with, as foundational concepts. It follows that an economic theory that bases its theoretical underpinning on classical mathematics can be freed from these foundations and can be made naturally algorithmic. This will make the subject face absolutely (algorithmically) undecidable decision problems. The thrust of the path towards an algorithmic revolution in economics lies, according to Velupillai, in pointing out that only a radically new mathematical vision of microeconomics, macroeconomics, behavioural economics, game theory, dynamical systems theory and probability theory can lead us towards making economic theory a meaningfully applied science and free of mysticism and subjectivism.

Sundar Sarukkai's penetrating contribution can be considered a meta-level aspect of the core of Velupillai's thesis. He considers mathematics itself as a complex system and makes the fertile point that the process of applying mathematics to models leads to (dynamic) complexities. Hence, using mathematics in modelling is a process of deciding what kinds of models to construct and what types of mathematics to use. Modelling, from Sarukkai's point of view, can be seen as a decision-making process where the scientists are the agents. However in choosing mathematical structures the scientist is not being optimally rational. In fact, fertile uses of mathematics in the sciences show a complicated use of mathematics that cannot be reduced to a method or to rational principles. This paper argues that the discourse of satisficing and bounded rationality well describes the process of choice and decision inherent in modelling.[10]

The innovative contributions by Shu-Heng Chen (jointly with George Wang) and Sami Al-Suwailem can be considered to be new and interesting applications of agent-based economic modelling in providing insights into behaviour, both from orthodox and non-orthodox theoretical points of view. Moreover, when used as in Sami Al-Suwailem's paper, agent-based modelling, coupled to a complexity vision, could expose some of the weaknesses in orthodox neoclassical theory. Emergence has become one of the much maligned buzzwords in the fashionable complexity literature. However the way Chen and Wang have generated it, in a variety of agent-based models, suggests new possibilities to go beyond sterile modelling exercises in conventional modern behavioural economics.

In a broad sense, Cassey Lee's approach is tied to an implicit belief in the fertility of agent-based modelling in giving content to the fertile concepts introduced by Simon, to model behaviour that is empirically meaningful. Lee's framework is more philosophical than epistemological and, therefore, somewhat tangential to what I consider is the hallmark of Simon's modelling strategy and epistemological stance. Yet, his reflective paper contributes to a kind of bridge between the mathematics of modelling bounded rational agents and the philosophy that must underpin such an exercise. In some ways, it is also a companion piece to Sarukkai's stimulating challenges to orthodoxy in mathematical modelling philosophy.

Asada *et al.*, contribute the latest version of their sustained research program of providing alternatives to the arid macrodynamics of the newclassicals and the newkeynesisans. Nonlinearities pervade the foundations of all their modelling exercises in macrodynamics and this paper follows that noble tradition with new insights and ingenuity, especially in the techniques harnessed for stability analysis.

Zambelli goes beyond the conventional nonlinear dynamic modelling emanating from the Kaldor, Hicks-Goodwin tradition by coupling, nonlinearly, economies to study their analytically untameable dynamic paths and behaviour. In a sense, this is an exercise in the grand tradition of the Fermi-Pasta-Ulam exercise and thus falls squarely within the defining themes of the conference. The forced nonlinear dynamics of coupled oscillators, linking nonlinear dynamics with randomness via ergodic theory, leads, in this case to definably complex dynamics, too. Characterising them remains a challenge for the future.

In a strong sense, there is a unifying theme in the contributions by Zambelli and McCauley, even though they appear to concentrate on modelling the dynamics of different aspects of an economic system: national economies in the aggregate in the former; financial markets, in the latter. However, of course, the stochastic dynamics of the latter and the nonlinear dynamics of the latter have ergodic theory to unify them. Eventually it should be possible to underpin both exercises in a theory of algorithmic randomness for coupled dynamical systems capable of computation universality.

3. Concluding Notes and Lessons for the Future

The notions of *Nonlinearity*, *Randomness* and *Complexity*, when underpinned by model of computation in the sense of *computability theory* may well provide the disciplining framework for the mathematical modelling of economic systems and economic agents in an age when the digital computer is all pervasive. Almost all mathematical modelling exercises in economic dynamics, even in the agent-based tradition, remain largely outside the computability tradition. Yet most exercises and discussions of complexity, whether of individual behaviour or of aggregate dynamics or of institutions and organizations, are not underpinned by a model of computation. Furthermore, no formal modelling exercise emphasizing nonlinear dynamic modelling in macroeconomics (or even microeconomics) is based on algorithmic formalisations.

Velupillai's fundamental modelling philosophy – and, indeed, also its epistemology – is that nonlinearity, complexity and randomness should be harnessed for the mathematical modelling of economic entitites, but based on algorithmic foundations. Computationally universal dynamical systems, computational complexity and algorithmic randomness are what he hopes the way to invoke the triptych of nonlinearity, complexity and randomness for the purposes of economic theory in the mathematical mode.

The contributions to this Special Issue try, each in their own way, with more and less success, to make some sense of Velupillai's fundamental stance against the arid visions of orthodoxy. In line with one of Velupillai's choice of quotations it is as if we were echoing that visionary call by Tennyson's Ulysses:

Come, my friends.
'T is not too late to seek a newer world.
. . . .
. . . .
Tho' much is taken, much abides; and tho'
We are not now that strength which in old days
Moved earth and heaven, that which we are, we are, –
One equal temper of heroic hearts,
Made weak by time and fate, but strong in will
To strive, to seek, to find, and not to yield.

Notes

1. To be precise, on exactly 24 February, 2009! However, there was a curious mistake in Velupillai's original e-mail, in that his suggested date for the conference, which was to lead to a set of papers for the Special Issue contents, was stated as 27/28 October, 2010 (and not 2009, which was when it was actually held)! Somehow, this mistake was never noticed, nor needed any special correction, in the ensuing correspondence and planning.
2. By the 23rd of April, 2009, Velupillai had received Donald's approval, with the consent of his fellow editors, for the publication of the proceedings of the envisaged conference in a 'Themed Issue' of the Journal, in 2011. Shortly thereafter it was also decided, after e-mail interchanges between Donald George, Vela Velupillai and Stefano Zambelli, that the Themed Issue would be Guest Edited by Zambelli, under the general editorial guidance of Donald. Now, in the most recent correspondence, Donald has informed me that the editorial board of *JOES* had finally decided to change the status from 'Themed' to 'Special', which also implies that this issue will be published, eventually, in book form by Blackwell Publishing.
3. Except in the case of the contributions by Chiarella *et al.* and Zambelli, where nonlinearity was the dominant theme, and McCauley's paper, where the emphasis was on the interaction between dynamics and randomness, especially via an invoking of the *Poincaré Recurrence theorem*.
4. Even as late as July, 2009 Velupillai and Puu were in correspondence, the former finalising the Conference structure with the latter expected to give the lead talk on the general topic of Nonlinearity in Economics. That our noble intentions were unable to be realised remains a source of deep sadness to us and, for now at least, all we can do is to offer our public apologies to Professor Puu and regrets to the readership of *JOES*, who have been prevented from the benefits of a panoramic view on a topic to which he has contributed enormously.
5. In his much more recent work he has 'expanded' the mathematical basis of computable economics to include, in addition to classical recursion theory, also Brouwerian Constructive Mathematics, itself underpinned by Intuitionistic logic,

especially because of the careful use of the teritum non datur in the latter and, hence, in the construction of implementable algorithms in economic decision problems. He deals with these issues in some detail in his lead contribution to this Special Issue: *Towards an Algorithmic Revolution in Economic Theory*.

6. After all, there have been the Seven Pillars of Wisdom, Seven Varieties of Convexity, Seven Schools of Macroeconomics and even the Seven Deadly Sins – so why not also Seven Varieties of Complexity? And, surely, a case can also be made for Seven Varieties of Randomness.

7. Which appeared, largely, as Velupillai (Op.cit), more than six years later.

8. In contrast to *Modern Behavioural Economics*, so called (cf., Camerer, et.al., 2004, pp. xxi-xxii), this characterizes Herbert Simon's kind of *computationally underpinned* behavioural economics.

9. 'More general' than the classical optimization paradigm of orthodox economic theory and, in particular, modern behavioural economics.

10. This contribution by Sarukkai is a refreshing antidote to the Panglossian platitudes of the rational expectations modeller in economics.

References

Bedford, T., Keane, M. and Series, C. (eds.) (1991) *Ergodic Theory, Symbolic Dynamics and Hyperbolic Spaces*. Oxford: Oxford University Press.

Camerer, C.F., Loewenstein, G. and Rabin, M. (eds.) (2004) *Advances in Behavioral Economics*. Princeton, New Jersey: Princeton University Press.

Downey, R.G. and Hirschfeldt, D.R. (2010) *Algorithmic Randomness and Complexity*. New York: Springer Science + Business Media LLC.

Lichtenberg, A.J. and Lieberman, M.A. (1983) *Regular and Stochastic Motion*. New York: Springer-Verlag.

Nies, A. (2009) *Computability and Randomness*. Oxford: Oxford University Press.

Nillson, R. (2010) *Randomness and Recurrence in Dynamical Systems, The Carus Mathematical Monographs*, Number 31. Washington, DC: The Mathematical Association of America.

Velupillai, K.V. (2000) *Computable Economics*. Oxford: Oxford University Press.

Velupillai, K.V. (2010a) *Computable Foundations for Economics*. Oxon, UK: Routledge.

Velupillai, K.V. (2010b) Foundations of boundedly rational choice and satisficing decisions, *Advances in Decision Sciences*.

2

TOWARDS AN ALGORITHMIC
REVOLUTION IN ECONOMIC THEORY

K. Vela Velupillai

1. A Foundational Preamble

Hilbert's vision of a universal algorithm to solve mathematical theorems[1] required a unification of Logic, Set Theory and Number Theory. This project was initiated by Frege, rerouted by Russell, repaired by Whitehead, derailed by Gödel, restored by Zermelo, Frankel, Bernays and von Neumann, shaken by Church and *finally demolished by Turing*. Hence, to say that the interest in algorithmic methods in mathematics or the progress in logic was engendered by the computer is wrong way around. For these subjects it is more correct to observe *the revolution in computing that was inspired by mathematics*.

Cohen (1991, p. 324; italics added)

It is in the above sense – of a 'revolution in computing that was inspired by mathematics' – that I seek to advocate an 'algorithmic revolution in economic theory inspired by mathematics'. I have argued elsewhere, (see Velupillai, 2010a), that a strong case can be made to the effect that 'the revolution in computing was inspired by mathematics' – more specifically by the *debates in the foundations of mathematics*, in particular those brought to a head by the *Grundlagenkrise* (see Section 3, below for a partial summary, in the context of the aims of this paper). Although this debate had the unfortunate by-product of 'silencing' Brouwer, *pro tempore*, it did bring about the 'derailing by Gödel', the 'shaking by Church' and the 'final demolition by Turing' of the Hilbert project of a *Universal Algorithm* to solve all mathematical problems.[2]

Before I proceed any further on a 'foundational preamble', let me make it clear that the path *towards an algorithmic revolution in economics* is not envisaged as one

Nonlinearity, Complexity and Randomness in Economics, First Edition.
Stefano Zambelli and Donald A.R. George.
© 2012 John Wiley & Sons. Published 2012 by John Wiley & Sons, Ltd.

on Robert Frost's famous '*Roads Not Taken*'. Algorithmic behavioural economics, algorithmic statistics, algorithmic probability theory, algorithmic learning theory, algorithmic dynamics and algorithmic game theory[3] have already cleared the initial roughness of the path for me.

In what sense, and *how*, did 'Turing demolish Hilbert's vision of a universal algorithm to solve mathematical [problems]'? – in the precise sense of showing, via the recursive unsolvability of the *Halting Problem for Turing Machines*, the impossibility of constructing any such universal algorithm to solve any given mathematical problem. This could be viewed as an example of *a machine demonstrating the limits of mechanisms*, but I shall return to this theme in the next section.

The resurgence of interest in *constructive mathematics*, at least via a far greater awareness that one possible rigorous – even if not entirely practicable – definition of an algorithm is in terms of its equivalence with a *constructive proof*, may lead to an alternative formalization of economic theory that could make the subject intrinsically algorithmic.

Equally inspirational, from what may, with much justification, be called a resurgence of interest in the possibilities for 'new' foundations for mathematical analysis – in the sense of replacing the 'complacent' reliance on set theory, supplemented by ZFC (Zermelo-Frankel plus the Axiom of Choice) – brought about by the development of *category theory* in general and, in particular, a category called a *topos*. The underpinning logic for a *topos* is entirely consistent with *intuitionistic logic* – hence no appeal is made to either the *tertium non datur* (the *law of the excluded middle*) or the *law of double negation* in the proof procedures of *topoi*.[4] This fact alone should suggest that *categories* are themselves intrinsically computational in the sense of constructive mathematics and the implications of such a realization is, I believe, exactly encapsulated in Martin Hyland's enlightened call for at least a 'radical reform' in mathematics education:

> Quite generally, the concepts of classical set theory are inappropriate as organising principles for much modern mathematics and *dramatically so for computer science*. The basic concepts of *category theory* are very flexible and prove more satisfactory in many instances. . . . .[M]uch *category theory is essentially computational* and this makes it particularly appropriate to the conceptual demands made by computer science. . . . .[T]he IT revolution has transformed [category theory] into a serious form of applicable mathematics. In so doing, it has revitalized logic and foundations. The old complacent security is gone. *Does all this deserve to be called 'a revolution' in the foundations of mathematics?* If not maybe it is something altogether more politically desirable: *a radical reform*.
>
> J.M.E. Hyland (1991, pp. 282–3; italics and quotes added)

As for independence from any reliance on the *tertium non datur*, this is a desirable necessity, not an esoteric idiosyncrasy, in any attempt to algorithmize even orthodox economic theory – whatever definition of algorithm is invoked. For example, the claims by computable general equilibrium theorists that they have devised a constructive algorithm to compute the (provably uncomputable) Walrasian equilibrium *is false* due to an appeal to the Bolzano–Weierstrass theorem[5] which, in turn, relies on an undecidable disjunction (i.e. an appeal is made to the *tertium non datur* in an infinitary context).

To place this last observation in its proper historical context, consider the following. There are at least 31 propositions[6] in Debreu's *Theory of Value* (Debreu, 1959), not counting those in chapter 1, of which the most important[7] are theorems 5.7 (existence of equilibrium), 6.3 (the 'optimality' of an equilibrium) and 6.4[8] (the 'converse' of theorem 6.3). None of these are algorithmic and, hence, it is impossible to implement their proofs in a digital computer, even if it is an ideal one (i.e. a Turing Machine, for example). As a matter of fact *none* of the proofs of the 31 propositions are algorithmic. On the contrary, there are at least 22 propositions in Sraffa (1960), and all – except possibly one – are endowed with algorithmic[9] proofs (or hints on how the proofs can be implemented algorithmically). In this sense one can refer to the theory of production in this slim classic as an algorithmic theory of production. The book, and its propositions are rich in algorithmic – hence, numerical and computational – content.[10]

Contrariwise, one can refer to the equilibrium existence theorem in Debreu (1959) as an uncomputable general equilibrium and *not* a Computable General Equilibrium (CGE) model; one can go even further: it is an *unconstructifiable* and *uncomputable* equilibrium existence theorem (cf. Velupillai, 2006, 2009). There is no numerical or computational content in the theorem.

Greenleaf (1991) summarized the 'insidious' role played by the *tertium non datur* in mathematical proofs[11]:

> Mathematicians use algorithms in their proofs, and many proofs are totally algorithmic, in that the triple [*assumption, proof, conclusion*] can be understood in terms of [*input data, algorithm, output data*]. Such proofs are often known as *constructive*, a term which provokes endless arguments about ontology.

> To 'understand' [any mathematical] theorem 'in algorithmic terms', represent the assumptions as *input data* and the conclusion as *output data*. Then try to convert the proof into an algorithm which will take in the input and produce the desired output. If you are unable to do this, it is probably because the proof relies essentially on the *law of the excluded middle*.

> Greenleaf (1991, pp. 222–3; quotes added)

What is the point of mathematizing economic theory in non-numerical, computationally meaningless, mode, as practised by Debreu and a legion of his followers – and all and sundry, of every school of economic thought? Worse, what is the justification of then claiming computational validity of theorems that are derived by non-constructifiable, uncomputable, mathematical formalisms?

The most serious and enduring mathematization of economic theory is that which took place in the wake of von Neumann's two pioneering contributions, in 1928 and

1938 (von Neumann, 1928, 1938), and in the related, *Hilbert-dominated*, mathematical activities of that period. To be sure, there were independent currents of mathematical economic trends – outside the confines of game theory and mathematical microeconomics – that seemed to be part of a *zeitgeist*, at least viewed with hindsight. Thus the germs and the seeds of the eventual mathematization of macroeconomics, the emergence of econometrics, and the growth of welfare economics and the theory of economic policy, in various *ad hoc* mathematical frameworks, were also 'planted' in this period.

Yet, in spite of all this, what has come to be the dominant mathematical methodology in economic theorizing is the intensely non-algorithmic, non-constructive, uncomputable one that is – strangely – the legacy of von Neumann. 'Strangely', because, after all, von Neumann is also one[12] of the pioneering spirits of the stored program digital computer. By aiming towards an algorithmic revolution in economic theory I am suggesting that there is much to be gained by shedding this legacy and its iron clasps that tie us to a non-numerical, computationally vacuous, framework of mathematical theorizing in economics.

What exactly is to be gained by this suggestion of adopting an alternative, algorithmic, mathematical framework for economic theorizing? There are at least three answers to this question. First, from an epistemological point of view, one is able to be precise about the limitations of mechanisms that can underpin knowledge, its acquisition and its utilization. Secondly, from a philosophical point of view, it will enable the economic theorist to acknowledge the limits to mathematical formalization and, hopefully, help return the subject to its noble humanitarian roots and liberate itself from the pseudo-status of being a branch of pure mathematics. Thirdly, methodologically, the algorithmic framework will not perpetuate the schizophrenia between an economic theorizing activity that is decidedly non-constructive and uncomputable and an applied, policy oriented, commitment that requires the subject to be uncompromisingly numerical and computational.

With these issues in mind, the paper is structured as follows. In the next section, largely devoted to definitional issues, an attempt is made to be precise about the relevant concepts that should play decisive roles in an algorithmic economics. Section 3 is devoted to an outline of the background to what I have called the von Neumann legacy in mathematical economic theorizing and the eventual, regrettable, dominance of 'Hilbert's Dogma' over Brouwer's algorithmic visions. There is much excitement about something called algorithmic game theory, these days; this is the obverse of computable general equilibrium theory. Both are plagued by the schizophrenia of doing the theory with one kind of mathematics and trying to compute the uncomputable and construct the non-constructive with another kind of mathematics. But there is also a genuinely alogorithmic statistics, free of schizophrenia, up to a point. And, there is also the noble case of classical behavioural economics, from the outset uncompromisingly algorithmic in the sense of computability theory. These issues are the subject matter of Section 4, the concluding section. It is also devoted to an outline of how I think *we should educate* the current generation of graduate students in economics so that they can become the harbingers of the algorithmic revolution in economics.

2. Machines, Mechanisms, Computation and Algorithms

There are several different ways of arriving at [the precise definition of the concept of *finite procedure*], which, however, all lead to exactly the same concept. The most satisfactory way, in my opinion, is that of reducing the concept of finite procedure to that of a machine with a finite number of parts, as has been done by the British mathematician *Turing*.

Gödel (1951/1995, pp. 304–5; italics added)

I should have included a fifth concept, *mind*, to the above quadruple, machines, mechanisms, computation and algorithms, especially because much of the constructive and computable basis for the discussion in this section originates in what Feferman (2009, p. 209) has called Gödel's dichotomy:

[I]f the human mind were equivalent to a finite machine, then objective mathematics not only would be incompletable in the sense of not being contained in any well-defined axiomatic system, but moreover there would exist *absolutely* unsolvable diophantine problems.... where the epithet 'absolutely' means that they would be undecidable, not just within some particular axiomatic system, but by *any* mathematical proof the human mind can conceive. So the following disjunctive conclusion is inevitable: *Either mathematics is incompletable in this sense, that its evident axioms can never be compromised in a finite rule, that is to say the human mind (even within the realm of pure mathematics) infinitely surpasses the powers of any finite machine, or else there exist absolutely unsolvable Diophantine problems ...* (where the case that both terms of the disjunction are true is not excluded, so that there are, strictly speaking, three alternatives).

Gödel (1951/1995, p. 310; italics in the original)

It goes without saying that I subscribe to the view that 'there exist absolutely unsolvable Diophantine problems', especially because I have maintained that Diophantine decision problems are pervasive in economics, from the ground up: basic supply–demand analysis, classical behavioural economics, economic dynamics and game theory. The nature of the data types in economics make it imperative that the natural mathematical modelling framework, from elementary supply–demand analysis to advanced decision theoretic behavioural economics, of the kind practised by Herbert Simon all his intellectual life, should be in terms of Diophantine decision problems.[13]

A 'machine[14] with a finite number of parts', in common sense terms, embodies a *mechanism*. Is it possible to envision, or imagine, a mechanism not *embodied* in a machine? This is neither a frivolous question, nor analogous to the deeper question whether the mind is embodied in the brain. I ask it because there is a respectable theory of mechanisms in economics without any implication that the economic system, its institutions or agents, are machines that embody it.

An *algorithm* is a finite procedure in the precise mathematical sense of the formalism of a *Turing Machine*, in terms of one kind of mathematics: *recursion* or *computability* theory. The 'several different ways of arriving at the precise definition of the concept of finite procedure', which all lead to 'the same concept' is summarized in the form of the *Church–Turing thesis*.

But there is another kind of mathematics, *constructive* mathematics, where finite proof procedures encapsulate, rigorously, the notion of an algorithm.[15] However, in constructive mathematics there is *no* attempt, formally or otherwise, to work with a 'precise definition of the concept of a finite procedure'. Yet:

> The interesting thing about [Bishop's *Constructive* mathematics] is that it reads essentially like ordinary mathematics, yet *it is entirely algorithmic in nature* if you look between the lines.[16]

> Donald E. Knuth (1981, p. 94)

However, unlike recursion theory with its non-embarrassment of reliance on classical logic and free-swinging set theoretic methods,[17] the constructive mathematician's underlying logic satisfies first-order *intuitionistic* or *constructive* logic and hence explicitly denies the validity of the *tertium non datur*. This elegant philosophy of a mathematics where the *proof-as-algorithm* vision is underpinned by a logic free of any reliance on the *tertium non datur* should be contrasted with the ruling mathematical paradigm based on *Hilbert's Dogma* – i.e. *proof-as-consistency = existence* – and unrestricted appeal to the *tertium non datur*.

The question of why economic theory, in its mathematical mode, shunned the proof-as-algorithm vision, underpinned by an intuitionistic logic, is addressed in the next section. Here my restricted aim is only to outline the implications of adopting the proof-as-algorithm vision, coupled to an adherence to intuitionistic logic, from the point of view of formal notions of *machines*, *mechanisms* and *computation*, thus linking it with computability theory, even if their underpinning logics are different. I believe that considerations of such implications are imperative for a sound mathematical basis for the path towards an algorithmic revolution in economics is to be constructed. This is especially so because the existing successes on paving paths towards algorithmic revolutions in probability, statistics, learning, induction and dynamics are based, almost without exception, on the foundations of computability theory in its recursion theoretic mode.

I want to ask four questions: *what* are *machines*, *mechanisms*, *computations* and *algorithms*? *How* interdependent are any answers to the questions? What are the *limitations* of mechanisms? Can a machine, encapsulating mechanisms, *know* its limitations. I ask these questions – and seek answers – in the spirit with which Warren McCulloch asked and answered his famous *experimental* epistemological question: *What is a Number, that a Man May Know It, and a Man, that He May Know a Number* (McCulloch, 1961/1965).

Before I continue in the 'McCulloch mode', finessed (I hope) by *Kant's deeper questions* as a backdrop to my suggested answers, two apparently 'simple', almost straightforward, questions must be faced squarely: '*What is a Computation?*' and '*What is an Algorithm?*'

The first of these two questions, 'What is a Computation?', was answered with exceptional clarity and characteristic depth and conviction, in the spirit and philosophy with which this essay is written, by that modern master of computability theory: Martin Davis. His elegant answer to the question is given in Davis (1978) (and my embellishment to that answer is detailed in Velupillai and Zambelli (2010)):

> What Turing did around 1936 was to give a cogent and complete logical analysis of the notion of 'computation'. Thus it was that although people have been computing for centuries, it has only been since 1936 that we have possessed a satisfactory answer to the question: 'What is a computation'?.....
>
> Turing's analysis of the computation process led to the conclusion that it should be possible to construct 'universal' computers which could be programmed to carry out any possible computation. The existence of a logical analysis of the computation process also made it possible to show that certain mathematical problems are incapable of computational solution, that they are, as one says, undecidable.
>
> Davis (1978, pp. 241–242; italics in the original)

At this point I could answer the second question – '*What is an Algorithm*'? – simply by identifying it with the (computer) *programme* which *implements* a computation on a (Universal) Turing Machine, but I shall not do so.[18] However, instead of the 'programme-as-algorithm' paradigm, I shall choose the 'proof-as-algorithm' route for a definition, mainly because my ultimate aim is a basis for economic theory in constructive mathematics.

In a series of important and exceptionally interesting – even with an unusual dose of humour, given the depth of the issues discussed in them – articles, Yiannis Moschovakis (1998, 2001) and Moschovakis and Paschalis (2008, p. 87) have proposed an increasingly refined, set-theoretic, notion of algorithm, with the aim 'to provide a traditional foundation for the theory of algorithms, ... within axiomatic set theory on the basis of the set theoretic modelling of their basic notions'. In my reading, and understanding, of this important line of research, it is closely related to the attempt in Blum *et al.* (1998), where algorithms are defined within a 'model of computation which postulates exact arithmetic on real numbers'. Because my twin aims are to found a notion of algorithms consistent with constructive mathematics and its proof-as-programme vision, underpinned by an intuitionistic logic which eschews any reliance on the *tertium non datur*, I shall by-pass this path towards a definition of a mathematical notion of algorithm. Moreover, I would also wish to respect the natural data-types that we are faced with in economics, in any definition of algorithms, and, hence, seek also some sort of *modus vivendi* with the notion that arises in recursion theory.

I am, on the other hand, somewhat relieved that the view of algorithms-as-(constructive) proofs is not entirely dismissed by Moschovakis, even if he does have serious doubts about any success along this path. His views on this matter are worth quoting in some detail, for they are the path I think economists should choose, if we are to make the subject seriously algorithmic with a meaningful grounding also in computability theory. In subsection '3.4 (IIb) Algorithms as Constructive Proofs', Moschoavakis (1998, pp. 77–78; italics in the original), points out that:

> Another, more radical proposal which also denies independent existence to algorithms is the claim that *algorithms are implicitly defined by constructive proofs* . . . . . .

> Although I doubt seriously that algorithms will ever be eliminated in favour of constructive proofs (or anything else for that matter), I think that this view is worth pursuing, because it leads to some very interesting problems. With specific, precise definitions of algorithms and constructive proofs at hand, one could investigate whether, in fact, every algorithm can be extracted (in some concrete way) from some associated, constructive proof. Results of this type would add to our understanding of the important connection between *computability and constructivity*.

In an 'aside' to the above observation, as a footnote, Moschovakis also points out that there is the possibility simply to 'define "algorithm" to be [a] constructive proof', but goes on to remark that he 'cannot recall seeing this view explained or defended'. It is this view that I subscribe to, especially because it is in line with the way, for example, Bishop (1967) is written, as observed by Knuth (1981), which I have quoted earlier in this section.

In passing, it may be apposite to point out that Moschovakis (2001, p. 919, footnote 2) refers to Knuth's monumental work on *The Art of Computer Programming* (Knuth, 1973) as 'the only standard reference [he knows] in which algorithms are defined where they should be, in Sect.1.1'. Somehow, Moschovakis seems to have overlooked Knuth's handsome acknowledgement (Knuth, 1973, p. 9) that his – i.e. Knuth's 'formulation [definition of algorithms] is virtually the same as that given by A.A. Markov in 1951, in his book *The Theory of Algorithms*'. This is doubly interesting, in the current context. First of all, Markov 'defines' algorithms even before 'Sect. 1.1' of his book, in fact in the Introduction to his classic book. Secondly, Markov endorses, although at that embryonic stage of the resurgence of constructive foundations for mathematics it could only have been a 'hope', the nexus 'algorithms' – constructive proof quite explicitly (Markov, 1954/1961):

> The entire significance for mathematics of rendering more precise the concept of algorithm emerges, however, in connection with the problem of a constructive foundation for mathematics. On the basis of a more precise concept of algorithm one may give the constructive validity of an arithmetical expression. On its basis one may set up also a constructive mathematical logic – a constructive propositional calculus and a constructive predicate calculus. Finally, the main field of application of the more precise concept of algorithm will undoubtedly be constructive analysis – the constructive theory of real numbers and functions of a real variable, which are now in a stage of intensive development.

These Markovian thoughts and suggestions were the embryonic *algorithmic visions* from which what came to be called *Russian Constructive Mathematics* (cf. chapter 3 of Bridges and Richman, 1987) and the influential work of Oliver Aberth (1980, 2001) emerged.[19]

I return now to the spirit of Warren McCulloch, deepened by Kant's famous themes. Kant's deeper question was: *What is man*, which he then proceeded to answer by subdividing it into three more limited queries: *What can I know*? *What must I do*? *What may I hope*? If I substitute, not entirely fancifully, machine for man, in Kant's question, then, the issues I try to discuss in terms of McCulloch's epistemological vision, must come to terms with at least the following: *What can a machine know about the limitations of the mechanisms it embodies*? The answer(s) depend crucially on Gödel's incompleteness theorems, the Turing Machine and Turing's famous result on the Unsolvability of the Halting Problem for Turing Machines.

However, in terms of *any* mathematical formalism, validity of mathematical theorems are claimed on the basis of *proof*, which are, in turn, the only *mechanism* for expressing *truth* effectively – in the precise sense of recursion theory – in mathematics. Then, with Kant:

- The mathematician can *hope* all *provable* mathematical statements are *true*;
- Conversely, the mathematician can also *hope* that all – and only – the true statements are provable;
- And, following Hilbert's vision, the mathematician's task – Kant's 'what must I do' – is to build a machine to *discover* – Kant's 'what must I know' – valid proofs of every possible theorem in any given formal system.

The first two hopes were 'derailed' by Gödel's incompleteness theorems, by the demonstration that in any reasonably strong formal system there are *effectively* presentable mathematical statements that are *recursively undecidable* – i.e. neither *algorithmically* provable nor unprovable. The third was 'shaken by Church and *finally demolished by Turing*', i.e. that no such machine can be 'built', shown in a precisely effective way.

Because, however, Gödel's theorems were presented recursively and proved constructively – hence within the proof-as-algorithm paradigm – it must be possible to build a *machine*, with an effective *mechanism*, to *check* the validity of the existence of *undecidable* statements. This, then, will be an instance of a mechanical verification of Gödel's proof and, hence, a demonstration that *a machine can establish the limitations of its own mechanism*.[20]

This is where computation, computability theory and constructive mathematics intersect and interact felicitously, via the Turing Machine, to unify the four notions of machines, mechanisms, computations and algorithms. The mechanism encapsulated in the Turing Machine implements the effective (finite) procedure that is an algorithm in its proof-as-algorithm role. Finally, because all the effectivizations are in terms of Gödel's arithmetization – i.e. via Gödel numberings – the implementations are all in number-theoretic terms and, thus, within the domain of computability theory.

What exactly is such a mechanism? And, given any such mechanism, does it have a universal property? By this is meant whether there are effectively definable – and constructible – alternative mechanisms, in machine mode or otherwise, that are as 'powerful' in some precise sense? For example, is there a closure property such that all calculable number-theoretic functions can be evaluated by one such mechanism?

The answer to this question is given by the Church–Turing thesis (cf. Velupillai, 2000, for a precise statement of this notion).

Surely, the obvious question an economist should ask, in view of these results, is the following: if the economic system is a mechanism, can the machine which encapsulates it demonstrate its set of undecidable statements? A frontier topic in economics, particularly in its mathematical mode and policy design variants, is *mechanism theory*. Strangely, though, mechanism theory has completely ignored the whole of the above development. *A fortiori*, therefore, the *Limitations of Mechanisms*, whether in thought processes, which lead up to theory building – in the sense in which Peirce used the term *abduction* or *retroduction* – or in the actual analysis of so-called *economic mechanisms*, are not explicitly considered.[21]

3. The Legacy of *Hilbert's Dogma* in Mathematical Economics

[Hilbert] won politically. . . . . Brouwer was devastated, and his active research career effectively came to an end.

[Hilbert] won mathematically. Classical mathematics remains intact, intuitionistic mathematics was relegated to the margin. . . . . .

And [Hilbert] won polemically. Most importantly . . . Hilbert's agenda set the context of the controversy both at the time and, largely, ever since.

Carl J. Posy (1998, pp. 292–293)

Suppose economics, in particular game theory, had been mathematized, say by von Neumann, in 1928 (von Neumann, 1928), in the *constructive* mode that was being vigorously advocated by Brouwer just in those years; or, in terms of *recursion theory*, which came into being, as a result of the pioneering works by Gödel, Church, Turing, Post, Rosser and Kleene, just as von Neumann's growth model (von Neumann, 1938) was made known to the wider mathematical and economics academic world, in 1936. What would we now, some eighty years later, be teaching as mathematics for economics to our graduate students?

To answer this obviously counterfactual question, let me backtrack a little, but on the basis of a strangely unscholarly remark made in a recent, respectable, almost encyclopaedic tract on *Real Analysis with Economic Applications* (Ok, 2007):

It is worth noting that in later stages of his career, he [Brouwer] became the most forceful proponent of the so-called intuitionist philosophy of mathematics, which not only forbids the use of the Axiom of Choice but also rejects the axiom that a proposition is either true or false (thereby disallowing the method of proof by contradiction). The consequences of taking this position are dire. For instance, an intuitionist would not accept the existence of an irrational number! In fact, in his later years, Brouwer did not view the Brouwer Fixed Point Theorem as a theorem. (he had proved this result in 1912, when he was functioning as a 'standard' mathematician).

If you want to learn about intuitionism in mathematics, I suggest reading – *in your spare time, please* – the four articles by Heyting and Brouwer in Benacerraf and Putnam (1983).

Efe. A. Ok (2007, p. 279; italics added)

The von Neumann (1928) paper introduced, and etched indelibly, to an unsuspecting and essentially non-existent Mathematical Economics community and tradition what has eventually come to be called Hilbert's Dogma,[22] 'consistency ⇔ existence'. This became – and largely remains – the mathematical economist's credo and hence, the resulting inevitable schizophrenia of 'proving' existence of equilibria first, and looking for methods to *construct* or *compute* them at a second, entirely unconnected, stage. Thus, too, the indiscriminate appeals to the *tertium non datur* – and its implications – in 'existence proofs', on the one hand, and the ignorance about the nature and foundations of constructive mathematics or recursion theory, on the other.

But it was not as if von Neumann was not aware of Brouwer's opposition to Hilbert's Dogma, even at that early stage, although there is reason to suspect – given the kind of theme I am trying to develop in this paper – that something peculiarly 'subversive' was going on. Hugo Steinhaus observed, with considerable perplexity (Steinhaus, 1965, p. 460; italics added):

> [My] inability [to prove the minimax theorem] was a consequence of the ignorance of Zermelo's paper in spite of its having been published in 1913. . . . . J von Neumann was aware of the importance of the minimax principle [in von Neumann (1928)]; it is, however, *difficult to understand the absence of a quotation of Zermelo's lecture in his publications.*

Why did not von Neumann refer, in 1928, to the Zermelo-tradition of (alternating) arithmetical games? van Dalen, in his comprehensive, eminently readable, scrupulously fair and technically and conceptually thoroughly competent biography of Brouwer, (van Dalen, 1999, p. 636; italics added), noted, without additional comment that:

> In 1929 there was another publication in the intuitionistic tradition: an intuitionistic analysis of the game of chess by Max Euwe. It was a paper in which the game was viewed as a spread (i.e., a tree with the various positions as nodes). Euwe carried out *precise constructive estimates* of various classes of games, and considered the influence of the rules for draws. When he wrote his paper he was not aware of the earlier literature of Zermelo and Dénès König. *Von Neumann called his attention to these papers, and in a letter to Brouwer von Neumann sketched a classical approach to the mathematics of chess, pointing out that it could easily be constructivized.*

Why did not von Neumann provide this 'easily constructivized' approach – then, or later?

Perhaps it was easier to derive propositions appealing to the *tertium non datur*, and to Hilbert's Dogma, than to do the hard work of constructing estimates of an algorithmic solution, as Euwe did?[23] Perhaps it was easier to continue using the axiom of choice *than to construct new axioms* – say the axiom of determinacy.[24] Whatever the reason, the fact remains, that von Neumann's legacy was, indisputably, a legitimization of *Hilbert's Dogma* (and the indiscriminate use of the axiom of choice in mathematical economics).

This is worth emphasizing, in the context of a discussion on an *Algorithmic Revolution in Economics*, especially because Walras and Pareto, Marshall and Edgeworth, Wicksell and Irving Fisher, strived to find methods to construct solutions than to prove existence via an appeal to consistency. Paradigmatic examples of this *genre* are, of course, *tâtonnement* as a device to solve a system of equations, the appeal to *the market as a computer* – albeit an *analogue* one – to solve large systems of equations by Pareto (and, later, taking centre stage in the *socialist calculation debate*), Irving Fisher's construction of an (analogue) hydraulic computer to measure and calibrate utility functions, and so on. I shall return to this theme in the concluding section.

It is against such a background that one must read, and not be surprised, at the kind of preposterously ignorant and false assertions in Ok's above observations and claims. These are made in a new advanced text book on mathematics for graduate (economic) students, published under the imprint of an outstanding publishing house – *Princeton University Press* – and peddled as a text treating the material it does contain 'rigorously', although the student is not warned that there are many yardsticks of 'rigour' and that which is asserted to be 'rigorous' in one kind of mathematics could be considered 'flippant' and slippery' in another kind (see van Dalen's point in footnote 22, above).

Yet, every one of the assertions in the above quote is false, and also severely misleading. Brouwer did not 'become the most forceful proponent of the so-called intuitionist philosophy of mathematics *in later stages of his career*'; he was an intuitionist long before he formulated and proved what came, later, to be called the Brouwer fix-point theorem (cf. Brouwer, 1907,[25] 1908a, b); for the record, even the fixed-point theorem came earlier than 1912. It is nonsensical to claim that Brouwer did not consider *his* 'fixed point theorem as *a theorem*'; he did *not* consider it a valid theorem in intuitionistic constructive mathematics, and he had a very cogent reason for it, which was stated with admirable and crystal clarity when he finally formulated and proved it, forty years later, *within* intuitionistic constructive mathematics (Brouwer, 1952). On that occasion he identified the reason why his original theorem was unacceptable in intuitionistic constructive – indeed, in almost any kind of constructive – mathematics, for example, in Bishop-style constructivism, which was developed without any reliance on a philosophy of intuitionism:

> [T]he validity of the Bolzano–Weierstrass theorem [in intuitionism] would make the classical and the intuitionist form of fixed-point theorems equivalent.

> Brouwer (1952, p. 1)

Note how Brouwer refers to a 'classical...form of the fixed-point theorem'. The invalidity of the Bolzano–Weierstrass theorem in any form of constructivism is due to its reliance on the law of the excluded middle in an infinitary context of choices (cf. also, Dummett, pp. 10–12). The part that invokes the Bolzano–Weierstrass theorem entails *undecidable disjunctions* and as long as any proof invokes this property, it will remain *unconstructifiable* and *non-computable*.

It is worse than nonsense – if such a thing is conceivable – to state that 'an intuitionist would not accept the existence of an irrational number'. Moreover, the law of
the excluded middle is not a mathematical axiom; it is a logical law, accepted even by
the intuitionists so long as meaningless – precisely defined – infinities are not being
considered as alternatives from which to 'choose'[26] This is especially to be remembered in any context involving intuitionism, particularly in its Brouwerian variants,
because he – more than anyone else, with the possible exception of Wittgenstein –
insisted on the *independence of mathematics from logic*.

As for the un-finessed remark about the axiom of choice being forbidden, the
author should have been much more careful. Had this author done his elementary
mathematical homework properly, Bishop's deep and thoughtful clarifications of the
role of a choice axiom in varieties of mathematics may have prevented the appearance
of such nonsense (Bishop, 1967, p. 9):

> When a classical mathematician claims he is a constructivist, he probably means
> he avoids the axiom of choice. This axiom is unique in its ability to trouble the
> conscience of the classical mathematician, but in fact it is not a real source of the
> unconstructivities of classical mathematics. A choice function exists in constructive
> mathematics, because a choice is implied by the very meaning of existence.[27]
> Applications of the axiom of choice in classical mathematics either are irrelevant or
> are combined with a sweeping appeal to the principle of omniscience.[28] The axiom
> of choice is used to extract elements from equivalence classes where they should
> never have been put in the first place.

4. Reconstructing Economic Theory in the Algorithmic Mode[29]

> I am sure that the power of vested interests is vastly exaggerated compared with
> the gradual encroachment of ideas. Not, indeed, immediately, but after a certain
> interval; for in the field of economic and political philosophy *there are not many
> who are influenced by new theories after they are twenty-five or thirty years of age*,
> so that the ideas which civil servants and politicians and even agitators apply to
> current events are not likely to be the newest. But, soon or late, it is ideas, not
> vested interests, which are dangerous for good or evil.

J. Maynard Keynes (1936, pp. 3833–3834; italics added)

I believe, alas, in this melancholy observation by the perceptive Keynes and I think
only a new generation of graduate students can bring forth an algorithmic revolution
in economics. Hence, this concluding section is partly a brief retrospective on what
has been achieved 'towards an algorithmic revolution in economics' and partly a
manifesto, or a program – decidedly not an algorithm – for the education of a new
generation of graduate students in economics who may be the harbingers of the
revolution. I do not pretend to ground my 'manifesto' for an educational effort in any
deep theory of 'scientific revolution', inducement to a 'paradigm shift', and the like.

I should begin this concluding section with the 'confession' that I have not dealt with
the notion of algorithm in numerical analysis and so-called 'scientific computation'

in this paper. In relation to the issues raised in this paper, the most relevant reference on founding numerical analysis in a model of computation is the work of Smale and his collaborators. An excellent source of their work can be found in (Blum *et al.*, 1998). My own take on their critique of the Truing Machine Model as a foundation for 'scientific computation' is reported in (Velupillai, 2009a; Velupillai and Zambelli, 2010). It may, however, be useful – and edifying – to recall what may be called the defining theme of *Complexity and Real Computation* (Blum *et al.*, 1998, p. 10): 'Newton's Method is the "search algorithm" sine qua non of numerical analysis and scientific computation'. Yet, as they candidly point out (Blum *et al.*, 1998, p. 153; italics added): '...even for a polynomial of one complex variable we cannot *decide* if Newton's method will converge to a root of the polynomial on a given input'. The 'decide' in this quote refers to recursive or algorithmic decidability.

At least six 'dawns' can be discerned in the development of the algorithmic social sciences, all with direct ramifications for the path towards an algorithmic revolution in economics: algorithmic behavioural economics,[30] algorithmic probability theory, algorithmic finance theory,[31] algorithmic learning theory,[32] algorithmic statistics,[33] algorithmic game theory[34] and algorithmic economic dynamics. Yet, there is no recognisable, identifiable, discipline called algorithmic economics. Why not?

Before I try to answer this question let me clarify a couple of issues related to *Algorithmic Statistics*, *Algorithmic Game Theory*, the theory of *Algorithmic Mechanism Design* and *Algorithmic Economic Dynamics*.

To the best of my knowledge 'Algorithmic Statistics' was so termed first by Gács, Tromp and Vitányi (Gács *et al.*, 2001, p. 2443; italics and quotes added):

> While Kolmogorov complexity is the expected absolute measure of information content of an individual finite object, a similarly absolute notion is needed for the relation between an individual data sample and an individual model summarizing the information in the data, for example, a finite set (or probability distribution) where the data sample typically came from. *The statistical theory based on such relations between individual objects can be called 'algorithmic statistics'*, in contrast to classical statistical theory that deals with relations between probabilistic ensembles.

Algorithmic statistics, still an officially young field, is squarely founded on recursion theory, but not without a possible connection with intuitionistic or constructive logic, at least when viewed from the point of view of Kolmogorov complexity and its foundations in the kind of frequency theory that von Mises tried to axiomatize. This is a chapter of intellectual history, belonging to the issues discussed in Section 2, above, on the (constructive) proof-as-program vision, with an underpinning in intuitonistic logic. An admirably complete, and wholly sympathetic, account of the story of the way an algorithmic foundations for the (frequency) theory of probability was subverted by orthodoxy wedded to the Hilbert Dogma is given in van Lambalgen (1987).

I began to think of Game Theory in algorithmic modes – i.e. *Algorithmic Game Theory* – after realizing the futility of algorithmizing the uncompromisingly subjective von Neumann–Nash approach to game theory and beginning to understand the importance of Harrop's theorem (Harrop, 1961), in showing the indeterminacy of even finite games. This realization came after an understanding of *effective playability in arithmetical games*, developed elegantly by Michael Rabin more than fifty years ago (Rabin, 1957). This latter work, in turn, stands on the tradition of *alternative games* pioneered by Zermelo (1913), and misunderstood, misinterpreted and misconstrued by generations of orthodox game theorists.

The brief, rich and primarily recursion theoretic framework of Harrop's classic paper requires a deep understanding of the rich interplay between recursivity and constructive representations of *finite sets* that are recursively enumerable. There is also an obvious and formal connection between the notion of a *finite combinatorial object*, whose complexity is formally defined by the uncomputable Kolmogorov measure of complexity, and the results in Harrop's equally pioneering attempt to characterize the recursivity of finite sets and the resulting indeterminacy – undecidability – of a Nash equilibrium even in the finite case. To the best of my knowledge this interplay has never been mentioned or analysed. This will be an important research theme in the path towards an algorithmic revolution in economics.

However, *algorithmic game theory*, at least so far as such a name for a field is concerned, seems to have been first 'defined' by Christos Papadimitriou (2007, pp. xiii–xiv; italics added):

> [T]he Internet was the first computational artefact that was not created by a single entity (engineer, design team, or company), but emerged from the strategic inter-action of many. Computer scientists were for the first time faced with an object that they had to feel the same bewildered awe with which economists have always approached the market. And, quite predictably, they turned to game theory for in-spiration – in the words of Scott Shenker, a pioneer of this way of thinking . . . 'the Internet is an equilibrium, we just have to identify the game'. A fascinating fusion of ideas from both fields – game theory and algorithms – came into being and was used productively in the effort to illuminate the mysteries of the Internet. It has come to be called algorithmic game theory.

But, alternative games were there, long before the beginning of the emergence of recursion theory, even in the classic work of Gödel, later merging with the work that led to Matiyasevich's decisive (negative) resolution of *Hilbert's Tenth Problem* (Matiyasevich, 1993). Hence, the origins of algorithmic game theory, like those of algorithmic statistics, lie in the intellectual forces that gave rise to the *grundlagenkrise* of the 1920s. Simply put, in the battle between alternative visions on proof and logic (see, for example, the references to Max Euwe in Section 3, above).

The two cardinal principles of what I think should be called algorithmic and arith-metical games are *effective playability and (un)decidability*, even in *finite* realizations of such games, and *inductive inference from finite sequences* for algorithmic statis-tics. These desiderata cannot be fulfilled either by what has already become orthodox algorithmic game theory and classical statistical theory.

In footnote 22, above, and in the related, albeit brief text to which it is a note, I have indicated why the theory of mechanism design, a field at the frontiers of research in mathematical economics, may have nothing whatsoever to do with the notion of algorithm, and its underpinning logic, that is the focus in this paper. The concept of *algorithmic mechanism design* is defined, for example, in Nisan (2007, p. 210). The kind of algorithms required, to be implemented on the economic mechanisms in such a theory, are those that can compute the uncomputable, decide the undecidable and are underpinned by a logic that 'completes' the 'incompletable'.

At least since Walras devised the *tâtonnement* process and Pareto's appeal to the market as a computing device (albeit an *analogue* one, Pareto, 1927), there have been sporadic attempts to find mechanisms to solve a system of supply–demand equilibrium equations, going beyond the simple counting of equations and variables. But none of these enlightened attempts to devise mechanisms to solve a system of equations were predicted upon the elementary fact that the data types – the actual numbers – realized in, and used by, economic processes were, at best, rational numbers. The natural equilibrium relation between supply and demand, respecting the elementary constraints of the equally natural data types of a market economy – or any other kind of economy – should be framed as a *Diophantine decision problems* (cf. Velupillai, 2005), in the precise sense in which Gödel refers to such things (see, above, Section 2) and the way arithmetic games are formalized and shown to be effectively unsolvable in analogy with *Hilbert's Tenth Problem* (cf. Matiyasevich, 1993).

The Diophantine decision theoretic formalization is, thus, common to at least three kinds of algorithmic economics: classical behavioural economics (cf. Velupillai, 2010b), algorithmic game theory in its incarnation as arithmetic game theory (cf. Chapter 7 in Velupillai, 2000) and elementary equilibrium economics. Even those, like Smale (1976, 1981), who have perceptively discerned the way the problem of finding mechanisms to solve equations was subverted into formalizations of inequality relations which are then solved by appeal to (unnatural) non-constructive, uncomputable, fixed point theorems did not go far enough to realize that the data types of the variables and parameters entering the equations needed not only to be constrained to be non-negative, but also to be rational (or integer) valued. Under these latter constraints economics in its behavioural, game theoretic and microeconomic modes must come to terms with absolutely (algorithmically) undecidable problems. This is the cardinal message of the path towards a revolution in algorithmic economics.

Therefore, if orthodox algorithmic game theory, algorithmic mechanism theory and computable general equilibrium theory have succeeded in computing their respective equilibria, then they would have to have done it with algorithms that are not subject to the strictures of the Church–Turing thesis or do not work within the (constructive) proof-as-algorithm paradigm. This raises the mathematical meaning of the notion of algorithm in algorithmic game theory, algorithmic mechanisms theory and computable general equilibrium theory (and varieties of so-called computational economics). Either they are of the kind used in numerical analysis and so-called 'scientific computing' (as if computing in the recursion and constructive theoretic traditions are not 'scientific') and, if so, *their* algorithmic foundations are, in turn, constrained by either the Church–Turing thesis (as in Blum *et al.*, 1998) or the (constructive) proof-as-algorithm paradigm; or, the economic system and its agents and institutions are computing the formally uncomputable and deciding the algorithmically undecidable (or are formal systems that are inconsistent or incomplete).

The only way I know, for now, to link the two visions of algorithms – short of reformulating all the above problems in terms of analogue computing models (see also the next footnote) – is through Gandy's definition of mechanism so that his characterizations, when not satisfied, imply a mechanism that can compute the un-computable. Gandy enunciates four set-theoretic '*Principles for Mechanisms*' (Gandy, 1980) to describe discrete deterministic machines[35]:

1. The form of description;
2. The principle of limitation of hierarchy;
3. The principle of unique reassembly and
4. The principle of local causality.

He then derives the important result, as a theorem, that any device which satisfies the four principles jointly generates successive states that are computable, and conversely, for any formal weakening of any of the above four principles, then there exist mechanisms that compute the uncomputable (Gandy, 1980, p. 123; italics in the original):

> It is proved that that if a device satisfied the [above four] principles [simultaneously] then its successive states form a computable sequence. Counter-example are constructed which show that if the principles be weakened in almost any way, then there will be devices which satisfy the weakened principles and which can calculate *any* number-theoretic function.

It is easy to show that market mechanisms and, indeed, all orthodox theoretical resource allocation mechanisms violate one or more of the above principles. Therefore, there is a generic impossibility result, similar to that of Arrow's in Social Choice Theory, inherent in mechanism theory, when analysed from the point of view of algorithmic economics. Hence any claims about *constructing* mechanisms to depict the efficient functioning of a market economy, the rational behaviour of agents and the rational and efficient organization of institutions and the derivation of efficient policies, as made by orthodox economic theorists in micro and macro economics, IO theory and game theory, are based on non-mechanisms in the precise sense of algorithmic economics. The immediate parallel would be a claim by an engineer to have built a perpetual motion machine, violating the (phenomenological) laws of thermodynamics.

Finally, I come to the topic of *algorithmic economic dynamics*. In the same spirit of respecting the constraints on economic data types, I have now come round to the view that it is not sufficient to consider just computable economic dynamics, theorized in terms of the theory of one or another variety of computable or recursive analysis. This meant, in my work thus far, the dynamical system equivalent of a Turing Machine had to be a discrete dynamical system acting on rational numbers (or the natural numbers).

Even if such is possible – i.e. constructing a discrete dynamical system acting on rational numbers – the further requirement such a dynamical system must satisfy is the capability of encapsulating three additional properties:

- The dynamical system should possess a relatively simple global attractor;
- It should be capable of meaningfully and measurably long – and extremely long – transients;[36]
- It should possess not just ordinary sensitive dependence on initial conditions (SDIC) that characterize 'complex' dynamical systems that generate strange

attractors. It should, in fact, possess *Super Sensitive Dependence on Initial Conditions (SSDIC)*. This means that the dynamical system *appears* to possess the property that distances between neighbouring trajectories diverge too fast to be encapsulated by even partial recursive functions.

Is it possible to construct such rational valued dynamical systems or, equivalently, algorithms that imply such dynamical systems? The answer, mercifully, is yes. In Velupillai (2010c), I have discussed how, for a Clower-Howitt 'Monetary Economy' (cf. Clower-Howitt, 1978), with rational valued, saw-tooth like monetary variables, it is possible to use the '*Takagi function*' to model its dynamics, while preserving its algorithmic nature. But in this case, it is necessary to work with computable – or recursive – analysis. It would be more desirable to remain within classical algorithmic formalizations and, hence, working with rational- or integer-valued dynamical systems that have a clear algorithmic underpinning.

I believe *Goodstein's algorithm* (cf. Goodstein, 1944) could be the paradigmatic example for modelling rational – or integer – valued algorithmic (nonlinear) economic dynamics (Paris and Tavakol, 1993). In every sense in which the notion of algorithm has been discussed above, for the path towards an algorithmic revolution in economics, is most elegantly satisfied by this line of research, a line that has by passed the mathematical economics and nonlinear macrodynamics community. This is the only way I know to be able to introduce the algorithmic construction of an integer-valued dynamical system possessing a very simple global attractor, and with immensely long, effectively calculable, transients, whose existence is *unprovable* in Peano arithmetic. Moreover, this kind of nonlinear dynamics, subject to super sensitive dependence on initial conditions (SSDIC), ultra-long transients and possessing simple global attractors whose existence can be encapsulated within a classic Gödelian, Diophantine, decision theoretic framework, makes it also possible to discuss effective *policy* mechanisms (cf. Kirby and Paris, 1982).

Diophantine decision problems emerge in the unifying theoretical framework, and the methodological and epistemological bases, for the path towards an algorithmic revolution in economics. Algorithmic economics – in their (classical) behavioural), microeconomic, macroeconomic, game theoretic, learning, finance and dynamic theoretical frameworks when the constraints of the natural data types of economics is respected – turns out to be routinely faced with absolutely undecidable (algorithmic) problems, at every level. In the face of this undecidability, indeterminacy of a kind that has nothing to do with a probabilistic underpinning for economics at any level, is the rule. Unknowability, undecidability, uncomputability, inconsistency and incompleteness endow every aspect of economic decision making with algorithmic indeterminacy.

The completion of the epistemological and methodological basis for economics given by the framework of Diophantine decision theoretic formalization, in the face of absolutely (algorithmically) undecidable problems, should, obviously, require a sound philosophical grounding, too. This, I believe, is most naturally provided by harnessing the richness of Husserlian phenomenology for the philosophical underpinning of algorithmic economics. This aspect remains an entirely virgin research direction, in the path towards an algorithmic revolution in economics, where indeterminacy and ambiguity underpin perfectly rational decision making.

How, then, can a belief in the eventual desirability and necessity of an algorithmic revolution in economics be fostered and furthered by educators and institutions that may not shy away from exploring alternatives? After all, whatever ideological underpinnings the mathematization of economics may have had, if not for the possibility of mathematical modelling of theoretical innovations, we would, surely, not have had any of the advances in economic theory at any kind of policy level?

In this particular sense, then, I suggest that a program of graduate education – eventually trickling downwards towards a reformulation of the undergraduate curriculum, too – is devised, in a spirit of adventure and hope, to train students in economics, finance and business in the tools, concepts and philosophy of algorithmic economics. It is easy enough to prepare a structured program for an intensive doctoral course in algorithmic economics, replacing traditional subjects with economic theory, game theory, behavioural economics, finance theory, nonlinear dynamics, learning and induction, stressing education – learning and teaching – from the point of view of algorithmic mathematics, methodologically – in the form of mathematical methods – and epistemologically – in the sense of knowledge and its underpinnings. Given that the nature of algorithmic visions is naturally dynamic, computational and experimental, these aspects would form the thematic core of the training and education program.

No mathematical theorem would be derived, in any aspect of economics, without explicit algorithmic content, which automatically means with computational and dynamic content, naturally amenable to experimental implementations. The schizophrenia between one kind of mathematics to devise, derive and prove theorems in economic theory and another kind of mathematics when it is required to give the derived, devised and proved results numerical and computational content, would forever be obliterated – at least from the minds of a new and adventurous generation of economists.

A decade ago, after reading my first book on computable economics (Velupillai, 2000), Herbert Simon wrote, on 25 May, 2000, to one of my former colleagues as follows:

> I think the battle has been won, at least the first part, although it will take a couple of academic generations to clear the field and get some sensible textbooks written and the next generation trained.

The 'battle' that 'had been won' against orthodox, non-algorithmic, economic theory had taken Simon almost half a century of sustained effort in making classical behavioural economics and its algorithmic foundations the centrepiece of his research at the theoretical frontiers of computational cognitive science, behavioural economics, evolutionary theory and the theory of problem solving. Yet, he still felt that more time was needed, in the form of 'two [more] academic generations to clear the field and get some sensible textbooks written and the next generation trained'.

For the full impact of a complete algorithmic revolution in economics, I am not sure orthodoxy will permit 'the clearing of the field', even if 'sensible textbooks' are written to get the 'next generation trained'. All the same, it is incumbent upon us to make the attempt to prepare for an algorithmic future, by writing the 'sensible textbooks' for the next – or future – generations of students, who will be the harbingers of the algorithmic revolution in economics.

There are no blueprints for writing textbooks for the harbingers of revolutions. Paul Samuelson's *Foundations of Economic Analysis* brought forth a serious revolution in the training of students with a level of skill on mathematics that was an order of magnitude much greater than previous generations – much sooner than did *The Theory of Games and Economic Behaviour*. The former will be my 'model' for pedagogical success; the latter for the paradigm shift, to be utterly banal about the choice of words, in theories, in the sense in which Keynes meant it, in the opening quote of this section. The non-numerical content and the pervasive use of the *tertium non datur* in the *Theory of Games and Economic Behaviour*, all the way from its rationality postulates to the massively complex many-agent, multilayered, institutional context, can only be made clear when an alternative mathematics is shown to be possible for problems of the same sort. This means a reformulation of mathematical economics in terms of Diophantine decision theory as the starting point and it is, ultimately, the equivalent of the revolution in vision wrought by von Neumann and Morgenstern, for the generations that came before us.

They had a slightly easier task, in a peculiarly subversive sense: they were confronted, largely, with an economics community that had not, as yet, been permanently 'contaminated' by an orthodox mathematics. Those of us, following Simon and others who believe in the algorithmic revolution in economics, face a community that is almost over-trained and overwhelmed by the techniques of classical mathematics and non-intuitionistic logic and, therefore, allow preposterous assertions, claims and 'accusations', like those by Efe Ok, to students who are never made aware of alternative possibilities of formalization respecting the computational and numerical prerogatives of economics.

Two simple examples will suffice to show the enormous task facing the textbook writer of algorithmic economics. The notion of function, in addition to that of sets, is all pervasive in the mathematical economics tradition that comes down from the revolutions that were set in their paces by the Foundations of Economic Analysis and The Theory of Games and Economic Behaviour. To disabuse a young, mathematically trained graduate student in economics, of a reliance on these seemingly all-pervasive notions – long before even beginning to frame economic problems as Diophantine decision problems – cannot be easy, but it is possible. This new generation is computer-literate in a way that was unimaginable at the time Samuelson and von Neumann–Morgenstern began their journeys on a new path. It should be easy to introduce the λ-*calculus* as the natural function concept for computation and *categories* (on which basis *toposes* can be introduced) as the basic mathematical entity, replacing sets. From these basic conceptual innovations it is easy to make clear, at a very elementary pedagogical level, why the *teritum non datur* is both unnecessary and pernicious for a subject that is intrinsically computational, numerical – and phenomenological.

The strategy would be the Wittgensteinian one of letting those mesmerized by Hilbert's invitation to stay in Cantor's paradise leave it of their own accord:

Hilbert (1925 [1926], p. 191): 'No one shall drive us out of the paradise which Cantor has created for us'.

Wittgenstein, (1939, p. 103): I would say, 'I wouldn't dream of trying to drive anyone out of this paradise'. I would try to do something quite different: I would try to show you that it is not a paradise – so that you'll leave of your own accord. I would say, 'You're welcome to this; just look about you'.

I do not envisage the slightest difficulty in gently replacing the traditional *function* concept and the abandonment of the reliance on the notion of *set* by, respectively the λ-*notation* and the λ-*calculus*, on the one hand, and *categories*, on the other. But disabusing the pervasive influence of reliance on the *tertium non datur* is quite another matter – replacing *Hilbert's Dogma* with (*constructive*) *proof-as-algorithm* vision as the natural reasoning basis. This is where one can only hope, by sustained pedagogy, to persuade students to 'leave' *Hilbert's paradise* 'of their own accord.

I fear that just two generations of text book writing will not suffice for this.

The part that will require more gentle persuasion, in its implementation as well as in its dissemination pedagogically, will be the philosophical part, the part to be underpinned by something like Husserlian phenomenology, extolling the virtues of indeterminacies and unknowability. This part is crucial in returning economics to its humanistic origins, away from its increasingly vacuous tendencies towards becoming simply a branch of applied mathematics.

The ghost, if not the spirit, of Frege looms large in the epistemology that permeates the themes in this paper. I can think of no better way to conclude this paean to an algorithmic revolution in economics than remembering Frege's typically perspicacious reflections on *Sources of Knowledge of Mathematics and the Mathematical Natural Sciences*[37] (Frege, 1924/1925, p. 267):

When someone comes to know something it is by his recognizing a thought to be true. For that he has first to grasp the thought. Yet I do not count the grasping of the thought as knowledge, but only the recognition of its truth, the judgement proper. What I regard as a source of knowledge is what justifies the recognition of truth, the judgement.

Acknowledgments

This paper is dedicated to the three *Honorary Patrons* of the *Algorithmic Social Science Research Unit* (*ASSRU*): Richard Day, John McCall and Björn Thalberg who, each in their own way, instructed, inspired and influenced me in my own algorithmic intellectual journeys. As a tribute also to their pedagogical skills in making intrinsically mathematical ideas of natural complexity available to non-mathematical, but sympathetic, readers, I have endeavoured to eschew any and all formalisms of any mathematical sort in writing this paper. The title of this paper should have been *Towards a Diophantine Revolution in Economics*. It was with considerable reluctance that I resisted the temptation to do so, mainly in view of the fact that graduate students in economics – my intended primary audience – are almost blissfully ignorant of the meaning of a *Diophantine Decision Problem*, having been overwhelmed by an overdose of optimization economics. An earlier paper, titled *The Algorithmic Revolution in the Social Sciences: Mathematical Economics, Game Theory and Statistical Inference*, was given as an Invited Lecture at the *Workshop on Information Theoretic Methods in Science and Engineering* (WITMSE), August 17–19, 2009, Tampere, Finland. This paper has *nothing in common* with that earlier one, except for a few words in the title. I am, as always, deeply indebted to my colleague and friend, Stefano Zambelli, for continuing encouragement along these 'less-travelled' *algorithmic* paths, often against considerable odds. Refreshing conversations with our research students, V. Ragupathy and Kao Selda, helped me keep at least some of my left toes firmly on mother earth. *None of them*, alas, are responsible for the remaining errors and infelicities in the paper.

Notes

1. I suspect Cohen means 'solve mathematical *problems*', because 'solving mathematical *theorems*' seems a meaningless phrase.
2. Whether this was, in fact, 'Hilbert's project' and 'vision' I am not sure and am not prepared to endorse that it was so. My own take on this is partially summarized in Section 3 below and Velupillai (2010a).
3. However, as I shall try to show in Section 4, below, the status of algorithmic game theory is more in line with computable general equilibrium theory than with the other fields mentioned above, which are solidly grounded in some form of computability theory.
4. See Bell (1998, especially chapter 8) for a lucid, yet rigorous, substantiation of this claim, although presented in the context of *Smooth Infinitesimal Analysis*, which is itself of relevance to the mathematical economist over-enamoured by orthodox analysis and official non-standard analysis. As in constructive analysis, in smooth infinitesimal analysis, all functions in use are continuous. A similar – though not exactly equivalent – case occurs also in computable analysis. Incidentally, I am not quite sure whether the plural of a *topos* is *topoi* or *toposes*!
5. See Section 3 for further discussion of this point.
6. Some, but not all, of them are referred to as theorems; none of the 'propositions' in Sraffa (1960) are referred to as theorems, lemmas, or given any other formal, mathematical, label.
7. I hope in saying this I am reflecting the general opinion of the mathematical economics community.
8. Debreu refers to this as a 'deeper theorem', without suggesting in what sense it is 'deep'. Personally, I consider it a trivial – even an 'apologetic' – theorem, and I am quite prepared to suggest in what sense I mean 'trivial'.
9. For many years I referred to Sraffa's proofs as being constructive in the strict mathematical sense. I now think it is more useful to refer to them as algorithmic proofs.
10. Herbert Simon, together with Newell and Shaw (1957), in their work leading up to the monumental work on *Human Problem Solving* (Newell and Simon, 1972), and Hao Wang (1960), in particular, automated most of the theorems in the first 10 chapters of *Principia Mathematica* (Whitehead and Russell, 1927). Surely, it is time one did the same with von Neumann-Morgenstern (1947)? I am confident that none of the theorems of this classic are proved constructively, in spite of occasional claims

to the contrary. If I was younger – but, then, much younger – I would attempt this task myself!

11. In the same important collection of essays that includes the previously cited papers by Cohen and Hyland.

12. Alan Turing arrived at a similar definition prior to von Neumann.

13. Practically all my research and teaching activities for the past decade has tried to make this point, from every possible economic point of view. One representative reference, choosing a mid-point in the decade that has passed, is Velupillai (2005), where the way to formalize even elementary supply–demand systems as Diophantine decision problems is outlined. The point here, apart from remaining faithful to the natural data types and problem focus – solvability of Diophantine equations – is to emphasize the roles of ambiguity, unsolvability, undecidability and uncomputability in economics and de-throne the arrogance of mathematical determinism of orthodox economic theory. Economists have lost the art of solving equations at the altar of Hilbert's Dogma, i.e. proof-as-consistency = existence, the topic of the next section.

14. It would be useful to recall Robin Gandy's somewhat 'tongue-in-cheek' attempt at a 'precise' characterization of this term (Gandy, 1980, p. 125; italics in the original):

> 'For vividness I have so far used the fairly nebulous term "machine." Before going into details I must be *rather* more precise. Roughly speaking I am using the term with its 19th century meaning; the reader may like to imagine some glorious contraption of gleaming brass and polished mahogany, or he may choose to inspect the parts of Babbage's "Analytical Engine" which are preserved in the Science Museum at South Kensington'.

It is refreshing to read, in the writing of a logician of the highest calibre, someone being '*rather* more precise' doing so in 'roughly speaking' mode!

15. Sometimes this approach is referred to as the 'proofs-as-program paradigm' (cf. Maietti and Sambin, 2005, chapter 6, especially pp. 93–95).

16. The trouble is that almost no one, outside the somewhat small circle of the constructive mathematical community, makes much of an effort to read or 'look between the lines'.

17. However, the unwary reader should be made aware that the appeal to the *tertium non datur* by the recursion theorist is usually for the purpose of deriving *negative universal assertions*; *positive existential assertions* are naturally constructive, even within recursion theory.

18. In posing, and trying to answer, this question, I am not addressing myself to flippant assertions in popularized nonsense – as distinct from pretentious nonsense, an example of which is discussed in the next section – such as Beinhocker (2006), for example, p12: 'Evolution is an *algorithm*'.

19. Aberth's important work was instrumental in showing the importance of integrating Ramon Moore's pioneering work in *Interval Analysis* and *Interval Arithmetic* (Moore, 1966) in algorithmic implementations (cf. Hayes, 2003).

20. For an exceptionally lucid demonstration and discussion of these issues, see Shankar (1994).

21. In other words, the rich literature on the formal characterization of a *mechanism* and its *limitations*, have played no part in economic theory or mathematical economics (cf. Gödel, 1951; Kreisel, 1974; Gandy, 1980, 1982; Shapiro, 1998). This is quite similar to the way the notion of information has been – and is being – used in economic theory, in both micro and macro, in game theory and industrial

organization (IO). None of the massive advances in, for example, *algorithmic information theory*, unifying Claude Shannon's pioneering work with those of Kolomogorov and Chaitin, have had the slightest impact in formal economic theorizing, except within the framework of *Computable Economics* (Velupillai, 2000), a phrase I coined more than 20 years ago, to give content to the idea of an economic theory underpinned by recursion theory (and constructive mathematics).

22. In van Dalen's measured, studied, scholarly, opinion, (van Dalen, 2005, pp. 576–577; italics added): 'Because Hilbert's yardstick was calibrated by the continuum hypothesis, Hilbert's dogma, "consistency ⇔ existence," and the like, he was by definition right. But *if one is willing to allow other yardsticks*, no less significant, but based on alternative principles, then Brouwer's work could not be written off as obsolete 19th century stuff'.

23. At the end of his paper Euwe reports that von Neumann brought to his attention the works by Zermelo and Konig, after he had completed his own work (Euwe, 1929, p. 641). Euwe then goes on (italics added):

   '*Der gegebene Beweis is aber nicht konstruktive*, d.h. es wird keine Methode angezeigt, mit Hilfe deren der gewinnweg, wenn überhaupt möglich, in *endlicher Zeit konstruiert werden kann*'.

24. Gaisi Takeuti's important observation is obviously relevant here (Takeuti, 2003, pp. 73–74; italics added):

   'There has been an idea, which was originally claimed by Gödel and others, that, if one added an axiom which is a strengthened version of the existence of a measurable cardinal to existing axiomatic set theory, then various mathematical problems might all be resolved. Theoretically, nobody would oppose such an idea, but, in reality, *most set theorists felt it was a fairy tale and it would never really happen. But it has been realized by virtue of the axiom of determinateness, which showed Gödel's idea valid*'.

25. Brouwer could not have been clearer on this point, when he wrote, in his 1907 thesis (Brouwer, 1907, p. 45; quotes added):

   '*[T]he continuum as a whole* was given to us by 'intuition'; *a construction* for it, an action which would create 'from the mathematical intuition' "all" its points as individuals, is inconceivable and impossible. *The* 'mathematical intuition' is unable to create other than denumerable sets of individuals'.

26. Even as early as in 1908, we find Brouwer dealing with this issue with exceptional clarity (cf. Brouwer 1908b, pp. 109–110; quotes added):

   'Now consider the principium *tertii exclusi*: It claims that every supposition is either true or false; . . . Insofar as only 'finite discrete systems' are introduced, the investigation whether an imbedding is possible or not, can always be carried out and admits a definite result, so in this case the principium tertii exclusi is reliable as a principle of reasoning. [I]n infinite systems the principium tertii exclusi is as yet not reliable'.

27. See, also, Bishop and Bridges (1985, p. 13, 'Notes').

28. Bishop (1967, p. 9), refers to a version of the law of the excluded middle as the *principle of omniscience*.

29. A timely conversation with Brian Hayes, who happened to be in Trento while this paper was being finalized, on the λ-calculus, and an even more screndipitous event

in the form of a seminar on, *How Shall We Educate the Computational Scientists of the Future* by Rosalind Reid, on the same day, helped me structure this concluding section with pedagogy in mind.

30. Which I have, in recent writings, referred to also as 'classical behavioural economics' and outlined its algorithmic basis in Velupillai (2010b).

31. Most elegantly, pedagogically and rigorously summarized in Shafer and Vovk (2001), although I trace the origins of research in algorithmic finance theory in the extraordinarily perceptive work by Osborne (1977).

32. In Velupillai (2000), chapters 5 and 6, I discussed both algorithmic probability theory and algorithmic learning theory as *The Modern Theory of Induction* and *Learning in a Computable Setting*, respectively.

33. In my *'Tampere Lecture'* (Velupillai, 2009b), I tried to outline the development of algorithmic statistics.

34. Again, in Velupillai (2009b) and Velupillai (1997) I referred to algorithmic game theory as arithmetic game theory and discussed its origins and mathematical framework is some detail.

35. However, Gandy adds the important explicit caveat that he (Gandy, 1982, p. 125; italics in the original): '[E]xcludes from consideration devices which are *essentially* analogue machines'. The use of isolated probabilistic elements in the implementation of an algorithm does not make it – the algorithm – a random mechanism; and, even if they did, there is an adequate way of dealing with them within the framework of both recursion and constructive mathematical theories of algorithms.

36. It was in a footnote in chapter 17 of the *General Theory* (Keynes, 1936) stressed the importance of *transition regimes* and made the reference to *Hume as the progenitor of the equilibrium concept in economics* (p. 343, footnote 3; italics added):

   '[H]ume began the practice amongst economists of stressing the importance of *the equilibrium position* as compared with the ever-shifting transition towards it, though he was still enough of a mercantilist not to overlook the fact *that it is in the transition that we actually have our being*: . . .'.

37. Naturally, I believe he would have added 'mathematical social sciences' had he been writing these thoughts today.

References

Aberth, Oliver (1980) *Computable Analysis*. New York: McGraw-Hill Book Company.

Aberth, Oliver (2001) *Computable Calculus*. San Diego, CA: Academic Press.

Beinhocker, Eric. D. (2006) *The Origin of Wealth: The radical Remaking of Economics and What It Means for Business and Society*. Boston, MA: Harvard Business School Press.

Bell, John L. (1998) *A Primer of Infinitesimal Analysis*. Cambridge, UK: Cambridge University Press.

Bishop, Errett. A. (1967) *Foundations of Constructive Analysis*. New York: McGraw-Hill Book Company.

Bishop, Errett and Douglas Bridges (1985) *Constructive Analysis*. Heidelberg, Germany: Springer-Verlag.

Blum, Lenore, Felipe Cucker, Michael Shub and Steve Smale (1998) *Complexity and Real Computation*. New York: Springer Verlag.

Bridges, Douglas and Fred, Richman (1987) *Varieties of Constructive Mathematics*. Cambridge, UK: Cambridge University Press.

Brouwer, Lutizen E.J. (1907/1975) Over de grondslagen der wiskunde [On the foundations of mathematics], Academic Thesis. In Arend Heyting (ed.), *L.E.J. Brouwer Collected Works: Vol. 1 – Philosophy and Foundations of Mathematics* (pp. 11–104). Amsterdam, Netherlands: North-Holland; New York: American Elsevier.

Brouwer, Lutizen E.J. (1908a/1975) Over de grondslagen der wiskunde [On the foundations of mathematics], Academic Thesis. In Arend Heyting (ed.), *L.E.J. Brouwer Collected Works: Vol. 1 – Philosophy and Foundations of Mathematics* (pp. 105–106). Amsterdam, Netherlands: North-Holland; New York: American Elsevier.

Brouwer, Lutizen E.J. (1908b/1975) De onbetrouwbaarheid der logische principes [The unreliability of the logical principles]. In Arend Heyting (ed.), *L.E.J. Brouwer Collected Works: Vol. 1 – Philosophy and Foundations of Mathematics* (pp. 197–111). Amsterdam, Netherlands: North-Holland; New York: American Elsevier.

Brouwer, Luitzen E.J. (1952) An intuitionist correction of the fixed-point theorem on the sphere. *Proceedings of the Royal Society*, London, UK, Vol. 213, 1–2, 5 June 1952.

Clower, Robert. W. and Peter W. Howitt (1978) The transaction theory of the demand for money: a reconsideration. *Journal of Political Economy* 86(3): 449–466.

Cohen, Daniel I.A. (1991) The superfluous paradigm. In J.H. Johnson and M.J. Loomes (eds), *The Mathematical Revolution Inspired by Computing* (pp. 323–329). Oxford: Oxford University Press.

Davis, Martin (1978) What is a computation? In Lynn Arthur Steen (ed.), *Mathematics Today – Twelve Informal Essays* (pp. 242–267). New York: Springer-Verlag.

Debreu, Gerard (1959) *Theory of Value: An Axiomatic Analysis of Economic Equilibrium*. London, UK: John Wiley & Sons, Inc.

Dummett, Michael (1977) *Elements of Intuitionism*. Oxford: Clarendon Press.

Euwe, Max (1929) *Mengentheoretische Betrachtungen über das Schachspiel*, Communicated by Prof. R. Weizenböck (May 25, 1929), *Proc. Koninklijke Nederlandse Akademie Van Wetenschappen*, Amsterdam, 32(5): 633–642.

Feferman, Solomon (2009) Gödel, Nagel, minds, and machines. *The Journal of Philosophy* 106(4): 201–219.

Frege, Gottlob (1924/1925/1970) Sources of knowledge of mathematics and the mathematical natural sciences. In Hans Hermes, Friedrich Kambartel and Friedrich Kaulbach (eds), with the assistance of Gottfried Gabriel and Walburgs Rödding, *Posthumous Writings* (pp. 267–277). Oxford: Basil Blackwell.

Gács, Péter, John T. Tromp and Paul Vitányi (2001) Algorithmic statistics. *IEEE Transactions on Information Theory* 47(6): 2443–2463.

Gandy, Robin. O. (1980) Church's thesis and principles for mechanisms. In J. Barwise, H.J. Keisler and K. Kunen (eds), *The Kleene Symposium* (pp. 123–148). Amsterdam, Netherlands: North-Holland.

Gandy, Robin. O. (1982) Limitations to mathematical knowledge. In D. van Dalen, D. Lascar and J. Smiley (eds), *Logic Colloquium'80* (pp. 129–146). Amsterdam, Netherlands: North-Holland.

Gödel, Kurt (1951/1995) Some basic theorems on the foundations of mathematics and their implications. In Solomon Feferman, John W. Dawson, Jr., Warren Goldfarb, Charles Parsons and Robert N. Solovay (eds), *Kurt Gödel – Collected Works, Volume III, Unpublished Essays and Lectures* (pp. 304–323). Oxford: Oxford University Press.

Goodstein, Reuben. L. (1944) On the restricted ordinal theorem. *Journal of Symbolic Logic* 9(2): 33–41.

Harrop, Ronald (1961) On the recursivity of finite sets, Zeitschrift für Mathematische Logik und Grundlagen der Mathematik, Bd, 7, pp. 136–140.

Hayes, Brian (2003) A lucid interval. *American Scientist* 91(6): 484–488.

Hilbert, David (1925 [1926]), On the infinite. In Paul Benacerraf and Hilary Putnam (eds) *Philosophy of Mathematics – Selected Readings*, 2nd edn (pp. 183–201), 1983. Cambridge, UK: Cambridge University Press.

Hyland, J.M.E. (1991) Computing and foundations. In J.H. Johnson and M.J. Loomes (eds), *The Mathematical Revolution Inspired by Computing* (pp. 269–284). Oxford: Oxford University Press.

Keynes, John Maynard (1936) *The General Theory of Employment, Interest and Money*. London, UK: Macmillan and Co., Limited.

Kirby, Laurie and Jeff Paris (1982) Accessible independence results for Peano arithmetic. *Bulletin of the London Mathematical Society* 14: 285–293.

Knuth Donald E. (1973) *The Art of Computer Programming: Volume 1/Fundamental Algorithms*, 2nd edn. Reading, MA: Addison-Wesley Publishing Company.

Knuth, Donald E. (1981) Algorithms in modern mathematics and computer science. In A.P. Ershov and Donald E Knuth (eds), *Algorithms in Modern Mathematics and Computer Science* (pp. 82–99). Berlin, Germany: Springer-Verlag.

Kreisel, Georg (1974) A notion of mechanistic theory. *Synthese* 29: 11–26.

Maietti, Maria Emilia and Giovanni Sambin (2005) Toward a minimalist foundation for constructive mathematics. In L. Crosilla and P. Schuster (eds), *From Sets and Types to Topology and Analysis: Towards Practicable Foundations for Constructive Mathematics* (Chapter 6, pp. 91–114). Oxford: Clarendon Press.

Markov, A.A. (1954/1961) Theory of Algorithms, Academy of Sciences of the USSR, Moscow and Leningrad, translated by Jacques J. Schorr-Kon and PST Staff and published for The National Science Foundation, Washington, D.C., and The Department of Commerce, USA, by The Israel Program for Scientific Translations, Jerusalem.

Matiyasevich, Yuri M. (1993) *Hilbert's Tenth Problem*. Cambridge, MA: The MIT Press.

McCulloch, Warren S. (1961/1965) *What is a Number, that a Man May Know It, and a Man, that He May Know a Number*, The Ninth Alfred Korzybski Memorial Lecture, reprinted in: *Embodiments of Mind* by Warren S. McCulloch Chapter 1, pp. 1–18. Cambridge, MA: The M.I.T. Press.

Moore, Ramon E. (1966) *Interval Analysis*. Englewood Cliffs, NJ: Prentice-Hall.

Moschovakis, Yiannis N. (1998) On founding the theory of algorithms. In H.G. Dales and G. Oliveri (eds), *Truth in Mathematics* (Chapter 4, pp. 71–104). Oxford: Clarendon Press.

Moschovakis, Yiannis N. (2001) What is an algorithm? In B. Engquist and W. Schmid (eds), *Mathematics Unlimited – 2001 and Beyond* (pp. 919–936). Berlin, Germany: Springer-Verlag.

Moschoavakis, Yiannis N. and Vasilis Paschalis (2008) Elementary algorithms and their implementations. In S. Barry Cooper, Benedikt Löwe and Andrea Sorbi (eds), *New Computational Paradigms: Changing Conceptions of What is Computable* (pp. 87–118). New York: Springer Science and Business Media LLC.

Newell, Allen and Herbert A. Simon (1972) *Human Problem Solving*. Englewood Cliffs, NJ: Prentice-Hall, Inc.

Newell, Allen, J.C. Shaw and Herbert A. Simon (1957) Empirical explorations of the logic theory machine: a case study in heuristics. *Proceeding of the Western Joint Computer Conference* 11: 218–239.

Nisan, Noam (2007) Introduction to mechanism design (for computer scientists). In Noam Nisan, Tim Roughgarden, Éva Tardos and Vijay V. Vazirani (eds), *Algorithmic Game Theory* (Chapter 9, pp. 209–241). New York: Cambridge University Press.

Ok, Efe A. (2007) *Real Analysis with Economic Applications*. Princeton, NJ: Princeton University Press.

Osborne, Maury (1977) *The Stock Market and Finance from a Physicist's Viewpoint*. Minneapolis, MN: Crossgar Press.

Papadimiriou, Christos H. (2007) Forward. In Noam Nisan, Tim Roughgarden, Éva Tardos and Vijay V. Vazirani (eds), *Algorithmic Game Theory* (pp. 29–51). New York: Cambridge University Press.

Pareto, Vilfredo (1927/1971) *Manual of Political Economy, translated from the French Edition of 1927 by Ann S. Schwier*, Ann S. Schwier and Alfred N. Page (eds). London: The Macmillan Press Ltd.

Paris, Jeff and Reza Tavakol (1993) Goodstein algorithm as a super-transient dynamical system. *Physics Letters A* 180(1–2): 83–86.

Posy, Carl J. (1998) Brouwer versus Hilbert: 1907–1928. *Science in Context* 11(2): 291–325.

Rabin, Michael O. (1957) Effective computability of winning strategies. In M. Dresher, A.W. Tucker and P. Wolfe (eds), *Annals of Mathematics Studies, No. 39: Contributions to the Theory of Games, Vol. III* (pp. 147–157). Princeton, New Jersey: Princeton University Press.

Shafer, Glenn and Vladimir Vovk (2001) *Probability and Finance: It's Only a Game*. New York: John Wiley & Sons, Inc.

Shankar, N. (1994) *Metamathematics, Machines, and Gödel's Proof*. Cambridge, UK: Cambridge University Press.

Shapiro, Stewart (1998) Incompleteness, mechanism, and optimism. *The Bulletin of Symbolic Logic* 4(3): 273–302.

Smale, Steve (1976) Dynamics in general equilibrium theory. *American Economic Review* 66(2): 288–294.

Smale, Steve (1981) Global analysis and economics. In Kenneth J. Arrow and Michael D. Intrilligator (eds), *Handbook of Mathematical Economics* (Vol. I, Chapter 8, pp. 331–370). Amsterdam, Netherlands: North-Holland Publishing Company.

Sraffa, Piero (1960) *Production of Commodities by Means of Commodities: Prelude to a Critique of Economic Theory*. Cambridge, UK: Cambridge University Press.

Steinhaus, Hugo (1965) Games, an informal talk. *The American Mathematical Monthly* 72(5): 457–468.

Timpson, Christopher G. (2004) Quantum computers: the Church-Turing hypothesis versus the turing principle. In Christof Teuscher (ed.), *Alan Turing – Life and Legacy of a Great Thinker* (pp. 213–240). Berlin, Germany: Springer-Verlag.

van Dalen, Dirk (1999) Mystic, geometer and intuitionist: the life of L.E.J. Brouwer – Volume 2: *Hope and Disillusion*. Oxford: Clarendon Press.

van Lambalgen, Michiel (1987) Random sequences, Doctoral Dissertation, University of Amsterdam, 16 September, 1987.

Velupillai, K. Vela (1997) Expository notes on computability and complexity in (arithmetical) games. *Journal of Economic Dynamics and Control* 21(6): 955–979.

Velupillai, K. Vela (2000) *Computable Economics*. Oxford: Oxford University Press.

Velupillai, K. Vela (2005) The unreasonable ineffectiveness of mathematics in economics. *Cambridge Journal of Economics* 29(6): 849–872.

Velupillai, K. Vela (2006) The algorithmic foundations of computable general equilibrium theory. *Applied Mathematics and Computation* 179(1): 360–369.

Velupillai, K. Vela (2009) Uncomputability and undecidability in economic theory. *Applied Mathematics and Computation* 215(4): 1404–1416.

Velupillai, K. Vela (2009a) A computable economist's perspective on computational complexity, J. Barkley Rosser, Jr. (ed.), *The Handbook of Complexity Research* (Chapter 4, pp. 36–83). Cheltenham, Gloucestershire, UK: Edward Elgar Publishing Ltd.

Velupillai, K. Vela (2009b) *The Algorithmic Revolution in the Social Sciences: Mathematical Economics, Game Theory and Statistics*. Invited Lecture, presented at the Workshop on Information Theoretic Methods in Science and Engineering, Tampere, Finland, August, 17/19, 2009. Published in the Proceedings of WITMSE 2009.

Velupillai, K. Vela (2010a) In praise of anarchy in research and teaching. *Economic and Political Weekly* XLV(14): 51–55.

Velupillai, K. Vela (2010b) Foundations of boundedly rational choice and satisfying decisions. *Advances in Decision Sciences*, April, 2010.

Velupillai, K. Vela (2010c) Reflections on mathematical economics in the algorithmic mode. *New Mathematics and Natural Computation* Forthcoming in, Vol. 6.

Velupillai, K. Vela and Stefano Zambelli (2010) Computation in economics. Forthcoming In John Davis and Wade Hands (eds), *The Elgar Companion to Recent Economic Methodology*, Cheltenham: Edward Elgar, 2011.

von Neumann, John (1928) Zur theorie der gesellsschaftsspiele. *Mathematische Annalen* 100: 295–320.

von Neumann, John (1938/1945–6) A model of general economic equilibrium. *Review of Economic Studies* XIII(1): 1–9.

Wang, Hao (1960/1970) Toward mechanical mathematics, In *Logic, Computers and Sets* (Chapter IX, pp. 224–268). New York, NY: Chelsea Publishing Company.

Whitehead, Alfred North and Bertrand Russell (1927) *Principia Mathematica* (Vol. I–III). Cambridge, UK: Cambridge University Press.

Wittgenstein, Ludwig (1939) Wittgenstein's Lectures on the Foundations of Mathematics – Cambridge, 1939. In Cora Diamond (ed.). *From the Notes of R.G. Bosanquet, Norman Malcolm, Rush Rhees, and Yorick Smuthies*. Chicago, IL: The University of Chicago Press.

Zermelo, Ernst (1913) Über ein anwendung der mengenlehre auf die theorie des schachspiels. In E.W. Hobson and A.E.H. Love (eds). *Proceedings of the Fifth International Congress of Mathematicians* (11–28 August, 1912, Vol. 2, pp. 501–504). Cambridge, UK: Cambridge University Press.

3

AN ALGORITHMIC INFORMATION-THEORETIC APPROACH TO THE BEHAVIOUR OF FINANCIAL MARKETS

Hector Zenil and Jean-Paul Delahaye

1. Introduction

One of the main assumptions regarding price modelling for option pricing is that stock prices in the market behave as stochastic processes, that is, that price movements are log-normally distributed. Unlike classical probability, algorithmic probability theory has the distinct advantage that it can be used to calculate the likelihood of certain events occurring based on their information content. We investigate whether the theory of algorithmic information may account for some of the deviation from log-normal of the data of price movements accumulating in a power-law distribution.

We think that the power-law distribution may be an indicator of an information-content phenomenon underlying the market, and consequently that departures from log-normality can, given the accumulation of simple rule-based processes – a manifestation of hidden structural complexity – be accounted for by Levin's universal distribution, which is compatible with the distribution of the empirical data. If this is true, algorithmic probability could supply a powerful set of tools that can be applied to the study of market behaviour. Levin's distribution reinforces what has been empirically observed, viz. that some events are more likely than others, that events are not independent of each other and that their distribution depends on their information content. Levin's distribution is not a typical probability distribution inasmuch as it has internal structure placing the elements according to their structure specifying their exact place in the distribution, unlike other typical probability distributions that may indicate where some elements accumulate without specifying the particular elements themselves.

The methodological discipline of considering markets as algorithmic is one facet of the algorithmic approach to economics laid out in (Velupillai, 2000). The focus is

Nonlinearity, Complexity and Randomness in Economics, First Edition.
Stefano Zambelli and Donald A.R. George.

not exclusively on the institution of the market, but also on agents (of every sort), and on the behavioural underpinnings of agents (rational or otherwise) and markets (competitive or not, etc.).

We will show that the algorithmic view of the market as an alternative interpretation of the deviation from log-normal behaviour of prices in financial markets is also compatible with some common assumptions in classical models of market behaviour, with the added advantage that it points to the iteration of algorithmic processes as a possible cause of the discrepancies between the data and stochastic models.

We think that the study of frequency distributions and the application of algorithmic probability could constitute a tool for estimating and eventually understanding the information assimilation process in the market, making it possible to characterise the information content of prices.

The paper is organised as follows: In Section 2 a simplified overview of the basics of the stochastic approach to the behaviour of financial markets is introduced, followed by a section discussing the apparent randomness of the market. In Section 4, the theoretic-algorithmic approach we are proposing herein is presented, preceded by a short introduction to the theory of algorithmic information and followed by a description of the hypothesis testing methodology 5.4. In Section 6.2.1, tables of frequency distributions of price direction sequences for five different stock markets are compared to equiprobable (normal independent) sequences of length 3 and 4 to length 10 and to the output frequency distributions produced by algorithmic means. The alternative hypothesis, that is that the market has an algorithmic component and that algorithmic probability may account for some of the deviation of price movements from log-normality is tested, followed by a backtesting Section 6.2 before introducing further considerations in Section 7 regarding common assumptions in economics. The paper ends with a short section that summarises conclusions and provides suggestions for further work in Section 8.

2. The Traditional Stochastic Approach

When events are (random) independent of each other they accumulate in a normal (Gaussian) distribution. Stock price movements are for the most part considered to behave independently of each other. The random-walk like evolution of the stock market has motivated the use of Brownian motion for modelling price movements.

Brownian motion and financial modelling have been historically tied together (Cont and Tankov, 2003), ever since Bachelier (1900) proposed to model the price S_t of an asset on the Paris stock market in terms of a random process of Brownian motion W_t applied to the original price S_0. Thus $S_t = S_0 + \sigma W_t$.

The process S is sometimes called a *log* (or *geometric*) *Brownian motion*. Data of price changes from the actual markets are actually too *peaked* to be related to samples from normal populations. One can get a more convoluted model based on this process introducing or restricting the amount of randomness in the model so that it can be adjusted to some extent to account for some of the deviation of the empirical data to the supposedly log-normality.

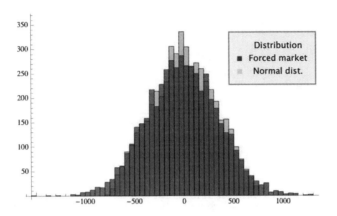

Figure 1. In a Normal Distribution any Event Is More or Less Like any Other.

A practical assumption in the study of financial markets is that the forces behind the market have a strong stochastic nature (see Figure 1 of a normal distribution and how a simulated market data may be forced to fit it). The idea stems from the main assumption that market fluctuations can be described by classical probability theory. The multiplicative version of Bachelier's model led to the commonly used Black–Scholes model, where the log-price S_t follows a random walk $S_t = S_0 \exp [\sigma\, t + \sigma W_t]$.

The kind of distribution in which price changes actually accumulate (see Figure 2) is a power law in which high-frequency events are followed by low-frequency events, with the short and very quick transition between them characterised by asymptotic behaviour. Perturbations accumulate and are more frequent than if normally distributed,

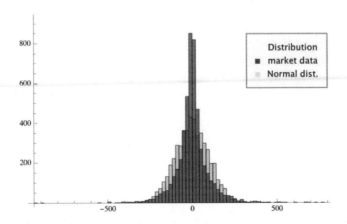

Figure 2. Events in a Long-Tailed (Power-Law) Distribution Indicate that Certain Days Are Not Like any Others.

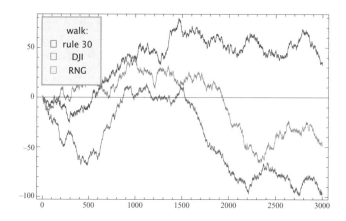

Figure 3. Simulated Brownian Walks Using a CA, an RNG and only one True Segment of Daily Closing Prices of the DJI.

as happens in the actual market, where price movements accumulate in long-tailed distributions. Such a distribution often points to specific kinds of mechanisms, and can often indicate a deep connection with other, seemingly unrelated systems.

As found by Mandelbrot (Mandelbrot, 1963) in the 1960s; prices do not follow a normal distribution; suggesting as it seems to be the case that some unexpected events happen more frequently than predicted by the Brownian motion model (see Figure 3). On the right one walk was generated by taking the central column of a rule 30 cellular automaton (CA), another walk by using the RandomInteger[] random number function built in *Mathematica*. Only one is an actual sequence of price movements for 3 000 closing daily prices of the Dow Jones Index (DJI).

3. Apparent Randomness in Financial Markets

The most obvious feature of essentially all financial markets is the apparent randomness with which prices tend to fluctuate. Nevertheless, the very idea of chance in financial markets clashes with our intuitive sense of the processes regulating the market. All processes involved seem deterministic. Traders do not only follow hunches but act in accordance with specific rules, and even when they do appear to act on intuition, their decisions are not random but instead follow from the best of their knowledge of the internal and external state of the market. For example, traders copy other traders, or take the same decisions that have previously worked, sometimes reacting against information and sometimes acting in accordance with it. Furthermore, nowadays a greater percentage of the trading volume is handled electronically, by computing systems (conveniently called algorithmic trading) rather than by humans. Computing systems are used for entering trading orders, for deciding on aspects of an order such as the timing, price and quantity, all of which cannot but be algorithmic by definition.

Algorithmic however, does not necessarily mean *predictable*. Several types of irreducibility, from non-computability to intractability to unpredictability, are entailed in most non-trivial questions about financial markets, as shown with clear examples in (Velupillai, 2000) and (Wolfram, 2002).

In (Wolfram, 2002) Wolfram asks whether the market generates its own randomness, starting from deterministic and purely algorithmic rules. Wolfram points out that the fact that apparent randomness seems to emerge even in very short timescales suggests that the randomness (or a source of it) that one sees in the market is likely to be the consequence of internal dynamics rather than of external factors. In economists' jargon, prices are determined by endogenous effects peculiar to the inner workings of the markets themselves, rather than (solely) by the exogenous effects of outside events.

Wolfram points out that pure speculation, where trading occurs without the possibility of any significant external input, often leads to situations in which prices tend to show more, rather than less, random-looking fluctuations. He also suggests that there is no better way to find the causes of this apparent randomness than by performing an almost step-by-step simulation, with little chance of beating the time it takes for the phenomenon to unfold – the timescales of real world markets being simply too fast to beat. It is important to note that the intrinsic generation of complexity proves the stochastic notion to be a convenient assumption about the market, but not an inherent or essential one.

Economists may argue that the question is irrelevant for practical purposes. They are interested in decomposing time series into a non-predictable and a presumably predictable signal in which they have an interest, what is traditionally called a trend. Whether one, both or none of the two signals is deterministic may be considered irrelevant as long as there is a part that is random-looking, hence most likely unpredictable and consequently worth leaving out.

What Wolfram's simplified model shows, based on simple rules, is that despite being so simple and completely deterministic, these models are capable of generating great complexity and exhibit (the lack of) patterns similar to the apparent randomness found in the price movements phenomenon in financial markets. Whether one can get the kind of crashes in which financial markets seem to cyclicly fall into depends on whether the generating rule is capable of producing them from time to time. Economists dispute whether crashes reflect the intrinsic instability of the market, or whether they are triggered by external events. In a model, in Lamper et al. (2002) for example, sudden large changes are internally generated suggesting large changes are more predictable – both in magnitude and in direction as the result of various interactions between agents. If Wolfram's intrinsic randomness is what leads the market one may think one could then easily predict its behaviour if this were the case, but as suggested by Wolfram's Principle of Computational Equivalence it is reasonable to expect that the overall collective behaviour of the market would look complicated to us, as if it were random, hence quite difficult to predict despite being or having a large deterministic component.

Wolfram's Principle of Computational Irreducibility (Wolfram, 2002) says that the only way to determine the answer to a computationally irreducible question is to

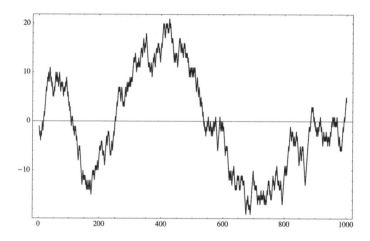

Figure 4. Patterns out of Nothing: Random Walk by 1 000 Data Points Generated Using the *Mathematica* Pseudo-Random Number Generator Based on a Deterministic Cellular Automaton.

perform the computation. According to Wolfram, it follows from his Principle of Computational Equivalence (PCE) that *'almost all processes that are not obviously simple can be viewed as computations of equivalent sophistication: when a system reaches a threshold of computational sophistication often reached by non-trivial systems, the system will be computationally irreducible'*.

Wolfram's proposal for modelling market prices would have a simple programme generating the randomness that occurs intrinsically (see Figure 4). A plausible, if simple and idealised behaviour is shown in the aggregate to produce intrinsically random behaviour similar to that seen in price changes. In Figure 4, one can see that even in some of the simplest possible rule-based systems, structures emerge from a random-looking initial configuration with low information content. Trends and cycles are to be found amidst apparent randomness.

An example of a simple model of the market as shown in (Wolfram, 2002), where each cell of a cellular automaton corresponds to an entity buying or selling at each step (see Figure 5). The behaviour of a given cell is determined by the behaviour of its two neighbours on the step before according to a rule. The plot on the left gives as a rough analog of a market price differences of the total numbers of black and white cells at successive steps. A rule like rule 90 is additive, hence reversible, which means that it does not destroy any information and has 'memory' unlike the random walk model. Yet, due to its random looking behaviour, it is not trivial shortcut the computation or foresee any successive step. There is some *randomness* in the initial condition of the cellular automaton rule that comes from outside the model, but the subsequent evolution of the system is fully deterministic. The way the series plot is calculated is written in *Mathematica* as follows: `Accumulate[Total/@(CA/.{0 → -1})]` with *CA* the output evolution of rule 90 after 100 steps.

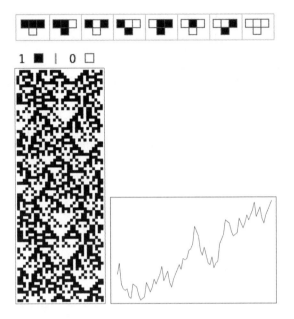

Figure 5. On the Top, the Rule 90 Instruction Table. On the Left the Evolution of Rule 90 from a Random Initial Condition for 100 Steps. On the Right the Total Differences at Every Step between Black and White Cells.

4. An Information-Theoretic Approach

From the point of view of cryptanalysis, the algorithmic view based on frequency analysis presented herein may be taken as a hacker approach to the financial market. While the goal is clearly to find a sort of password unveiling the rules governing the price changes, what we claim is that the password may not be immune to a frequency analysis attack, because it is not the result of a true random process but rather the consequence of the application of a set of (mostly simple) rules. Yet that doesn't mean one can crack the market once and for all, since for our system to find the said password it would have to outperform the unfolding processes affecting the market, which, as Wolfram's PCE suggests, would require at least the same computational sophistication as the market itself, with at least one variable modelling the information being assimilated into prices by the market at any given moment. In other words, the market password is partially safe not because of the complexity of the password itself but because it reacts to the cracking method.

Whichever kind of financial instrument one looks at, the sequences of prices at successive times show some overall trends and varying amounts of apparent randomness. However, despite the fact that there is no contingent necessity of true randomness behind the market, it can certainly look that way to anyone ignoring the generative processes, anyone unable to see what other, non-random signals may be driving market movements.

von Mises' approach to the definition of a random sequence, which seemed at the time of its formulation to be quite problematic, contained some of the basics of the modern approach adopted by Per Martin-Löf (Löf, 1966). It is during this time that the Keynesian (Keynes, 1936) kind of induction may have been resorted to as a starting point for Solomonoff's seminal work (Solomonoff, 1964) on algorithmic probability.

Martin-Löf gave the first suitable definition of a random sequence. Intuitively, an algorithmically random sequence (or random sequence) is an infinite sequence of binary digits that appears random to any algorithm. This contrasts with the idea of randomness in probability. In that theory, no particular element of a sample space can be said to be random. Martin-Löf's randomness has since been shown to admit several equivalent characterisations in terms of compression, statistical tests and gambling strategies.

The predictive aim of economics is actually profoundly related to the concept of predicting and betting. Imagine a random walk that goes up, down, left or right by one, with each step having the same probability. If the expected time at which the walk ends is finite, predicting that the expected stop position is equal to the initial position, it is called a martingale. This is because the chances of going up, down, left or right, are the same, so that one ends up close to one's starting position, if not exactly at that position. In economics, this can be translated into a trader's experience. The conditional expected assets of a trader are equal to his present assets if a sequence of events is truly random.

Schnorr (1971) provided another equivalent definition in terms of martingales (Downey and Hirschfeldt, 2010). The martingale characterisation of randomness says that no betting strategy implementable by any computer (even in the weak sense of constructive strategies, which are not necessarily computable) can make money betting on a random sequence. In a true random memory-less market, no betting strategy can improve the expected winnings, nor can any option cover the risks in the long term.

Over the last few decades, several systems have shifted towards ever greater levels of complexity and information density. The result has been a shift towards Paretian outcomes, particularly within any event that contains a high percentage of informational content.[1]

Departures from normality could be accounted for by the algorithmic component acting in the market, as is consonant with some empirical observations and common assumptions in economics, such as rule-based markets and agents.

If market price differences accumulated in a normal distribution, a rounding would produce sequences of 0 differences only. The *mean* and the *standard deviation* of the market distribution are used to create a normal distribution, which is then subtracted from the market distribution. Rounding by the normal distribution cover, the elements in the tail are *extracted* as shown in Figure 6.

4.1 *Algorithmic Complexity*

At the core of algorithmic information theory (AIT) is the concept of algorithmic complexity,[2] a measure of the quantity of information contained in a string of digits. The algorithmic complexity of a string is defined as the length (Kolmogorov, 1965;

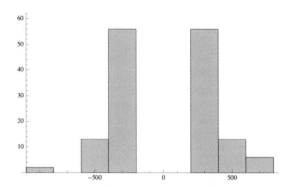

Figure 6. By Extracting a Normal Distribution from the Market Distribution, the Long-Tail Events Are Isolated.

Chaitin, 2001) of the shortest algorithm that, when provided as input to a universal Turing machine or idealised simple computer, generates the string. A string has maximal algorithmic complexity if the shortest algorithm able to generate it is not significantly shorter than the string itself, perhaps allowing for a fixed additive constant. The difference in length between a string and the shortest algorithm able to generate it is the string's degree of compressibility. A string of low complexity is therefore highly compressible, as the information that it contains can be encoded in an algorithm much shorter than the string itself. By contrast, a string of maximal complexity is incompressible. Such a string constitutes its own shortest description: there is no more economical way of communicating the information that it contains than by transmitting the string in its entirety. In AIT a string is algorithmically random if it is incompressible.

Algorithmic complexity is inversely related to the degree of regularity of a string. Any pattern in a string constitutes redundancy: it enables one portion of the string to be recovered from another, allowing a more concise description. Therefore highly regular strings have low algorithmic complexity, whereas strings that exhibit little or no pattern have high complexity.

The algorithmic complexity $K_U(s)$ of a string s with respect to a universal Turing machine U is defined as the binary length of the shortest programme p that produces as output the string s.

$$K_U(s) = \min\{|p|, U(p) = s\}$$

Algorithmic complexity conveys the intuition that a random string should be incompressible: no programme shorter than the size of the string produces the string.

Even though K is uncomputable as a function, meaning that there is no effective procedure (algorithm) to calculate it, one can use the theory of algorithmic probability to obtain exact evaluations of $K(s)$ for strings s short enough for which the halting problem can be solved for a finite number of cases due the size (and simplicity) of the Turing machines involved.

4.2 *Algorithmic Probability*

What traders often end up doing in turbulent price periods is to leave aside the 'any day is like any other normal day' rule, and fall back on their intuition, which leads to their unwittingly following a model we believe to be better fitted to reality and hence to be preferred at all times, not just in times of turbulence.

Intuition is based on weighting past experience, with experience that is closer in time being more relevant. This is very close to the concept of algorithmic probability and the way it has been used (and was originally intended to be used (Solomonoff, 1964)) in some academic circles as a theory of universal inductive inference (Hutter, 2007).

Algorithmic probability assigns to objects an *a priori* probability that is in some sense universal (Kirchherr and Li, 1997). This *a priori* distribution has theoretical applications in a number of areas, including inductive inference theory and the time complexity analysis of algorithms. Its main drawback is that it is not computable and thus can only be approximated in practise.

The concept of algorithmic probability was first developed by Solomonoff (1964) and formalised by Levin (1977). Consider an unknown process producing a binary string of length k bits. If the process is uniformly random, the probability of producing a particular string s is exactly 2^{-k}, the same as for any other string of length k. Intuitively, however, one feels that there should be a difference between a string that can be recognised and distinguished, and the vast majority of strings that are indistinguishable to us as regards whether the underlying process is truly random.

Assume one tosses a fair coin 20 three times and gets the following outcomes:

$$00000000000000000000$$

$$01100101110101001011$$

$$11101001100100101101$$

The first outcome would be very unlikely because one would expect a pattern-less outcome from a fair coin toss, one that resembles the second and third outcomes. In fact, it would be far more likely that a simple deterministic algorithmic process has generated this string. The same could be said for the market: one usually expects to see few if any patterns in its main indicators, mostly for the reasons set forth in Section 3. Algorithmic complexity captures this expectation of patternlessness by defining what a random-looking string looks like. On the other hand, algorithmic probability predicts that random-looking outputs are the exception rather than the rule when the generating process is algorithmic.

There is a measure which describes the expected output of an abstract machine when running a random programme. A process that produces a string s with a programme p when executed on a universal Turing machine U has probability $m(s)$. As p is itself a binary string, $m(s)$ can be defined as being the probability that the output of a universal Turing machine[3] U is s when provided with a sequence of fair coin flip inputs interpreted as a programme.

$$m(s) = \Sigma_{U(p)=s} 2^{-|p|} = 2^{-K(s)+O(1)}$$

That is, the sum over all the programmes p for which the universal Turing machine U outputs the string s and halts.

Levin's universal distribution is so called because, despite being uncomputable, it has the remarkable property (proven by Leonid Levin himself) that among all the lower semi-computable semi-measures, it dominates every other.[4] This makes Levin's universal distribution the optimal prior distribution when no other information about the data is available, and the ultimate optimal predictor (Solomonoff's original motivation (Solomonoff, 1964) was actually to capture the notion of learning by inference) when assuming the process to be algorithmic (or more precisely, carried out by a universal Turing machine). Hence the adjective 'universal'.

The algorithmic probability of a string is uncomputable. One way to calculate the algorithmic probability of a string is to calculate the universal distribution by running a large set of abstract machines producing an output distribution, as we did in (Delahaye and Zenil, 2007).

5. The Study of the Real Time Series versus the Simulation of an Algorithmic Market

The aim of this work is to study the direction and eventually the magnitude of time series of real financial markets. To that mean, we first develop a codification procedure translating financial series into binary digit sequences. Despite the convenience and simplicity of the procedure, the translation captures several important features of the actual behaviour of prices in financial markets. At the right level, a simplification of finite data into a binary language is always possible. Each observation measuring one or more parameters (e.g. price, trade name) is an enumeration of independent distinguishable values, a sequence of discrete values translatable into binary terms.[5]

5.1 *From AIT Back to the Behaviour of Financial Markets*

Different market theorists will have different ideas about the likely pattern of 0's and 1's that can be expected from a sequence of price movements. Random walk believers would favour random-looking sequences in principle. Other analysts may be more inclined to believe that patterned-looking sequences can be spotted in the market, and may attempt to describe and exploit these patterns, eventually deleting them.

In an early anticipation of an application of AIT to the financial market (Mansilla, 2001), it was reported that the information content of price movements and magnitudes seem to drastically vary when measured right before crashes compared to periods where no financial turbulence is observed. As described in Mansilla (2001), this means that sequences corresponding to critical periods show a qualitative difference compared to the sequences corresponding to periods of stability (hence prone to be modelled by the traditional stochastic models) when the information content of the market is very low (and when looks random as carrying no information). In Mansilla (2001), the concept of conditional algorithmic complexity is used to measure these differences in the time series of price movements in two different financial markets

(NASDAQ and the Mexican IPC), here we use a different algorithmic tool, that is the concept of algorithmic probability.

We will analyse the complexity of a sequence s of encoded price movements, as described in Section 6.2.1 We will see whether this distribution approaches one produced artificially – by means of algorithmic processes – in order to conjecture the algorithmic forces at play in the market, rather than simply assume a pervasive randomness. Exploitable or not, we think that price movements may have an algorithmic component, even if some of this complexity is disguised behind apparent randomness.

According to Levin's distribution, in a world of computable processes, patterns which result from simple processes are relatively likely, while patterns that can only be produced by very complex processes are relatively unlikely. Algorithmic probability would predict, for example, that consecutive runs of the same magnitude, that is, runs of pronounced falls and rises, and runs of alternative regular magnitudes have greater probability than random-looking changes. If one fails to discern the same simplicity in the market as is to be observed in certain other real world data sources (Zenil and Delahaye, 2010), it is likely due to the dynamics of the stock market, where the exploitation of any regularity to make a profit results in the deletion of that regularity. Yet these regularities may drive the market and may be detected upon closer examination. For example, according to the classical theory, based on the average movement on a random walk, the probability of strong crashes is nil or very low. Yet in actuality they occur in cycles over and over.

What is different in economics is the nature of the dynamics some of the data are subject to, as discussed in Section 3, which underscores the fact that patterns are quickly erased by economic activity itself, in the search for an economic equilibrium.

Assuming an algorithmic hypothesis, that is that there is a rule-based – as opposed to a purely stochastic – component in the market, one could apply the tools of the theory of algorithmic information, just as assuming random distributions led to the application of the traditional machinery of probability theory.

If this algorithmic hypothesis is true, the theory says that Levin's distribution is the optimal predictor. In other words, one could run a large number of machines to simulate the market, and m, the algorithmic probability based on Levin's universal distribution would provide accurate insights into the particular direction and magnitude of a price based on the fact that the market has a rule-based element. The correlation found in the experiments described in the next section 6.2.1 suggests that Levin's distribution may turn out to be a way to calculate and approximate this potentially algorithmic component in the market.

5.2 *Unveiling the Machinery*

When observing a certain phenomenon, its outcome f can be seen as the result of a process P. One can then ask what the probability distribution of P generating f looks like. A probability distribution of a process is a description of the relative number of times each possible outcome occurs in a number of trials.

In a world of computable processes, Levin's semi-measure (a.k.a universal distribution) establishes that patterns which result from simple processes (short programmes)

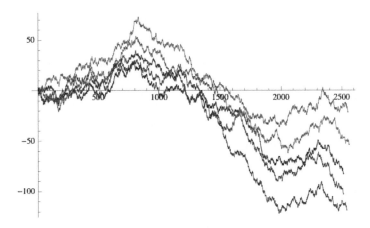

Figure 7. Series of Daily Closing Prices of Five of the Largest Stock Markets from 01/01/2000 to January 01/01/2010. The Best Sequence Length Correlation Suggests that Markets Catch Up with Each Other (Assimilate Each Others' Information) in about 7–10 Days on Average.

are likely, while patterns produced by complicated processes (long programmes) are relatively unlikely. Unlike other probability measures, Levin's semi-measure (denoted by m) is not only a probability distribution establishing that there are some objects that have a certain probability of occurring according to said distribution, it is also a distribution specifying the order of the particular elements in terms of their individual information content.

Figure 7 suggests that by looking at the behaviour of one market, the behaviour of the others may be predicted. But this cannot normally be managed quickly enough for the information to be of any actual use (in fact the very intention of succeeding in one market by using information from another may be the cause rather than the consequence of the correlation).

In the context of economics, if we accept the algorithmic hypothesis (that price changes are algorithmic, not random), m would provide the algorithmic probability of a certain price change happening, given the history of the price. An anticipation of the use of this prior distribution as an inductive theory in economics is to be found in Velupillai (2000). But following that model would require us to calculate the prior distribution m, which we know is uncomputable. We proceed by approaching m experimentally in order to show what the distribution of an algorithmic market would look like, and eventually use it in an inductive framework.

Once m is approximated, it can be compared to the distribution of the outcome in the real world (i.e. the empirical data on stock market price movements). If the output of a process approaches a certain probability distribution, one accepts, within a reasonable degree of statistical certainty, that the generating process is of the nature suggested by the distribution. If it is observed that an outcome s occurs with probability $m(s)$, and the data distribution approaches m, one would be persuaded, within the same degree of certainty, to accept a uniform distribution as the footprint of a random process (where events are independent of each other), that is, that the source of the data is suggested by the distribution *m*.

What Levin's distribution implies is that most rules are simple because they produce simple patterned strings, which algorithmically complex rules are unlikely to do. A simple rule, in terms of algorithmic probability, is the average kind of rule producing a highly frequent string, which according to algorithmic probability has a low random complexity (or high organised complexity), and therefore looks patterned. This is the opposite of what a complex rule would be, when defined in the same terms – it produces a pattern-less output, and is hence random-looking.

The outcomes of simple rules have short descriptions because they are less algorithmically complex, means that in some sense *simple* and *short* are connected, yet large rules may also be simple despite not being short in relative terms. And the outcomes of the application of simple rules tend to accumulate exponentially faster than the outcomes of complicated rules. This causes some events to occur more often than others and therefore to be dependent on each other. Those events happening more frequently will tend to drastically outperform other events and will do so by quickly beginning to follow the irregular pattern and doing so closely for a while.

The first task is therefore to produce a distribution by purely algorithmic means using abstract computing machines[6] – by running abstract computational devices like Turing machines and cellular automata (CA).

It is not only in times of great volatility that one can see that markets are correlated to each other (see Figure 7). This correlation means that, as may be expected, markets systematically react to each other. One can determine the information assimilation process time by looking at the correlations of sequences of daily closing prices of different lengths for five of the largest European and U.S. stock markets. It is evident that they react neither immediately nor after an interval of several days. As suggested by the table in Section 6.1.2, over a period of 20 years, from January 1990 to January 2010, the average assimilation time is about a week to a week and a half. For one thing, the level of confidence of the correlation confirms that even if some events may be seen as randomly produced, the reactions of the markets follow each other and hence are neither independent of each other nor completely random. The correlation matrix 6.1.2 exhibits the Spearman rank correlation coefficients, followed by the number of elements compared (number of sequence lengths found in one or another market), underlining the significance of the correlation between them.

5.3 *Binary Encoding of the Market Direction of Prices*

Market variables have three main indicators. The first is whether there is a significant price change (i.e. larger than, say, the random walk expectation), the second is the direction of a price change (rising or falling), and third, there is its magnitude. We will focus our first attempt on the direction of price changes, since this may be the most valuable of the three (after all whether one is likely to make or lose money is the first concern, before one ponders the magnitude of the possible gain or loss).

In order to verify that the market carries the algorithmic signal, the information content of the non-binary tuples can be collapsed to binary tuples. One can encode the price change in a single bit by 'normalizing' the string values, with the values of the entries themselves losing direction and magnitude but capturing price changes.

Prices are subject to such strong forces (interests) in the market that it would be naive to think that they could remain the same to any decimal fraction of precision, even if they were meant to remain the same for a period of time. In order to spot the algorithmic behaviour one has to provide some stability to the data by getting rid of precisely the kind of minor fluctuations that a random walk may predict. If not, one notices strong biases disguising the real patterns. For example, periods of price fluctuations would appear less likely than they are in reality if one allows decimal fluctuations to count as much as any other fluctuation.[7]

This is because from one day to another the odds that prices will remain exactly the same up to the highest precision is extremely unlikely, due to the extreme forces and time exposure they are subject to. Even though it may seem that at such a level of precision one or more decimal digits could represent a real price change, for most practical purposes there is no qualitative change when prices close to the hundreds, if not actually in the hundreds, are involved. Rounding the price changes to a decimal fraction provides some stability, for example, by improving the place of the 0^n tuple towards the top, because as we will see, it turns out to be quite well placed at the top once the decimal fluctuations have been gotten rid of. One can actually think of this as using the Brownian motion expectation to get rid of meaningless changes. In other words, the Brownian movement is stationary in our analysis, being the predictable (easy) component of the minor fluctuations, while the actual objects of study are the wilder dynamics of larger fluctuations. We have changed the focus from what analysts are used to considering as the signal, to noise, and recast what they consider noise as the algorithmic footprint in empirical data.

5.3.1 Detecting Rising versus Falling

As might be expected given the apparent randomness of the market and the dynamics to which it is subject, it would be quite difficult to discern clear patterns of rises versus falls in market prices.

The asymmetry in the rising and falling ratio is explained by the pattern deletion dynamic. While slight rises and falls have the same likelihood of occurring, making us think they follow a kind of random walk bounded by the average movement of Brownian motion, significant rises are quickly deleted by people taking advantage of them, while strong drops quickly worsen because of people trying to sell rather than buy at a bargain. This being so, one expects to see longer sequences of drops than of rises, but actually one sees the contrary, which suggests that periods of optimism are actually longer than periods of pessimism, though periods of pessimism are stronger in terms of price variation. In Mansilla (2001) it was reported that the information content of price movements and magnitudes seem to drastically vary when measured to intervals of high volatility (particularly right before crashes) compared to periods where no financial turbulence is observed.

We construct a binary series associated to each real time series of financial markets as follows. Let $\{p_t\}$ be the original time series of daily closing prices of a financial market for a period of time t. Then each element $b_i \in \{b_n\}$, the time series of price differences, with $n = t - 1$, is calculated as follows:

$$b_i = \begin{cases} 1 & p_{i+1} > p_i \\ 0 & p_{i+1} \leq p_i \end{cases}$$

The frequency of binary tuples of short lengths will be compared to the frequency of binary tuples of length the same length obtained by running abstract machines (deterministic Turing machines and one-dimensional CA).

5.4 Calculating the Algorithmic Time Series

Constructing Levin's distribution m from abstract machines is therefore necessary in order to strengthen the algorithmic hypothesis. In order to make a meaningful comparison with what can be observed in a purely rule-governed market, we will construct from the ground up an experimental distribution by running algorithmic machines (Turing machines and CA). An abstract machine consists of a definition in terms of input, output and the set of allowable operations used to turn the input into the output. They are of course algorithmic by nature (or by definition).

The Turing machine model represents the basic framework underlying many concepts in computer science, including the definition of algorithmic complexity. In this paper we use the output frequency distribution produced by running a finite, yet very large set of Turing machines with empty input as a means to approximate m. There are 11 019 960 576 four-state two-symbol Turing machines (for which the halting condition is known, thanks to the Busy Beaver game). The conception of the experiment and further details are provided in Delahaye and Zenil (2007) and Zenil and Delahaye (2010). These Turing machines produced an output, from which a frequency distribution of tuples was calculated and compared to the actual time series from the market data produced by the stock markets encoded as described in 5.3.1. A forthcoming paper provides more technical details (Delahaye and Zenil, 2011).

Also, a frequency distribution from a sample of 10 000 four-colour totalistic CA was built from a total of 1 048 575 possible four-colour totalistic CA, each rule starting from an random initial configuration of 10–20 black and white cells, and running for 100 steps (hence arbitrarily halted). Four-colour totalistic CA produce four-symbol sequences. However only the binary were taken into consideration, with the purpose of building a binary frequency distribution. The choice of this CA space was dictated by the fact that the smallest CA space is too small, and the next smallest space too large to extract a significant enough sample from it. Having chosen a sample of four-colour totalistic CA, the particular rules sample was randomly generated.

For all the experiments, stock market data sets (of daily closing prices) used covered the same period of time: from January 1990 to January 2010. The stock market code names can be readily connected with their full index names or symbols.

Spearman's rank coefficient was the statistical measure of the correlation between rankings of elements in the frequency distributions. As is known, if there are no repeated data values, a perfect Spearman correlation of $+1$ or -1 occurs when each of the variables is a perfect monotone function of the other. While 1 indicates perfect correlation (i.e. in the exact order), -1 indicates perfect negative correlation (i.e. perfect inverse order).

6. Experiments and Results

It is known that for any finite series of a sequence of integer values, there is a family of countable infinite computable functions that fit the sequence over its length. Most of them will be terribly complicated, and any attempt to find the simplest accounting for the sequence will face uncomputability. Yet using the tools of AIT, one can find the simplest function for short sequences by deterministic means, testing a set of increasingly complex functions starting from the simplest and proceeding until the desired sequence assuring the simplest fit is arrived at. Even if the likelihood of remaining close to the continuation of the series remains low, one can recompute the sequence and find good approximations for short periods of time.

The following experiment uses the concept of algorithmic complexity to find the best fit in terms of the simplest model fitting the data, assuming the source to be algorithmic (rule-based).

6.1 *Rankings of Price Variations*

In the attempt to capture the price change phenomenon in the stock market, we have encoded price changes in binary strings. The following are tables capturing the rise and fall of prices and their occurrence in a ranking classification.

6.1.1 *Carrying an Algorithmic Signal*

Some regularities and symmetries in the sequence distribution of price directions in the market may be accounted for by an algorithmic signal, but they also follow from a normal distribution. For example, the symmetry between the left- and right-hand sides of the Gaussian curve with zero skewness means that reverted and inverted strings (i.e. consecutive runs of events of prices going up or down) will show similar frequency values, which is also in keeping with the intuitive expectation of the preservation of complexity invariant to certain basic transformations (a sequence of events 1111... are equally likely to occur as 0000..., or 0101... and 1010...).

This means that one would expect n consecutive runs of rising prices to be as likely as n consecutive runs of falling prices. Some symmetries, however, are broken in particular scenarios. In the stock market for example, it is very well known that sequences of drastic falls are common from time to time, but never sequences of drastic price increases, certainly not increases of the same magnitude as the worst price drops. And we witnessed such a phenomenon in the distributions from the Dow Jones Index (DJI). Some other symmetries may be accounted for by business cycles engaged in the search for economic equilibrium.

6.1.2 Correlation Matrices

With algorithmic probability in hand, one may predict that alternations and consecutive events of the same type and magnitude are more likely, because they may be algorithmically more simple. One may, for example, expect to see symmetrical events occurring more often, with reversion and complementation occurring together in groups (i.e. a string 10^n occurring together with 0^n1 and the like). In the long-term, business cycles and economic equilibria may also be explained in information theoretic terms, because for each run of events there are the two complexity-preserving symmetries, reversion and complementation, that always follow their counterpart sequences (the unreversed and complement of the complement), producing a cyclic type of behaviour.

The correlations shown in Table 2 indicate what is already assumed in looking for cycles and trends, viz. that these underlying cycles and trends in the markets are more prominent when *deleting* Brownian *noise*. As shown later, this may be an indication that the tail of the distribution has a stronger correlation than the elements covered by the normal curve, as could be inferred from the definition of a random walk (i.e. that random walks are not correlated at all).

The entries in each comparison table (Table 1 to 7) consist of the Spearman coefficient followed by the number of elements compared. Both determine the level of confidence and are therefore essential for estimating the correlation. Rows compare different stock markets over different sequence lengths of daily closing prices, represented by the columns. It is also worth noting when the comparisons, such as in Table 2, displayed no negative correlations.

6.2 Backtesting

Applying the same methodology over a period of a decade, from 1980 to 1990 (old market), to three major stock markets for which we had data for the said period of time, similar correlations were found across the board, from weak to moderately weak – though the trend was always towards positive correlations.

6.2.1 Old Market versus CA Distribution

The distributions indicate that price changes are unlikely to rise by more than a few points for more than a few days, while greater losses usually occur together and over longer periods. The most common sequences of changes are alternations. It is worth noticing that sequences are grouped together by reversion and complementation relative to their frequency, whereas traditional probability would have them occur in no particular order and with roughly the same frequency values.

Table 1. Stock Market versus Stock Market.

Market vs. Market	4	5	6	7	8	9	10
CAC40 vs. DAX	0.059|16	0.18|32	0.070|62	0.37|109	0.48|119	0.62|87	0.73|55
CAC40 vs. DJIA	0.31|16	0.25|32	0.014|62	0.59|109	0.27|124	0.34|95	0.82|51
CAC40 vs. FTSE350	0.16|16	-0.019|32	-0.18|63	0.15|108	0.59|114	0.72|94	0.73|62
CAC40 vs. NASDAQ	0.30|16	0.43|32	0.056|63	0.16|111	0.36|119	0.32|88	0.69|49
CAC40 vs. SP500	0.14|16	0.45|31	-0.085|56	-0.18|91	0.16|96	0.49|73	0.84|45
DAX vs. DJIA	0.10|16	-0.14|32	0.13|62	0.37|110	0.56|129	0.84|86	0.82|58
DAX vs. FTSE350	0.12|16	-0.029|32	0.12|63	0.0016|106	0.54|118	0.81|89	0.80|56
DAX vs. NASDAQ	0.36|16	0.35|32	0.080|62	0.014|110	0.64|126	0.55|96	0.98|48
DAX vs. SP500	0.38|16	0.062|31	-0.20|56	-0.11|88	0.11|94	0.43|76	0.63|49
DJIA vs. FTSE350	0.35|16	-0.13|32	-0.022|63	0.29|107	0.57|129	0.76|99	0.86|56
DJIA vs. NASDAQ	-0.17|16	-0.13|32	0.0077|62	0.079|112	0.70|129	0.57|111	0.69|64
DJIA vs. SP500	-0.038|16	0.32|31	-0.052|55	0.14|89	0.37|103	0.32|86	0.60|59
FTSE350 vs. NASDAQ	0.36|16	0.38|32	-0.041|63	0.54|108	0.68|126	0.57|107	0.66|51
FTSE350 vs. SP500	0.50|16	0.50|31	0.12|56	-0.11|92	0.25|101	0.26|96	0.29|66
NASDAQ vs. SP500	0.70|16	0.42|31	0.20|56	0.024|91	0.41|111	0.23|102	0.42|61

Table 2. In Contrast, when the Markets are Compared to Random Price Movements, Which Accumulate in a Normal Curve, They Exhibit no Correlation or Only a Very Weak Correlation, as Shown in Section 6.1.2.

Market vs. Market	4	5	6	7	8	9	10
CAC40 vs. DAX	0.58|11	0.58|15	0.55|19	0.37|26	0.59|29	0.55|31	0.60|28
CAC40 vs. DJIA	0.82|11	0.28|15	0.28|21	0.29|24	0.52|29	0.51|32	0.33|36
CAC40 vs. FTSE350	0.89|11	0.089|15	0.41|20	0.17|22	0.59|30	0.28|28	0.30|34
CAC40 vs. NASDAQ	0.69|11	0.27|14	0.28|18	0.44|23	0.30|30	0.17|34	0.61|30
CAC40 vs. SP500	0.85|11	0.32|15	0.49|20	0.55|24	0.42|33	0.35|35	0.34|36
DAX vs. DJIA	0.76|11	0.45|16	0.56|20	0.35|26	0.34|28	0.25|35	0.24|33
DAX vs. FTSE350	0.61|11	0.30|16	0.58|19	0.14|25	0.30|29	0.34|30	0.21|31
DAX vs. NASDAQ	0.40|11	0.27|16	0.36|18	0.75|25	0.28|29	0.28|35	0.50|33
DAX vs. SP500	0.14|12	0.36|17	0.72|20	0.64|28	0.42|31	0.52|34	0.51|32
DJIA vs. FTSE350	0.71|11	0.30|16	0.63|20	0.71|22	0.21|28	0.28|31	0.35|33
DJIA vs. NASDAQ	0.58|11	0.52|15	0.33|19	0.58|23	0.46|29	0.49|37	0.51|35
DJIA vs. SP500	0.70|11	0.20|16	0.45|21	0.29|26	0.35|32	0.37|36	0.55|36
FTSE350 vs. NASDAQ	0.73|11	0.57|15	0.70|17	0.48|23	0.62|28	0.34|33	0.075|35
FTSE350 vs. SP500	0.66|11	0.65|16	0.56|19	0.18|24	0.64|32	0.32|32	0.52|38
NASDAQ vs. SP500	0.57|11	0.37|15	0.41|18	0.32|24	0.30|34	0.19|35	0.35|40

Table 3. When Random Price Movements Are Compared to Rounded Prices of the Market (Denoted by 'r. Market' to Avoid Accumulation in the Normal Curve) the Correlation Coefficient is too Weak, Possessing no Significance at all. This may Indicate that it is the Prices Behaving and Accumulating in the Normal Curve that Effectively Lead the Overall Correlation.

r. Market vs. Random	4	5	6	7	8	9	10
DJIA vs. random	−0.050|16	0.080|31	−0.078|61	0.065|96	0.34|130	0.18|120	0.53|85
SP500 vs. random	0.21|16	−0.066|30	0.045|54	−0.16|81	0.10|99	0.29|87	0.32|57
NASDAQ vs. random	0.12|16	−0.095|31	0.11|60	0.14|99	0.041|122	0.29|106	0.57|68
FTSE350 vs. random	0.16|16	−0.052|31	0.15|61	0.14|95	0.30|122	0.50|111	0.37|77
CAC40 vs. random	0.32|16	−0.15|31	−0.13|60	0.16|99	0.19|119	0.45|109	0.36|78
DAX vs. random	0.33|16	0.023|31	0.20|60	0.14|95	0.26|129	0.31|104	0.31|77

Table 4. Comparison between the Daily Stock Market Sequences versus an Hypothesised Log-Normal Accumulation of Price Directions.

Market vs. Random	4	5	6	7	8	9	10
DJIA vs. random	0.21|12	−0.15|17	0.19|23	−0.033|28	−0.066|33	0.31|29	0.64|15
SP500 vs. random	−0.47|12	−0.098|17	−0.20|25	0.32|31	0.20|38	0.41|29	0.32|20
NASDAQ vs. random	−0.55|11	−0.13|16	−0.093|20	0.18|26	0.015|37	0.30|35	0.38|25
FTSE350 vs. random	−0.25|11	−0.24|16	−0.053|22	−0.050|24	−0.11|31	0.25|23	0.49|13
CAC40 vs. random	−0.12|11	−0.14|15	0.095|22	0.23|26	0.18|30	0.36|23	0.44|14
DAX vs. random	0.15|12	−0.067|18	−0.12|24	0.029|31	0.31|32	0.27|27	0.59|15

Table 5. The Comparison to TM Revealed Day Lengths Better Correlated than other, Although their Significance Remained Weak and Unstable, with a Tendency, however, to Positive Correlations.

Market vs. TM	5	6	7	8	9	10
DJIA vs. TM	0.42|16	0.20|21	0.42|24	−0.021|35	−0.072|36	0.20|47
SP500 vs. TM	0.48|18	0.30|24	−0.070|32	0.32|39	0.26|47	0.40|55
NASDAQ vs. TM	0.67|17	0.058|25	0.021|32	0.26|42	0.076|49	0.17|57
FTSE350 vs. TM	0.30|17	0.39|22	0.14|29	0.43|36	0.013|41	0.038|55
CAC40 vs. TM	0.49|17	0.026|25	0.41|32	0.0056|38	0.22|47	0.082|56

Table 6. When Compared to the Distribution from Cellular Automata, the Correlation was Greater. Each Column had Pairs of Score means: (−0.09, 16), (0.17, 32), (0.09, 64), (0.042, 116), (0.096, 144), (0.18, 119), (0.41, 67) for 4 to 10 Days, for which the Last 2 (9 and 10 days Long) Have Significant Levels of Correlation According to their Critical Values and the Number of Elements Compared.

Market vs. CA	4	5	6	7	8	9	10
DJIA vs. CA	−0.14|16	0.28|32	−0.084|63	−0.049|116	0.10|148	0.35|111	0.51|59
SP500 vs. CA	−0.16|16	0.094|32	0.0081|64	0.11|116	0.088|140	0.17|117	0.40|64
NASDAQ vs. CA	0.065|16	0.25|32	0.19|63	0.098|116	0.095|148	0.065|131	0.36|65
FTSE350 vs. CA	−0.16|16	−0.15|32	0.12|64	−0.013|120	−0.0028|146	0.049|124	0.42|76
CAC40 vs. CA	−0.035|16	0.36|32	0.21|64	0.064|114	0.20|138	0.25|114	0.33|70

Table 7. Comparison Matrix of Frequency Distributions of Daily Price Directions of Three Stock Markets from 1980 to 1990.

Old Market vs. CA	4	5	6	7	8	9	10
DJIA vs. CA	0.33|10	0.068|16	0.51|21	0.15|28	−0.13|31	0.12|32	0.25|29
SP500 vs. CA	0.044|13	0.35|19	0.028|24	0.33|33	0.45|33	0.00022|30	0.37|34
NASDAQ vs. CA	0.45|10	0.20|17	0.27|24	0.16|30	0.057|31	0.11|34	0.087|32

Table 8. 3-Tuples Distribution from the DJI Price Difference Time Series for the Past 80 Years. 1 Means that a Price Rose, 0 that it Fell or Remained the Same as Described in the Construction of the Binary Sequence b_n as Described in Section 5.3.1 and Partitioned in 3-Tuples for this Example. By Rounding to the Nearest Multiple of .4 (i.e. Dismissing Decimal Fraction Price Variations of this Order) Some More Stable Patterns Start to Emerge.

Tuple	Prob.
000	0.139
001	0.130
111	0.129
011	0.129
100	0.129
110	0.123
101	0.110
010	0.110

Table 9. 3-Tuples from the Output Distribution Produced by Running all 4-state 2-Symbol Turing Machines Starting from an Empty Tape First on a Background of 0's and then Running it Again on a Background of 1's to Avoid Asymmetries Due to the Machine Formalism Convention.

Tuple	Prob.
000	0.00508
111	0.00508
001	0.00488
011	0.00488
100	0.00488
110	0.00468
010	0.00483
101	0.00463

Tables 8 and 9 illustrate the kind of frequency distributions from the stock markets (in this case for the DJI) over tuples of length 3 with which distributions from the market data were compared with and its statistical correlation evaluated section between four other stock markets and over larger periods of time up to 10 closing daily prices.

6.3 *Algorithmic Inference of Rounded Price Directions*

Once with the tuples distributions calculated and a correlation found, one can apply Solomonoff's (Solomonoff, 1964) concept algorithmic inference. Let's say that by looking two days behind of daily closing prices one sees two consecutive losses. The algorithmic inference will say that with probability 0.129 the third day will be a loss again. In fact, as we now know, algorithmic probability will suggest that with higher probability the next day will only repeat the last values of any run of 1's or 0's and the empirical distribution from the market will tell us that runs of 1 s (gains) are more likely than consecutive losses (before the rounding process deleting the smallest price movements) without taking into account their magnitude (as empirically known, losses are greater than gains, but gains are more sustainable), but runs of consecutive 0's (losses) will be close or even more likely than consecutive losses after the rounding process precisely because gains are smaller in magnitude.

To calculate the algorithmic probability of a price direction b_i of the next closing price by looking n consecutive daily rounded prices behind, is given by

$$P(b_i) = m(b_{i-n} \ldots b_i)$$

That is, the algorithmic probability of the string constituted by the n consecutive price directions of the days before followed by the possible outcome to be estimated, with m Levin's semi-measure described in equation (6.3). It is worth noting however that the inference power of this approach is limited by the correlation found between the market's long tails and the distributions calculated by means of exhaustive computation. Tables with distributions for several tuple lengths and probability values will be available in Delahaye and Zenil (2011), so that one can empirically calculate m by means of the results of exhaustive computation.

For example, the algorithmic model predicts a greater incidence of simple signatures as trends under the *noise* modelled by the Brownian motion model, such as signatures 000... of price stability. It also predicts that random-looking signatures of higher volatility will occur more if they are already occurring, a signature in unstable times where the Brownian motion no longer works in these kind of events outside the main Bell curve.

7. Further Considerations

7.1 *Rule-Based Agents*

For sound reasons, economists are used to standardising their discussions by starting out from certain basic assumptions. One common assumption in economics is that actors in the market are decision makers, often referred to as *rational agents*. According to this view, rational agents make choices by assessing possible outcomes and assigning a utility to each in order to make a decision. In this rational choice model, all decisions are arrived at by a *rational* process of weighing costs against benefits, and not randomly.

An agent in economics or a player in game theory is an actor capable of decision making. The idea is that the agent initiates actions, given the available information, and tries to maximise his or her chances of success (traditionally their personal or collective utilities), whatever the ultimate goal may be. The algorithm that each agent takes may be non-deterministic, which means that the agent may make decisions based on probabilities, not that at any stage of the process a necessarily truly random choice is made. It actually doesn't matter much whether their actions may be perceived as mistaken, or their utility questioned. What is important is that agents follow rules, or if any chance is involved there is another large part in it not random at all (specially when one takes into consideration the way algorithmic trading is done). The operative assumption is that the individual has the cognitive ability to weigh every choice he/she makes, as opposed to taking decisions stochastically. This is particularly true when there is nothing else but computers making the decisions.

This view, wherein each actor can be viewed as a kind of automaton following his or her own particular rules, does not run counter to the stance we adopt here, and it is in perfect agreement with the algorithmic approach presented herein (and one can expect the market to get more algorithmic as more automatization is involved). On the contrary, what we claim is that if this assumption is made, then the machinery of the theory of computation can be applied, particularly the theory of algorithmic information (AIT). Hence market data can be said to fall within the scope of algorithmic probability.

Our approach is also compatible with the emergent field of behavioural economics (Camerer et al., 2003), provided the set of cognitive biases remain grounded in rules. Rules followed by emotional (or non-rational) traders can be as simple as imitating behaviour, repeating from past experience, acting out of fear, taking advice from others or following certain strategy. All these are algorithmic in nature in that they are rule based, despite their apparent idiosyncrasy (assuming there are no real clairvoyants with true metaphysical powers). Even though they may look random, what we claim, on the basis of algorithmic probability and Levin's distribution, is that most of these behaviours follow simple rules. It is the accumulation of simple rules rather than the exceptional complicated ones which actually generate trends.

If the market turns out to be based on simple rules and driven by its intrinsic complexity rather than by the action of truly random external events, the choice or application of rational theory would be quite irrelevant. In either case, our approach remains consistent and relevant. Both the rational and, to a large extent, the behavioural agent assumptions imply that what we are proposing here is that algorithmic complexity can be directly applied to the field of market behaviour, and that our model comes armed with a natural toolkit for analysing the market, viz. algorithmic probability.

7.2 The Problem of Over-Fitting

When looking at a set of data following a distribution, one can claim, in statistical terms, that the source generating the data is of the nature that the distribution suggests. Such is the case when a set of data follows a model, where depending on certain variables, one can say with some degree of certitude that the process generating the data follows the model.

It seems to be well known and largely accepted among economists that one can basically fit anything to anything else, and that this has shaped most of the research in the field, producing a sophisticated toolkit dictating how to achieve this fit as well as how much of a fit is necessary for particular purposes, even though such a fit may have no relevance either to the data or to particular forecasting needs, being merely designed to produce an instrument with limited scope fulfilling a specific purpose.

However, a common problem is the problem of over-fitting, that is, a false model that may fit perfectly with an observed phenomenon. A statistical comparison cannot actually be used to categorically prove or disprove a difference or similarity, only to favour one hypothesis over another.

To mention one of the arbitrary parameters that we might have taken, there is the chosen rounding. We found it interesting that the distributions from the stock markets were sometimes unstable to the rounding process of prices. Rounding to the closest .4 was the threshold found to allow the distribution to stabilise. This instability may suggest that there are two different kinds of forces acting, one producing very small and likely negligible price movements (in agreement to the random walk expectation), and other producing the kind of qualitative changes in the direction of prices that we were interested in. In any case this simply results in the method only being able to predict changes of the order of magnitude of the rounding proceeding from the opposite direction, assuming that the data are not random, unlike the stochastic models.

Algorithmic probability rests upon two main principles: the principle of multiple explanations, which states that one should keep all hypotheses that are consistent with the data, and a second principle known as Occam's razor, which states that when inferring causes, entities should not be multiplied beyond necessity, or, alternatively, that among all hypotheses consistent with the observations, the simplest should be favoured. As for the choice of an *a priori* distribution over a hypothesis, this amounts to assigning simpler hypotheses a higher probability and more complex ones a lower probability. So this is where the concept of algorithmic complexity comes into play.

As proven by Levin and Solomonoff, the algorithmic probability measure (the universal distribution) will outperform any other, unless other information is available that helps to foresee the outcome, in which case an additional variable could be added to the model to account for this information. But since we've been suggesting that information will propagate fast enough even though the market is not stochastic in nature, deleting the patterns and making them unpredictable, any additional assumption only complicates the model. In other words, Levin's universal distribution is optimal over all non-random distributions (Levin, 1973), in the sense that the algorithmic model is by itself the simplest model fitting the data when these data are produced by a process (as opposed to being randomly generated). The model is itself ill-suited to an excess of parameters argument because it basically assumes only that the market is governed by rules.

As proven by Solomonoff and Levin, any other model will simply overlook some of the terms of the algorithmic probability sum. So rather than being more precise, any other model will differ from algorithmic probability in that it will necessarily end up overlooking part of the data. In other words, there is no better model taking into account the data than algorithmic probability. As Solomonoff has claimed, one can't do any better. Algorithmic inference is a time-limited optimisation problem, and algorithmic probability accounts for it simply.

8. Conclusions and Further Work

When looking at a large-enough set of data following a distribution, one can in statistical terms safely assume that the source generating the data is of the nature that the distribution suggests. Such is the case when a set of data follows a normal distribution, where depending on certain statistical variables, one can, for example, say with a high degree of certitude that the process generating the data is of a random nature. If there is an algorithmic component in the empirical data of price movements in financial markets, as might be suggested by the distribution of price movements, AIT may account for the deviation from log-normality as argued herein. In the words of Velupillai (Velupillai, 2000) – quoting Clower (Clower, 1994) talking about Putnam's approach to a theory of induction (Putnam, 1975, 1990) – *This may help ground 'economics as an inductive science'* again.

One may well ask whether a theory which assumes that price movements follow an algorithmic trend ought not to be tested in the field to see whether it outperforms the current model. The truth is that the algorithmic hypothesis would easily outperform the current model, because it would account for recurrent periods of instability. The current theory, with its emphasis on short-term profits, is inclined to overlook these, for reasons that are probably outside the scope of scientific inquiry. In our understanding, the profits attributed to the standard current model are not really owed to the model as such, but rather to the mechanisms devised to control the risk-taking inspired by the overconfidence that the model generates.

In a strict sense, this paper describes the ultimate possible numerical simulation of the market when no further information about it is known (or cannot be known in practise) assuming no other (neither efficient markets nor general equilibrium) but actors following a set of rules and therefore to behave algorithmically at least at some extent hence potentially modelled by algorithmic probability.

The simulation may turn out to be of limited predictive value – for looking no more than a few days ahead and modelling weak signals – due to the deleting patterns phenomenon (i.e. the time during which the market assimilates new information). More experiments remain to be done which carefully encode and take into consideration other variables, such as the magnitude of prices, for example, looking at consecutive runs of gains or loses.

Acknowledgments

Hector Zenil wishes to thank Vela Velupillai and Stefano Zambelli for their kind invitation to take part in the workshop on Nonlinearity, Complexity and Randomness at the Economics Department of the University of Trento, and for their useful comments. Jason Cawley, Fred Meinberg, Bernard François and Raymond Aschheim provided helpful suggestions, for which many thanks. And to Ricardo Mansilla for pointing us out to his own work and kindly provided some data sets. Any misconceptions remain of course the sole responsibility of the authors.

Notes

1. For example, if one plots the frequency rank of words contained in a large corpus of text data versus the number of occurrences or actual frequencies, Zipf showed that one obtains a power-law distribution.
2. Also known as programme-size complexity, or Kolmogorov complexity.
3. A universal Turing machine is an abstraction of a general-purpose computer. Essentially, as proven by Alan Turing, a universal computer can simulate any other computer on an arbitrary input by reading both the description of the computer to be simulated and the input thereof from its own tape.
4. Since it is based on the Turing machine model, from which the adjective *universal* derives, the claim depends on the Church–Turing thesis.
5. Seeing it as a binary sequence may seem an oversimplification of the concept of a natural process and its outcome, but the performance of a physical experiment always yields data written as a sequence of individual observations sampling certain phenomena.
6. One would actually need to think of one-way non-erasing Turing machines to produce a suitable distribution analogous to what could be expected from a sequence of events that have an unrewritable past and a unique direction (the future), but the final result shouldn't be that different according to the theory.
7. The same practise is common in time series decomposition analysis, where the sole focus of interest is the average movement, in order that trends, cycles or other potential regularities may be discerned.

References

Bachelier, L. (1900) Théorie de la spéculation. *Annales Scientifiques de l'Ecole Normale Supérieure* 3(17): 21–86.

Camerer, C., Loewenstein, G. and Rabin, M. (2003) *Advances in Behavioral Economics.* Princeton: Princeton University Press.

Chaitin, G.J. (2001) *Exploring Randomness*, London: Springer Verlag.

Clower, R.W. (1994) Economics as an inductive science. *Southern Economic Journal* 60: 805–814.

Cont, R. and Tankov, P. (2003) *Financial Modelling with Jump Processes.* Boca Raton, FL: Chapman & Hall/CRC Press.

Delahaye, J.P. and Zenil, H. (2007) In C.S. Calude (ed.) *On the Kolmogorov-Chaitin complexity for short sequences Complexity and Randomness: From Leibniz to Chaitin.* World Scientific.

Delahaye, J.P. and Zenil, H. (2011) *Numerical Evaluation of Algorithmic Complexity for Short Strings: A Glance into the Innermost Structure of Randomness* arXiv:1101.4795v1 [cs.IT].

Downey, R.G. and Hirschfeldt, D. (2010) *Algorithmic Randomness and Complexity.* Berlin: Springer Verlag.

Hutter, M. (2007) On universal prediction and Bayesian confirmation. *Theoretical Computer Science* 384(1): 33–48.

Thompson, J.E. (2003) *Probability Theory: The Logic of Science.* Cambridge: Cambridge University Press.

Keynes, J.M. (1936) *General Theory of Employment Interest and Money.* London: Macmillan (reprinted 2007).

Kirchherr, W. and Li, M. (1997) The miraculous universal distribution. In *Mathematical Intelligencer*.

Kolmogorov, A.N. (1965) Three approaches to the quantitative definition of information. *Problems of Information and Transmission* 1(1): 1–7.

Lamper, D., Howison, S. and Johnson, N.F. (2002) Predictability of large future changes in a competitive evolving population. *Physical Review Letters* 88:11.

Levin, L. (1973) *Universal Search Problems*, 9(3): 265–266, submitted: 1972, A Survey of Russian Approaches to Perebor (Brute-force Search) Algorithms. *Annals of the History of Computing* 6(4): 384–400.

Levin, L. (1977) On a concrete method of assigning complexity measures. *Doklady Akademii nauk SSSR* 18(3): 727–731.

Mansilla, R. (2001) Algorithmic complexity in real financial markets. *Physica A* 301: 483–492.

Martin-Löf P. (1966) The definition of random sequences. *Information and Control* 9(6): 602–619.

Putnam, H. (1990) *The Meaning of the Concept of Probability in Application to Finite Sequences*. New York: Garland Publishing.

Putnam, H. (1975) *Probability and Confirmation. Mathematics, Matter and Methods: Philosophical papers I*, Cambridge: Cambridge University Press.

Reis, R. (2006) Inattentive Consumers. *Journal of Monetary Economics* 53(8): 1761–1800.

Schnorr, C.-P. (1971) *Zufälligkeit und Wahrscheinlichkeit. Eine algorithmische Begründung der Wahrscheinlichkeitstheorie*. Berlin: Springer.

Solomonoff, R.J. (1964) A formal theory of inductive inference: Parts 1 and 2. *Information and Control* 7:1–22 and 224–254.

Vela Velupillai, K. (2000) *Computable Economics*. Oxford: Oxford University Press.

Wolfram, S. (2002) *A New Kind of Science*. Champaign, IL: Wolfram Media.

Zenil H. and Delahaye, J.P. (2010) On the Algorithmic Nature of the World. In *Information and Computation*. World Scientific.

4

COMPLEXITY AND RANDOMNESS IN MATHEMATICS: PHILOSOPHICAL REFLECTIONS ON THE RELEVANCE FOR ECONOMIC MODELLING

Sundar Sarukkai

Complexity is an important paradigm across disciplines in the sciences, including economics. This paper will explore some philosophical ideas related to complexity. In particular, I will attempt to understand the ideas of complexity present in mathematics. This complexity is present in mathematics as a symbolic system as well as in the way it is applied in models. In the final section, I will argue that choosing or deciding on appropriate mathematics for a model is a problem of bounded rationality. Such a view is relevant for a deeper understanding of the use of mathematics in economics.

Rescher (1998) discusses philosophical ideas relevant to the idea of complexity. For Rescher, the world itself is complex, in a technical sense of the word. Not only does the natural world exhibit complexity but so do social processes. He extends this analogy to argue that science becomes progressively more complex, part of which leads to greater technological complexity. In general, he identifies three different themes that defines complexities – first is the variety and quantity of constituent elements of a complex system along with their interrelations, second are three ontological levels of complexity and third is the increasing cognitive resources needed for making sense of more complex systems.

Rescher agrees with many other writers when he points out that while there are no clear definitions for what exactly constitutes complexity, there is however one maxim that is commonly accepted: that complexity is the opposite of simplicity. He also describes different modes of complexity. First is the epistemic mode under which are placed descriptive, generative and computational complexity. Under the ontological modes he has three subsections – compositional, structural and functional

Nonlinearity, Complexity and Randomness in Economics, First Edition.
Stefano Zambelli and Donald A.R. George.

complexity. Compositional has constitutional (variety of elements) and taxonomical (heterogeneity of kinds); structural has organisational (different ways of arranging pieces, for example) and hierarchical (levels of simpler to the complex); functional has operational (types of functioning) and nomic (complexity of the laws governing the complex phenomenon).

There is another domain of complexity which has not been studied as much as it should have been. Language illustrates great complexity. In this paper I will only gesture to one facet of this complexity: meaning as an emergent phenomenon. Mathematics, as a language, is also a complex system. Here I will restrict myself to an analysis of the question of meaning in mathematics in order to illustrate one aspect of this complexity.

1. The Complexity of Mathematics

Foote (2007) suggests that mathematics itself (or parts of it) may be a complex system. Just as physical systems show complex behaviour so too does mathematics: 'areas of mathematics itself may be viewed as complex systems exhibiting many of the characteristics of the physical structures, including discernible "layers" closely analogous to microscopic or macroscopic strata in physics, biology, and other sciences' (Foote, 2007, p. 410).

Finite group theory is a paradigm example of a complex system. Foote describes the basic outline of finite groups and their classification. He also notes that, although deep, finite group theory need not be seen as 'complex', particularly because it is deterministic. However, by looking at the complex as set of interrelated locals leading to global properties, he sees that there are three 'layers' in this theory. Classification of finite simple groups has been a long drawn process and eventually required, as he says, '10,000 to 15,000 journal pages spread over some 500 articles, written mostly between 1950 and 1980 by more than 100 mathematicians. This is the genome project of finite group theory!'

Foote argues that this classification is a 'prototype for the study of other complex systems'. Merely breaking a group into its simple factors does not capture the complexities of classification. Like a paradigm case of complexity, what is more important is how the simple factors bond. Thus, a given finite group cannot be determined just because its factors are given. Foote points out that in general the 'extension problem' ('constructing larger groups from smaller constituents') is common to mathematical structures and even in the case of finite groups is unattainable. Thus classification itself is an example of complexity in mathematics.

Foote also points out that defining complexity specifically – such as through emergence – might be too limited. More broadly, 'a legitimate hallmark' of complexity is 'unexpected behavior that leads to deeper understanding of the system or relationships to other phenomena not heretofore considered relevant to the system' (Foote, 2007, p. 412). His example of classification of finite groups is one such example of complexity.

However, in the way Foote characterises complexity in terms of 'unexpected behaviour', much, if not all, of mathematics will be complex. We can see this very clearly in the case of applied mathematics. Here, often unexpected behaviour is discovered. Usually, a deeper understanding of the system arises through some specific use of mathematics. For example, the use of fibre bundles to describe gauge fields in physics not only gave a much deeper understanding but it also opened up new interpretations. The claim that complexity has to do only with 'deeper' understanding makes it too subjective and also too universal. Foote might agree for he also notes: 'The human element is an essential agent in the evolution of mathematics as a complex system, and the "layers" of complexity mirror the "knowledge states" in this adaptive process' (Foote, 2007, p. 412).

The example of groups invoked by Foote is indeed relevant to illustrate the nature of complexity in mathematics. However alongside, the shift to the way mathematics is used and applied actually illustrates the mode of complexity in equal measure. I will discuss this theme of applicability in the last section of this paper.

We can extend Foote's insight about complexity in mathematics in many ways. First of all, what is the complexity in mathematics a reflection of? When we say that a phenomenon is complex in nature, we are characterising certain characteristics of that phenomenon as being complex. In the case of mathematics, what exactly is complex? Equivalently, what elements of mathematics – both as a linguistic system as well as in its use – exhibit complexity? Even assuming that the classification of simple groups is complex, what exactly carries the mark of complexity? The act of classification? The description inherent in classification? If so, is the complexity a consequence of the descriptive process, that is, a reflection of the complexity of language? In other words, when we say that mathematics is complex, what sense can we ascribe to it? I suggest that invocation of the idea of complexity in the context of mathematics can be usefully understood in one specific context, that of mathematics-as-language. Complexity of mathematics as language can have two aspects – one, complexity of the language in itself and two, complexity in the way this language is used to describe the world. Foote's example illustrates the former and in the final section, I will discuss the latter.

While there are different ways of characterising mathematics, the idea of mathematics as language is still not taken very seriously. One tends to view mathematics largely in terms of logic, models, symbolic manipulation, rule-following and so on. However there is a fundamental impulse to mathematics and that is in its linguistic character, in particular, as a semiotic system. The primary mark of a language is the semiotic structure, as a set of signs. A semiotic system has discursive strategies that create this semiotic universe. Once we emphasise the semiotic aspect of languages in general, it is quite easy to see how mathematics functions as a language.

First, it will be useful to go back to the philosophical description of complexity in terms of epistemic and ontological categories. Rescher's description given earlier can be a starting point. The epistemic modes were the descriptive, generative and computational complexity. In the ontological modes there were three kinds – compositional, structural and functional complexity. There were two kinds of compositional complexity – one is constitutional, which captures the quantity and variety of elements, and the other taxonomical, which is about the heterogeneity of kinds. Mathematics, as a semiotic system, also exhibits these different kinds of complexity. In mathematics, there are a variety of mathematical entities which can be classified into 'kinds': numbers, sets, functions, matrices, groups and so on. However, there is an impulse in mathematics which attempts to describe one kind in terms of another. For example, instead of considering sets and numbers to be different kinds, there is an attempt to reduce numbers to sets. For mathematics, there is indeed a large variety of kinds and new mathematics is primarily the creation of new 'kinds'. In the case of groups, there is not only a category called the group but there are also different sub-categories of different kinds of groups such as finite groups, Lie groups, homotopy groups, homology and cohomology groups, all of which have their own unique properties.

The structural view of mathematics has many supporters (Shapiro, 1997). As described earlier, Rescher classifies complexity in terms of structure also. Under structural complexity he suggests two types – organisational, which is about how elements can be organised and arranged, and hierarchical, which is basically complexity related to levels, moving from the simplest to the more complex. Organisation complexity has to do with pattern making. There is a long history of making sense of mathematics in terms of patterns and pattern formation. The complexity that arises out of creating new patterns or following the rules for making patterns adds to the complexity of mathematics.

While these are some avenues to explore the idea of complexity in mathematics, I will, in what follows, restrict myself to a special kind of a problem in mathematics, namely, its unique writing strategies. Often, when one talks of mathematics, we ignore the written aspect of it. However, what is so unique to mathematics is that it is primarily a written system and uses very interesting strategies of writing (Sarukkai, 2002). To motivate this discussion, consider the alphabetic system in English. All words in English are formed from a given set of 26 alphabets. These limited alphabets are enough to create an inexhaustible set of words and sentences. Even if we acknowledge that there is something mysterious in this capacity to create a potentially infinite combination of words and sentences (e.g. note the importance of the poverty stimulus and novelty argument in language), there is really little that is 'complex' about it. In contrast, mathematical writing illustrates something quite radically different. I will argue later that mathematical writing is concerned with creating endless 'alphabets'. Moreover, in the case of English, we might discover complexity in the phenomenon of meaning. I will first discuss the possibility that meaning is an emergent phenomenon and then consider the role of meaning in mathematics. Emergence, as is well known, is an important marker of complexity.

2. Emergence and Meaning

We can discover one example of potentially complex behaviour in a natural language, like English, in the emergence of meaning. Given a set of alphabets alone, we cannot predict what kind of words can be meaningfully formed. In this sense, formation of words from alphabets is random (although there seem to be 'rules' like u follows q). Alphabets do not have meanings in themselves but words do; for example, 'c', 'a' and 't' in themselves do not have a meaning but the combination of 'c-a-t' or 'a-c-t' does. How does meaning emerge when alphabets are put together? In philosophy of language, there is an important debate – are words the units of meaning or sentences? That is, does meaning depend only on words or in the context of sentences? While there are supporting arguments for both sides, we only need to note the emergence of meaning can occur at different levels – either at the level of a word or of a sentence.

However is meaning an emergent phenomenon like other emergent properties? At the first instance, it might not seem to be so since meaning is thought to be arbitrary. There is nothing natural about meaning. It is not a property in the way other natural properties are. However this argument is only partly correct. It is indeed true that meaning emerges through the putting together of alphabets, phonemes, etc. This meaning can be arbitrary but it only implies that we cannot say *which* meaning emerges; that meaning *emerges* is undisputed. While it may be true that particular meanings for a word are accepted through convention, nevertheless it is the case that 'meaning' as such is generated when alphabets are put together. However, it is obvious that just putting alphabets together is not enough to guarantee meaning. So although I can create meaningful words like 'cat' and 'act' from 'a', 'c' and 't', other words like 'cta' or 'tca' do not possess meaning in the language as of now. However note that even these two words have the potential for meaning; if these words get into circulation for some reason or the other, they will acquire a conventional meaning. So what is acquired are only 'particular' meanings and not 'meaning' as such: the potential for meaning is already present in 'cta' and 'tca'. Thus, combining alphabets seem to be necessary but not sufficient for the emergence of meaning.

There have been some attempts to understand how meaning is generated in language. Gardenfors (1993) discusses how social meaning emerges from individual meaning. Moreover, he bases conventional meaning on the emergence of this social meaning. In attempting to answer how individual meanings can come together to give a collective, social meaning, he invokes the idea of emergence. However he does not invoke the notion of emergence in the context of individual meanings. One theory of meaning, a realist theory, holds that meaning is out there in the world and is extra-linguistic in some sense. So when we make meaning we are primarily matching the meaning we make in our 'minds' with the external meaning. In this manner, meaning is not reduced to a subjective act but has an external correlate which makes it possible to say whether something has a correct meaning or not. Meaning, for the realists, 'cannot be in the head'. In contrast, a cognitive theory of meaning suggests that meaning 'resides' in, and is created by, the individual. As Gardenfors notes, the motto for cognitive semanticists is that 'meanings are in the head' (Gardenfors, 1993, p. 288). In this approach, meanings are thought to be 'mental entities' and making meaning is to map language terms to these entities (unlike the realist view which maps language terms to the external world).

The cognitive model explains how we are able to associate meanings to linguistic expressions by matching it with existing mental entities. However what are these mental entities? How are they generated? Are they hard wired or *a priori* in some sense? However, there is a process which has to be understood prior to this matching and this is the emergence of these mental entities associated with meaning. In a restricted sense, individual meaning itself is an emergent phenomenon.[1]

There is an interesting connection with this view and an important theory of meaning that was held by Indian grammarians called the sphoṭa theory of meaning. Consider how meaning arises when we listen to language. When we hear a word we hear one phoneme after another, although given the extremely short time duration it might seem as if we hear the word as a whole and at one instant. The word is 'formed' after we hear all the phonemes. It is also exactly at that moment after all the phonemes are heard that the meaning of the word also becomes known. Therefore, it is the sound of the last phoneme along with the memories of the other phonemes, which occurred before it, that completes the word and thus 'discovers' the meaning of that word. (One can see how a similar argument works for writing: meaning emerges when the last alphabet is written along with the traces of the earlier alphabets.) For the grammarian Bharthari, sphoṭa is a mental entity that is directly perceived. This perception of it is the realisation of meaning (Coward, 1980; Bhattacharyya, 1998). At first glance, it seems as if the sphoṭa are similar to these mental entities corresponding to meaning. While one can see intriguing parallels between these descriptions, nevertheless a proper judgement has to take into account the different metaphysics that is pre-supposed for these descriptions. My task here is not to do this comparison but to illustrate how a powerful idea of meaning as 'emergence' is available in some philosophical traditions. The sphoṭa theory clearly illustrates how meaning comes to be, how it originates in the acts of speaking and writing.

3. Meaning and Mathematics

Do mathematical expressions have meaning like natural language terms do? Are there elements in mathematics that are equivalent to alphabets in natural language? Are mathematical expressions created out of a combination of such alphabets? Is meaning an emergent phenomenon in mathematics?

There are different theories of meaning in mathematics. Ernst, for example, catalogues four of them: dual analysis of meaning, meaning as proof, holistic theory and syntactic relation (Ernst, 1990, p. 444). He argues that the dual analysis, that is, the sense/reference analysis of meaning, does not capture the cognitive processes of meaning because they cannot define the "sense of a compound expression explicitly" (Ernst, 1990, p. 446). He also rejects the view of proof as meaning, which, among other things, is based on mental representations as also the holistic theory of meaning for mathematical expressions. Finally, he draws upon the syntactic theory (derived from Chomsky) to explain how meaning in mathematics is cognitively generated. He suggests, albeit very briefly, a theory to explain the cognitive acquisition of meaning. This approach draws upon syntactic analysis and the ideas of surface structure (form) and deep structures (meaning). According to this view, the reader first sees the mathematical expression, then creates a representation of the surface structure, which is followed by a checking, iterative process. Similarly the representation of the deep structure is also created. I will not delve into the merits of this approach and instead offer a more simplified analysis of how meaning is cognised at the level of symbols.

Tymoczko (1998) does not accept the view that the meaning of mathematics is grounded in extra-linguistic reality or in the external world. Rather he situates meaning within the rationality of mathematical practice and our capacity to talk about it. In this sense, rationality is equivalent to meaningfulness. Results and proofs make sense to us; are available to us as being meaningful. One way to relate this position to what I argue below is to ask whether notations make sense to us in more meaningful ways than hitherto accepted. Wittgenstein (1974) associates meaning in mathematics with proof but also comments on the fact that mathematics is all about calculation and there is no meaning in it. Miller (1977, p. 543) points out how this understanding of meaning in mathematics doesn't really explain how meaning is different when different notational systems are used. How can such notational and stylistic changes create differences in meaning? In what follows, I will describe this process of notational meaning in some detail and explore its role in the creation of mathematical meaning.

The way mathematics is *written* illustrates a mark of complexity in mathematics. Natural languages like English begin with a set of alphabets. Words are formed from these alphabets and sentences from these words. In the case of mathematics, something unique happens: it is 'alphabets' that are created all the time. Most new mathematical entities that are created are at the level of an alphabet. This is what I have elsewhere called as 'alphabetisation' in mathematics (Sarukkai, 2002, p. 35). Interestingly, these alphabets are discovered through the way they are 'written'. The nature of writing is thus important to make sense of not only mathematics but also computability and calculation.

As far as writing is concerned, it is easy to distinguish between an alphabet and a word. A word is composed of more than one alphabet (with notable exceptions, of course, like 'a' and 'I'). In the way they are written, alphabets in English are graphemes – single, unitary marks on the paper. Putting two or more of these alphabets immediately creates a word. In the previous section, we discussed some aspects of the emergence of meaning in this context. In the case of mathematics, how do recognise an alphabet? Writing allows us to recognise the distinction between alphabets and words. Now if we look at mathematics, we discover something quite fascinating.

Mathematics is distinguished by the way it is written. It is primarily a written mode. In fact, speaking mathematics 'correctly' is impossible given the special nature of its writing. Unlike English which has a fixed set of 26 alphabets from which words are constructed, the task of mathematics is to keep creating new alphabets. How do we recognise an alphabet in mathematics? By looking for a grapheme – single, unitary marks. Now if we look at mathematical writing we see a remarkable attempt to create all kinds of graphemes. Consider a simple example like f(x). f(x) is not fx (which is a 'word'). The brackets are a writing tool to communicate the 'graphemic' nature of f(x). I have argued elsewhere (Sarukkai, 2002) that such strategies are integral to mathematics because of the association of these alphabets with mathematical 'objects'. The brackets when used in elementary representations of matrices also do this job of simulating a unitary 'object' called a matrix. Similarly superscripts, subscripts, bold fonts, Greek alphabets and so on are popular tools in creating new alphabets. Alphabets from English are not enough to capture the multiplicity in mathematics and although alphabets from other systems, such as the popular Greek alphabets, are used eventually none of them are enough. So an essential aspect of mathematical writing is to keep creating and constructing new alphabets.

The specialty of mathematics lies in this creation of potentially infinite alphabets as part of its language. Now here is an interesting possibility to consider: 'meaning' in mathematics does not fundamentally arise at the level of proof or even of reasonable mathematical practice but actually at the linguistic level of creating mathematical alphabets. This is remarkable because in English there is no meaning to alphabets but only to words. In mathematics, meaning is primarily present in its alphabets. Meaning in alphabets emerges not through convention (like words in English) but often through a 'natural' cognitive process. The process of creating alphabets in mathematics is indeed 'complex'. Let me take a random example – $H_c^i(\mathbf{R}^n)$, the compact cohomology groups of $\mathbf{R}^n$ (Bott and Tu, 1982). This is a grapheme in that it is a unitary mark and is not to be read as a temporal succession of symbols; so it is not equivalent to "HciRn". In writing this set of symbols in this integrated manner new meanings are generated. The meaning is encoded in the way it is written. By looking at this alphabet we know what it refers to, the order of the cohomology group, what kind of a manifold is involved and so on. There are different cognitive capacities including visual cognition that work together to create meaning in these alphabetic symbols. The act of symbolising encodes certain descriptions. This is not enough to make it mathematical. Once we begin calculating with these symbols, the form of these symbols influence the various results that are obtained in calculation – a good example of this is the now standard way of writing tensors using subscripts and superscripts. This pictorial representation of a tensor makes visual meaning possible in a powerful way. For example, the way the indices 'cancel' each other in scalar product of two vectors gives us a visual meaning of the process (Sarukkai, 2002). Calculating with the help of these alphabets creates a different set of meaning in ways similar to that created in the writing of natural language.

As discussed earlier, mathematics is a complex system at many levels and the notational complexity involved in its writing and calculating is one such component of this complexity. The way mathematics creates and uses the multiplicity of alphabets is something unique to it. The way meaning emerges in mathematical calculation is complex. The process of alphabetisation and the ways by which meaning is generated through the use of these alphabets as well as through calculation illustrate the operational complexity of mathematics. There is really no language in which such operational complexity occurs as compared to mathematics.

I will not add anything here on computational complexity but point the readers to Velupillai (2000). It is also interesting to read Chaitin's description of the complexity in mathematics:

"The Platonic world of mathematical ideas is infinitely complex, but what we can know is only a finite part of this infinite complexity, depending on the complexity of our theories.

Let's now compare math with biology. Biology deals with very complicated systems. There are no simple equations for your spouse, or for a human society. However math is even more complicated than biology. The human genome consists of 3×10^9 bases, which is 6×10^9 bits, which is large, but which is only finite. Math, however, is infinitely complicated, provably so.

An even more dramatic illustration of these ideas is provided by the halting probability Ω, which is defined to be the probability that a program generated by coin tossing eventually halts. In other words, each **K**-bit program that halts contributes 1 over 2^K to the halting probability Ω. To show that Ω is a well-defined probability between zero and one it is essential to use the 1970s version of AIT with self-delimiting programs." (Chaitin, 2010, p. 132)

Another unique kind of complexity in mathematics is the complex relation mathematics has with natural language. I will only make some brief remarks on this relation here and refer the reader to Sarukkai (2001) for more details. First of all, there is no mathematics without natural language – this is primarily a statement about the writing of mathematics as well as its linguistic reference. Mathematics derives from and departs away from natural language in complex ways. On the one hand, it is projected as a completely different activity as compared to natural language and it has largely succeeded in this – look at the difficulty in getting people to accept mathematics as a language! However on the other hand it draws upon natural language in very interesting ways – the way theorems are phrased, the ways by which the ambiguity of natural language is cleverly utilised in a mathematical statement and so on. The inherent contradiction in mathematical practice is that mathematics needs and does not need natural language. It engages with and at the same time disengages with the activity of meaning making in natural languages. For lack of space I do not want to add anything more except to suggest that important ideas of complexity are present in the relationship between mathematics and natural language.

The last example of complexity in mathematics lies in its applicability. Unlike other languages, the applicability of mathematics is unique to mathematics. Frege goes so far as to claim that without applicability mathematics is merely a game like chess. What adds value to mathematics is its unreasonable success in applying it to real problems, natural and social. However how should one apply mathematics? Is there a procedure for doing it most efficiently and optimally? In the last section I will argue that there are no such processes and successful application is one that is a 'complex' application in more ways than one.

For Chaitin, the idea of irreducible complexity in mathematics arises from other considerations. As mentioned above, Chaitin calls for a radical re-understanding of mathematics, one that will place it on "par" with physics. He calls his enterprise of mathematics "quasi-empirical". His concept of halting probability shows that mathematics "has infinite complexity, because the bits of Ω are infinitely complex" (Chaitin, 2007).

However, these are all some specific ideas of complexity. None of this explains what is so special to mathematics. In fact, because mathematics is so special we tend to understand it in terms of its complexity. Unless we show that there is a consequence of this complex nature this description of mathematics is not really significant. I do believe that there is one such consequence of the complexity of mathematics and this has to do with its applicability. I believe that we can use the 'complexity index' of mathematics to explain why it is so unreasonably effective as far as its use in describing the world is concerned.

4. Applicability of Mathematics and Complexity: Lessons from Economics

As I mentioned earlier, the mystery of mathematics lies in its fertile applicability. Philosophers have long puzzled over this aspect – what is so special to mathematics that makes it so effective in describing the natural world? Scientists, although they use mathematics across disciplines, are completely at a loss to explain why mathematics is necessary for the modern sciences or even why mathematics should 'work'.

One source of the puzzlement lies in the way mathematics is understood. Unlike natural languages, mathematics is seen to have no relationship with the real world. Mathematics arises independent of the real world and yet without it any useful description of the real world does not seem to be possible. Scientists from Galileo onwards, including Newton and Einstein, have commented on the mysteriousness of this applicability (Steiner, 1998). And yet we have little idea on the process of applying mathematics.

Applicability should not be confused with reducibility, although sometimes they are. In the early days of physics, it was felt that physics could be reduced to mathematics. Similar views on reduction of chemistry to physics or biology to chemistry are well entrenched in the scientific community, although there is increasing opposition to these views. Interestingly, these are claims of reduction and what they mean is that chemistry is reducible to physics and not that physics is applied to chemistry. Similarly, when it is said that physics is reducible to mathematics, as Descartes indeed believed, it means that all of physics can be reduced to some mathematics. The real liberation of physics came when it was realised that physics is not reducible to mathematics but mathematics should be applied to it. The point here is that the way physicists use mathematics is very different from the way mathematicians 'use' mathematics. Economics is an interesting example which straddles these two ways of 'using' mathematics. In economics the questions are how best to use mathematics, what kind of mathematics should be used and in which manner it should be used. In a response to Velupillai (2011), I had argued that the axiomatic approach in economics is akin to reduction of economics to mathematics (Sarukkai, 2011), more in the mistaken way of Descartes trying to reduce physics to mathematics. Following Velupillai's argument that economists must use mathematics like physicists do, I had explored the different ways of using mathematics in physics. And there is an important lesson in understanding the way physicists have used or misused mathematics. In fact, if there be a slogan for the applicability of mathematics in physics it should be: 'Misuse mathematics, not use it'.

Chaitin (1994, p. 3) notes that 'I've found mathematical truths that are true for no reason at all. These mathematical truths are beyond the power of mathematical reasoning because they are accidental and random'. He is suggesting that mathematics should be done more like physics, where one continues to use entities or structures without really understanding them and so 'elementary number theory should be pursued some-what more in the spirit of experimental science'. His aim is to show how randomness is an essential component of mathematics just as in physics. (This experimental nature is also emphasised in Velupillai (2011).)

Chaitin's argument that physicists use mathematics without knowing what they are doing is right on the mark. Students in physics, and the theoretical sciences in general, are taught to use mathematics without worrying about what it means or even what is formally allowed! The distinction between mathematicians and physicists is based on their view of mathematics – sacrosanct for one and exploitable for the other.

However the question that remains is this: why should such arbitrary use of mathe-matics work? Granted that physicists do not use mathematics like mathematicians do but it still does not answer this question: why then is it so effective?

In what follows, I will sketch an argument that attempts to answer these questions about applicability. This argument draws crucially on some aspects of economics or at least some ideas that have been inspired by economics. I refer to certain issues in the study of complexity in economics as well as Herbert Simon's seminal idea of satisficing.

The first point that should strike us about applicability, as also illustrated in Chaitin's comments, is that there seems to be some 'randomness' in this process; it is this that leads to expressions of surprise by so many leading scientists at the unreasonable effectiveness of mathematics. Chaitin notes that he has found mathematical truths which have no reason to be true. These are just accidental and random. Interest-ingly, the language of applicability follows very similar lines. Most scientists do not 'know why' a particular mathematical formalism should work. When physicists use mathematics, they often take potshots at different mathematical frameworks. Some work, some don't. And once a particular mathematical framework is chosen, this still doesn't guarantee effective applicability. How the results of that framework are inter-preted in the context of the problem is crucial to the success of applying mathematics. In all these senses, applicability is random like the randomness which Chaitin finds in mathematics. Take two celebrated examples of such random actions: the Feynman path integral formalism and Dirac's equation for an electron (which was an attempt to represent the 'square root' of a second order differential equation!).

However this randomness is the randomness of the action of an agent, the scientist in this case. How a scientist chooses which mathematical framework to use, and how to use it, is many times, particularly in paradigmatic cases, largely a matter of 'Hit and Miss'. These frameworks are not chosen with well-defined rationality nor do they represent optimal rational choices. They are chosen 'intuitively', often do not work and very creative manipulation of the original mathematics is required.

Consider the problem of choosing which mathematical structure to use to model a given problem. Part of the randomness in making mathematics applicable is that the outcome is rarely, if ever, predictable in advance. The application is often not the most 'efficient', at least in the initial moments of its use. The use of mathematics in physics is filled with examples that illustrate all these characteristics (Steiner, 1998).

Conventional accounts of science interpret the creation of mathematical models as a rational act. Scientists – in choosing their models or which mathematical structure is relevant – are rational optimisers. The scientists are supposed to evaluate, revise and choose mathematical structures based on maximum utility. However this is rarely the case. First of all, most scientists do not have the requisite understanding of the mathematical apparatus they use. There was a time a couple of decades back when topology suddenly became the rage in theoretical physics. So, many problems starting using the language of topology, independent of their understanding of that subject in detail as well as having any clear expectation that such pursuit would lead them to some success.

5. Satisficing, Bounded Rationality and Modelling

There is another way to understand the process of applying mathematics. This process is best understood as a decision-making problem.[2] The problem of applicability is also this: How does one choose which mathematics is most relevant for a given situation? The scientist who chooses mathematics to model her theory is often mistaken as an optimal rational agent. However the history of applied mathematics in the sciences shows exactly the opposite trend. Scientists choose mathematics not based on well-defined parameters of optimal rationality but more along the lines of bounded rationality. I believe that satisficing better describes the applicability of mathematics than any other process. The idea of satisficing, first suggested by Herbert Simon and then taken up in a variety of disciplines, offers a new way of understanding decision-making procedures. In contrast to the notion of the rational agent who decides based on notions of optimality, satisficing offers a more realistic view of decision making. It is no wonder then that this idea has been used with some success in fields such as economics, philosophy, management and the social sciences.

Satisficing is primarily about 'choosing what is satisfactory' instead of 'what is best' (Byron, 2004). Simon chose this concept in order to reflect how people really behave when they choose. We are not impersonal rational optimisers and do not possess the cognitive capacities to behave in that manner. We choose based on measures of satisfaction and not optimisation. Simon, while acknowledging that we do not possess the cognitive and computational apparatus required for optimal choice, nevertheless accounts for some kind of rational action which is limited and bound. Such bounded rationality only expects us to make decisions that lead to satisfactory outcomes. However, as Velupillai (2010) argues, bounded rationality should not be seen as a limit or approximation of the Olympian or the ideal form of rationality.

Byron (1998) suggests that satisficing is also a rational action. Traditional accounts of satisficing distinguish between the optimal conception and the satisficing conception. In the case of the former, the rational agent seeks 'the best means to their given ends' whereas in the latter 'to be rational we sometimes need only choose *satisfactory* means to our ends' (Byron, 1998, p. 69). Moreover, models based on satisficing are 'descriptively adequate' since they give a better account of how we actually make choices (Byron, 2004, p. 4).

Simon's original argument was that human agents are not supercomputing agents who can optimise rationality in decision making but instead choose criteria such as satisfaction. Later he emphasised that bounded rationality consisted essentially of 'procedural rationality' instead of 'substantive rationality' and finally added the notions of recognition and heuristic search to these procedures (Munier, 1999).

Modelling is an essential method in the sciences and has had a great impact in the development of economics. The notion of modelling is larger than that of mathematical modelling although often one is mistaken for the other. Suppose a scientist wants to model a phenomenon. How does she go about it? What are the procedures she follows in building a model – or should we say – in building a *satisfactory* model? What kind of decisions does she make in choosing various parameters, mathematical techniques and so on? Very often, scientists talk about modelling as an art. What they mean is that there are no set rules or methods of how and what to model. It is impossible to be optimally rational in deciding the various aspects of modelling. Neither is modelling completely random and arbitrary. In the regular practice of science, one chooses a model based on already established models which have been successful. However when new models are being created or when old models are being paradigmatically changed, what kind of decisions does the scientist make? There is no set procedure and hence, very often, a wide variety of heuristics is used to choose the elements of a model. For example, even the decision on which mathematical technique and what kind of mathematical structure to use are based more on 'satisfactory adequacy' (to modify the popular phrase 'empirical adequacy' used in philosophy of science) rather than strict rules of rational behaviour. I believe that the mechanics of, and the decision procedure for, modelling work on the principles of bounded rationality and exhibits not only 'satisfactory adequacy' but also 'procedural rationality' and heuristic search. These rich sets of ideas which define bounded rationality may also best describe the modelling process in general.

Somehow scholars have overlooked the dynamics of model creation since modelling seems apparently dictated by rational principles. An ironic illustration of this is from Simon's paper on systems modelling (Simon, 1990). I use the term 'ironic' because Simon is discussing some larger principles behind modelling and in doing so is deploying – subconsciously perhaps, since he doesn't make an explicit reference to it – measures of bounded rationality! His approach to modelling is a good example of why even somebody like Simon overlooks the dynamics of decision making and choice inherent in modelling.

Simon begins his analysis of models by first pointing out that the necessity of models for studying complex systems and then goes on to add that we are nowhere near achieving the computational capacity needed to capture the complexity in nature. He then suggests that modelling needs 'some basic principles' through which the 'essential' can be separated from the 'dispensable' so that models can represent 'simplified picture of reality'. Before models are 'built', there must be specified goals. Presumably based on these goals, one can choose how to build these models. His arguments are built around the themes of 'prediction' and 'prescription'.

Numerical computation is not only expensive in every sense of the term but it may also not lead to desired results. As Simon points out, the Club of Rome model, the nuclear winter model and seeding hurricane model were all problematical because of the excessive dependency on numerical modelling. In saying this, Simon makes a claim that models should be addressed to questions that can be answered 'more or less definitively'. He also points out that for effective modelling, 'intelligent approximation, not brute force computation, is the key' (Simon, 1990, p. 11). Another desired choice in modelling (although he doesn't refer to it as choice) is that complex systems are more easily handled when modelled through hierarchical structures. And finally, he also suggests the appropriate use of symbolic modelling instead of numerical modelling.

One can look at this general essay on modelling as a prescriptive model of modelling complex systems. There are points in this work to which many other modellers might object. The point I am making is not whether Simon's views on modelling are right or not, but only how any choice of models is a particular decision-making process with various assumptions and beliefs. These assumptions and beliefs may be different for different people. However even given the assumptions and information that Simon works under, I would still argue that his choice of models is dictated not by any sense of optimal rationality but by some sense of bounded rationality. In fact, the successes of many models in the natural sciences illustrate how far successful model making is from an optimal rational process.

We can thus argue that satisficing and models of bounded rationality can yield a 'truer' picture of the dynamics of mathematical applicability. Although not explicitly discussed in this context, there is an important relationship between bounded rationality and the 'making of meaning'. The meaning created through alphabetisation in mathematics described earlier is a model of meaning making which is more within the discourse of bounded rationality. The upshot of all this is that the process of mathematical applicability illustrates complexity in the following manner. Suppose we begin with a model of a phenomenon. In the first step, we choose some concepts, approximations and idealisations. We can then describe this model using mathematics – that is, we can apply mathematical description to this model. In doing so, something remarkable happens: the particular mathematical framework used in the model generates a *feedback* to the initial model. For effective applicability, and thus for a successful model, the feedback from the mathematical structures to the original model is non-monotonic and non-linear. So we can consider this hypothesis: mathematics is a 'complex' language and successful applicability exhibits characteristics of complexity in the process of application. The remarkable success of Dirac's equation, the strategies of creating mathematical alphabets, path integral formalism and renormalisability all point to the positive, non-linear feedback which the initial inputs have on the system.

Not all mathematical use in models leads to complex, non-linear feedback. Mathematics used in the sense of axiomatisation and not in the sense of creative application, tends to be 'linear'. Axiomatisation in economics mimics the optimal rationality model. It is more demanding and leads to potential problems in understanding real situations.

In the context of applicability, I have tried to address two questions. First, why is mathematics a privileged form of scientific description as compared to natural language? Second, why is applicability so unreasonably successful? (The phrase 'unreasonable effectiveness' coined by Wigner, which describes the mysterious success of mathematical applicability, has become one of the defining phrases in science.

Drawing on Simon, I would suggest that the phrase 'unreasonable satisfaction' is perhaps more apt for many mathematical models.)

The answers to the two questions are as follows: Mathematics is preferred over natural language because of the complexity inherent in mathematics (as described in the earlier sections). This complexity alone is not enough. In describing the world with the help of mathematics, there is a necessary positive feedback which arises in using mathematics. Such a positive feedback does not arise in the case of using only natural language. This non-linear, positive feedback from mathematics changes the original description to an extent that makes new knowledge possible. Not all use of mathematics is successful; we can speculate whether only the successful cases exhibit this relationship of complexity.

Second, to understand applicability we have to understand scientists as agents who are not rational optimisers of the mathematics they know. Instead they should be seen as cognitive agents, similar to those described in complexity economics, who use a variety of cognitive processes. Modelling applicability in this manner, understanding that applicability of mathematics is itself governed by ideas of complexity, will yield new insights into what specific mathematical framework would work most effectively for modelling in economics. If applicability of a mathematical framework is more complex, non-linear and unstable then the greater chance of 'creating' a better theory, whether in physics or economics.

Acknowledgements

I am grateful to Vela for inspiring me to search in places I have not gone before. I am also extremely thankful to Vela and Stefano Zambelli for very useful comments on an earlier draft.

Notes

1. For a discussion on emergent properties in the use of metaphors, see Wilson and Carston (2006).
2. Not in the strict sense of decision-making problems. For example, Velupillai (2010) describes decision making as follows: 'A decision problem asks whether there exists an algorithm to decide whether a mathematical assertion does or does not have a proof; or a formal problem does or does not have a solution'. Choosing the mathematical apparatus for a model will not be formal in this sense.

References

Bhattacharyya, S. (1998) *Language, Testimony and Meaning*. Delhi: ICPR.
Bott, R. and Tu, L.W. (1982) *Differential Forms in Algebraic Topology*. New York: Springer-Verlag.
Byron, M. (1998) Satisficing and optimality. *Ethics* 109: 67–93.
Byron, M. (2004) Introduction. In M. Byron (ed.), *Satisficing and Maximizing* (pp. 1–13). Cambridge: Cambridge University Press.
Chaitin, G.J. (1994) Randomness and complexity in pure mathematics. *International Journal of Bifurcation and Chaos* 4: 3–15.

Chaitin, G.J. (2007) The halting probability omega: irreducible complexity in pure mathematics. *Milan Journal of Mathematics* 75: 291–304.

Chaitin, G.J. (2010) Leibniz, complexity and incompleteness. In A. Carsetti (ed.), *Causality, Meaningful Complexity and Embodied Cognition* (pp. 127–134). Dordrecht: Springer.

Coward, H. (1980) *The Sphoṭa Theory of Language: A Philosophical Analysis.* Delhi: Motilal Banarsidass.

Ernst, P. (1990) The meaning of mathematical expressions: does philosophy shed any light on psychology? *British Journal of Philosophy of Science* 41: 443–460.

Foote, R. (2007) Mathematics and complex systems. *Science* 318: 410–412.

Gardenfors, P. (1993) The emergence of meaning. *Linguistics and Philosophy* 16: 285–309.

Miller, R. (1977) Wittgenstein in transition: a review of the philosophical grammar. *The Philosophical Review* 86: 520–544.

Munier, B., Selten, R., Bouyssou, D., Bourgine, P., Day, R., Harvey, N., Hilton, D., Machina, M.J., Parker, P., Sterman, H., Sterman, J., Weber, E., Wernerfelt, B. and Wensley, R. (1999) Bounded rationality modeling. *Marketing Letters* 10: 233–248.

Rescher, N. (1998) *Complexity: A Philosophical Overview.* New Brunswick: Transaction Publishers.

Sarukkai, S. (2001) Mathematics, language and translation. *META* 46: 664–674.

Sarukkai, S. (2002) *Translating the World: Science and Language.* Lanham: University Press of America.

Sarukkai, S. (2011) Mathematics in economics: reducibility and/or applicability? *New Mathematics and Natural Computation*, forthcoming.

Simon, H.A. (1990) Prediction and prescription in systems modeling. *Operations Research* 38: 7–14.

Shapiro, S. (1997) *Philosophy of Mathematics: Structure and Ontology.* New York: Oxford University Press.

Steiner, M. (1998) *The Applicability of Mathematics as a Philosophical Problem.* Cambridge: Harvard University Press.

Tymoczko, T. (1998) Gödel and the concept of meaning in mathematics. *Synthese* 114: 25–40.

Velupillai, K.V. (2000) *Computable Economics.* Oxford: Oxford University Press.

Velupillai, K.V. (2010) Foundations of boundedly rational choice and satisficing decisions. *Advances in Decision Sciences*, vol. 2010, Article ID 798030, 16 pages. doi:10.1155/2010/798030.

Velupillai, K.V. (2011) Taming the incomputable, reconstructing the nonconstructive and deciding the undecidable in mathematical economics. *New Mathematics and Natural Computation*, forthcoming.

Wilson, D. and Carston, R. (2006) Metaphor, relevance and the emergent property issue. *Mind & Language* 21: 404–433.

Wittgenstein, L. (1974) *Philosophical Grammar.* R. Rhees (ed.), Anthony Kenny (trans.), Oxford: Blackwell.

5

BEHAVIOURAL COMPLEXITY

Sami Al-Suwailem

1. Introduction

Studies of complexity economics (CE) have been growing increasingly in recent years. These studies emphasize how the economy is dynamic, innovative, adaptive and persistently in disequilibrium, as compared to the neoclassical view of equilibrium, stable and static economy (e.g. Beinhocker, 2006).

The list of differences between the two paradigms, however, might easily become arbitrary and subjective. A more precise and objective way to differentiate CE from neoclassical economics (NE) would be based on the existence, or absence, of a critical assumption regarding the economic landscape. NE assumes the world (i.e. consumption and production sets) to be *convex*. This is one of the most important assumptions in standard economic analysis (Debreu, 1959, p. 23; Takayama, 1993, p. 53; Newman, 1998). CE, in contrast, holds the view that nonconvexities cannot be ignored even as a first approximation. Nonconvexity of the choice set leads to dramatically different characteristics and behaviours. As we shall see, convexity (or lack thereof) serves as an organizing principle to clarify how the two paradigms compare and contrast to each other.

Section 2 highlights some major aspects of NE in contrast to CE. Section 3 examines the characteristics of complex systems, namely self-organization and emergence. Accordingly, Section 4 proposes a modelling framework of complex behaviour. The main mechanism of self-organization, relative behaviour, is further discussed and elaborated in Section 5. Section 6 presents an application of the model framework to consumption function using agent-based simulation. The results, presented in Section 7, lend support to the hypothesized nature of complex systems and how they contrast to NE. Conclusions are presented in Section 8.

Nonlinearity, Complexity and Randomness in Economics, First Edition.
Stefano Zambelli and Donald A.R. George.
© 2012 John Wiley & Sons. Published 2012 by John Wiley & Sons, Ltd.

2. Economics of a Nonconvex World

A set is said to be convex if the linear combination, or the weighted average, of any two points in the set, belongs to the same set (Debreu, 1959, p. 23). Visually, a convex set is like a disc or a solid ball. The strait line connecting any two points in the ball is still inside the ball. A star-shaped body is nonconvex: The line connecting any two points in the star does not always lie inside the star.

2.1 Novelty and Creativity

Probably the most fundamental property of a convex set is lack of novelty. Novelty describes a situation in which the combination of two (or more) elements results in properties that none of constituting elements possesses independently (Hargadon, 2003). It is not difficult to see that convexity substantially limits the room for novelty and innovation. Combining two substances or technologies frequently produces outcomes that have starkly different properties than either of the two.

This is probably one reason why innovation is absent from a neoclassical world. According to Arrow (1988, p. 281): 'Innovations, almost by definition, are one of the least analysed parts of economics, in spite of the verifiable fact that they have contributed more to per capita economic growth than any other factor'.

For the same reason, entrepreneurship is difficult to integrate with standard neoclassical theory. Baumol (1993, p. 12) points out that, for 50 years, he was particularly puzzled why formal economic theory has so little to say about entrepreneurs, where 'virtually all theoretical firms are entrepreneur-less'. He writes (p. 13):

> Explicitly or implicitly, the firm is taken to perform a mathematical calculation which yields optimal (i.e. profit-maximizing) values for all of its decision variables ... There matters rest, forever or until exogenous forces lead to an autonomous change in the environment. Until [then], the firm is taken to replicate precisely its previous decisions, day after day, year after year.

> Clearly, the entrepreneur has been read out of the model. There is no room for enterprise or initiative. The management group becomes a passive calculator that reacts mechanically to changes imposed on it by fortuitous external developments over which it does not exert ... any influence. One hears of no clever ruses, ingenious schemes, valuable innovations or any of the other stuff of which outstanding entrepreneurship is made; one does not hear of them because there is no way in which they can fit into the formal optimization model.

According to Freeman (1998, p. 860), 'empirical studies of innovations and their diffusion have provided mounting evidence that mainstream neoclassical theories of firm behaviour, competition, international trade and consumer behaviour, are seriously deficient in their assumptions and conclusions'.

Innovation not only affects production, it also affects consumption. Innovation introduces new goods and services that were not included in the consumption set. Accordingly, arguments in the utility function increase, which may upset existing preferences (Martens, 2000, p. 7). This implies that preferences must be at least partially endogenous to account for new goods, and not exogenously fixed as NE assumes.

The absence of innovation, creativity and entrepreneurship from standard NE is why it is associated with a mechanical, 'clock-work', world. This is not the world we live in, nor is it the one we enjoy belonging to. CE, in contrast, views the world as dynamic, alive and perpetually novel (Holland, 1988).

2.2 Increasing Returns

Convexity also excludes increasing returns to scale (Debreu, 1959, p. 41), which can produce economic effects starkly different from the world envisioned by NE, as surveyed by Heal (1999). Convexity thus becomes inconsistent with one of the most established economic facts of modern times: Specialization improves productivity and returns more than it costs. And based on this property, division of labour and production lines have been developed, which in turn were instrumental for the industrial advancement in the West. With specialization, the economy collectively behaves in a more sophisticated way than its components. 'This is the hallmark of complex systems', as Kirman (2011, p. 24) remarks. This result is excluded by convexity, which requires that intermediate points should be as good as either of the two endpoints. Specialization implies that returns to an endpoint are larger than to middle, half-way skills. In a convex world, therefore, specialization does not pay.

Decreasing returns do not apply to the most important assets in the society: knowledge and information, which clearly has increasing returns (Romer, 1986; Stiglitz, 2000). The more we build up knowledge, the higher the marginal return and marginal payoff we get. Because such processes are not permitted in a convex world, learning and accumulation of knowledge become foreign concepts in NE (Rothschild, 2000). According to Velupillai (2007, p. 486), constructing learning processes in a neoclassical world is 'either provably impossible or formally intractable'.

Nonconvexity also results in discontinuity of demand and supply functions (Rosser, 2000). If not properly accounted for, discontinuities may cause crashes of markets (Gennotte and Leland, 1990; Mandelbrot, 1997), and sudden 'freeze up' of liquidity, as happened in the recent global financial crisis (Baily et al., 2008).

2.3 Positive Feedback

Decreasing returns exclude the possibility of self-reinforcing mechanisms in economic processes. Economic processes are assumed to dampen out and reach equilibrium smoothly. But we know that the world is much different than that. If more consumers use mobile phones, they become more useful, which makes more consumers use them. Network structure creates self-reinforcing effects (e.g. Barabási, 2003), which are excluded by NE (Arthur, 1988, 1997). Further, science is abundant with examples of reinforcing feedback mechanisms. In other words, nonconvexity is abundant in both natural and social systems. According to Paul Samuelson (1947) 'the fine garments [of NE are] sometimes achieved fit only by chopping off some real arms and legs. The theory of cones, polyhedra and convex sets made possible 'elementary' theorems and lemmas. But they seduced economists away from the phenomena of increasing returns to scale and nonconvex technology that lie at the heart of oligopoly problems and many real-world maximizing assignments' (p. xix; cited in Auyang, 1998, p. 140).

We shall see later how the two features, novelty and positive feedback, are essential for the behaviour of complex systems.

2.4 *Path Dependence, Integrability and Non-Economic Factors*

Positive feedback may make final outcomes sensitive to initial conditions. Choice therefore becomes 'path dependent'. But this is not what NE dictates. NE assumes agents make their choices solely based on economic factors, namely prices and income. Although it is clear that choice is influenced by a myriad of other factors, social and psychological, these factors are subsumed into the market.

With this view, economic choice is determined purely by market signals. From observed economic choices, preferences under NE assumptions can be inferred. This is the well-known 'integrability problem' (e.g. Varian, 1992, pp. 125–131); namely, demand functions can be integrated to recover the underlying preference function if certain requirements are satisfied (symmetry and negative semi-definiteness of the substitution matrix of demand functions). These properties follow from convexity of preferences. If preferences are nonconvex, integrating demand functions recovers only the convex portions of preferences; nonconvex portions are lost (Mas-Colell *et al.*, 1995, pp. 75–78; Deaton and Muelbauer, 1980, p. 48).

Integrability implies that the process of choice, or how preferences are translated into actions, is ignored (Mirowski, 1989, p. 371). Accordingly, choice is *path in-dependent* – i.e. it does not matter how one arrives at choosing a given bundle of commodities, or what were the initial conditions or past experiences; utility or sat-isfaction is the same regardless. According to Akira Takayama (1993, pp. 632–633), path independence follows almost trivially from the existence of the neoclassical utility function; conversely, path independence requires integrability, which in turn ensures the recoverability of NE utility function.

Because the choice process is irrelevant in NE, it becomes of little significance how one earns his or her income, whether by hard work or by blind luck; by honesty or by cheating. Utility is insensitive to these aspects. Moral values and ethics therefore have no formal place in NE; a result that many economists find difficult to accept (e.g. Ben-Ner and Putterman, 1998; Gintis *et al.*, 2005).

Further, with increasing returns and positive feedback mechanisms, past events and initial conditions may have significant impact on present decisions. The fact that 'history matters' clearly indicates that many fundamental economic processes are path dependent (Puffert, 2003; David, 2005).

Empirically, conditions required for integrability are poorly supported by applied studies (e.g. Deaton and Muelbauer, 1980, chapter 3). Experimental tests (e.g. Camerer *et al.*, 2004) consistently show that choice is influenced by endowment, loss aversion, framing and similar context-sensitive factors. This makes choice *reference dependent*, which invalidates integrability conditions (Hands, 2006).

2.5 *Indivisibility*

One reason why nonconvexities arise is indivisibility. In our daily life, we deal with things in a discrete manner. One can buy an integral number of automobiles; say 1 or 2, but not 1.78. Similarly, a company cannot hire 3.51 employees. One cannot earn 0.42 degree in business and 0.58 degree in engineering. That is, the nature of choices in real life requires dealing with integers rather than 'real' numbers with infinitely long decimal representations. Indivisibility leads to economies of scale which makes production set nonconvex (Scarf, 1981, 1994). These nonconvexities are fundamental in economic activities and usually cannot be 'convexified' through aggregation (Romer, 1990).

Indivisibility does not arise because of physical barriers; even nucleus of the atom can be shattered into smaller particles. Rather, indivisibility arises because the function and behaviour of an object changes dramatically when decomposed into its parts. This is just another way to say that 'the whole is greater than the sum', a distinguishing property of complex systems, as shall be discussed later.

2.6 *Rational Choice*

Given that numbers used in economic life are predominantly integers, Velupillai (2005a, 2005b) argues that economic relations should be represented by 'Diophantine equations': polynomials whose solutions are integers (or ratios of integers). Accordingly, economic choice is represented as a Diophantine decision problem. However, Diophantine problems are not always solvable, i.e. there is no procedure or algorithm that systematically determines whether or not a particular problem has a solution.

A Diophantine problem can still be solved but through trial and error (induction), and other non-deductive means. From this angle, unsolvability opens the door for learning, discovery and innovation, that are absent from NE. Further, it allows for non-economic factors to affect the decision process, which again is ruled out by NE. In this context, it is easy to see the rationale behind Herbert Simon's 'satisficing' criterion (Simon, 1997). When deductive means are of limited value due to undecidabilities and unsovlabilities, agents consciously resort to non-deductive means for solving decision problems. This arises not because agents' intelligence is necessarily bounded; it is the nature of the world they live in (Velupillai, 2005a, p. 173; 2010, p. 383).

2.7 *Summary*

Table 1 summarizes some of the main differences between NE and CE.

Table 1. Neoclassical Economics vs. Complexity Economics.

	NE	CE
Choice set	Convex	Nonconvex
Novelty	Severely limited	Perpetual novelty
Dynamics	Decreasing returns only	Decreasing *and* increasing returns
Choice process	Irrelevant – path independent	Relevant – path dependent
Decision rule	Maximization	Satisficing

3. Nature of Complex Systems

Now we know that complexity assumes a nonconvex world, we need to move a step further to examine the characteristics and structure of complex systems. Although there are many definitions of complexity (see Rosser, 1999; Mitchell, 2009, chapter 7), two important features generally constitute a complex system:

1. Self-organization, and
2. Emergence.

3.1 *Self-Organization*

This term indicates that a system consisting of a (large) number of interacting units, is able to show order at the system macroscopic level when units only locally interact and have no access to global variables or a central control. In other words, self-organization is global order arising from local interactions. It is a decentralized order. It is also called 'spontaneous order' (e.g. Barry, 1982; Sugden, 1989).

A widely cited example is a flock of birds moving together in an ordered manner. Scientists found that such flocks do not have leaders; rather, birds are self-organized into flocks through local interactions only. Other examples include fireflies that flash in unison without a particular leader (Strogatz, 2003, pp. 11–14). Further examples are provided in Camazine *et al.* (2001).

3.2 *Emergence*

There are many definitions of 'emergence' (see Lee, 2005; Sawyer, 2005). Here, emergence implies that the system is able to perform functions or solve problems that individual parts cannot achieve separately. The brain, for example, can perform functions a collection of independent neurons never can. Other examples include the immune system and ant colonies (Mitchell, 2009, pp. 172–178).

Frequently, emergence is defined to be the case when the 'whole is greater than the sum' (e.g. Holland, 1996, 1999). Although this is true for complex systems, it also applies to other systems as well. Any man-made machine performs functions that cannot be performed by the sum of its components. But the machine does not arise spontaneously. Thus emergence is more specific than mere inequality of the whole to the sum; it is the ability of the self-organized system to perform functions that independent parts cannot.

The two terms, self-organization and emergence, describe structure and function, respectively, of complex systems. In the literature on complexity, however, writers frequently use them interchangeably.

Self-organization depends on positive feedback mechanisms, as will be discussed later. Emergence reflects the novelty the system brings into existence. These two features cannot be obtained in a convex world, and thus, they are excluded by construction from NE, as discussed earlier. Although the economy is a complex system par excellence (Holland, 1988), we shall see later that NE fails to capture the essential mechanisms that makes the economy as such.

3.3 Why Complex Systems?

Complex systems attain complexity through local interactions of agents with local information. Further, the interactions occur through simple rules rather than complicated processes. The logic behind this structure is consistent with the underlying worldview. Because the world is assumed highly rich and novel, and choice problems are frequently unsolvable, there is no reliable mechanism for agents to achieve desired outcomes individually. Rather, through interactions and cooperation of agents, the system as a whole can achieve desirable outcomes and solve hard computational problems much more efficiently (Markose, 2005).

NE in contrast assumes the world to be quite simple, but assumes agents to have unusual powers to analyse all market signals and compute all equilibrium quantities instantly. As Axel Leijonhufvud points out, NE assumes 'incredibly smart people in unbelievably simple situations', whereas in reality we find 'believably simple people with incredibly complex situations' (cited in Beinhocker, 2006, p. 52). If agents were equipped with the computational power to process all information on all aspects of the economy, then, as Arrow (1987, p. 208) rightly notes, 'the hand running the economy is very visible indeed'. To have an *invisible* hand, agents should behave much more simply, yet their local interactions produce the complex and rich phenomena we observe in real world. Complex systems therefore economize on computation as well as information in order to reach the desired solution, because 'mind is a scarce resource' as Simon (1978, p. 9) rightly observes. From this angle, complexity is more relevant to economics than neoclassical theory.

'Swarm Intelligence' refers to intelligence of the group of interacting agents in solving complex problems, where no single agent is able to do so alone. Ants, for example, are able to find the shortest distance to resources even though no single ant is able to solve this problem (Bonabeau *et al.*, 1999; Bonabeau and Meyer, 2001; Kennedy and Eberhart, 2001). Vilfredo Pareto argued about a century ago that only markets are able to work out the solutions for market equilibrium (cited in Velupillai, 2007, pp. 469–470). Intelligence therefore is a characteristic of the system, but not necessarily of individual agents (Brooks, 1991). Accordingly, individual rationality is complemented and supplemented by 'ecological rationality' (Gigerenzer *et al.*, 1999; Smith, 2007).

3.4 *Chaos versus Complexity*

Complexity has evolved from research in various fields of knowledge, including mathematics, physics and biology. It has been advanced throughout the 20th century via several movements with an interdisciplinary approach, including general systems theory, cybernetics, catastrophe theory, chaos and synergetics (Rosser, 1999; Abraham, 2002). They share the view that natural and social systems have common structures that defeat reductionism and show rich and unexpected behaviour. The history of the concept of 'emergence' however, goes back to the John Stewart Mill and George Henry Lewes in the 19th century (Sawyer, 2005, chapter 2; Velupillai, 2005c, pp. 9–10).

3.4.1 *Comparison*

The two concepts, chaos and complexity, have some common properties, including nonlinearity, irreducibility and universality. Differentiating the two thus may not be very obvious, and it would be difficult therefore to draw a dividing line. Tentatively, however, the following differences could be highlighted (Williams, 1997, p. 234; Brock, 2000, p. 29; Sawyer, 2005, p. 15):

1. A complex system usually requires a large number of interacting parts. In contrast, a system can be chaotic with only a single variable. A system with a large number of parts may also be chaotic, but a system with only one variable cannot be complex. Another way to say it is that a complex system is a network of some sort. This is not necessarily true for a chaotic system.
2. A chaotic system shows a behaviour that is apparently indistinguishable from purely random processes. In contrast, a complex system shows recognizable patterns of organization and behaviour, e.g. the brain, the economy, ant colonies, etc., that clearly differs from random processes.
3. A complex system is adaptive, that is to say, it self-organizes within its changing environment. A chaotic system need not be adaptive.
4. A chaotic system is ergodic (Flake, 1998, pp. 155–156). A complex system is usually (but not always) non-ergodic (Kauffman, 2000, chapter 7; Durlauf, 2005, p. 226).
5. A complex system might be capable of universal computation; a chaotic system is not capable of universal computation (Velupillai, 2010, pp. 454–455).
6. The behaviour of a complex system (its basin of attraction) cannot be systematically characterized in advance. But the behaviour of a chaotic system, in principle, can be characterized (Velupillai, 2010, p. 455; Markose, 2002). For this reason simulation is important for complex systems, since it might be the only way to know exactly how the system behaves.
7. A complex system is path dependent; that is, the impact of initial conditions lasts for prolonged periods. A chaotic system, while sensitive to initial conditions, is driven to the same attractor set regardless. May be that's why differences between economies, which are complex systems, persist over time. But bubbles and crashes, which represent chaos, look similar regardless of their origins.

8. Accordingly, for a complex system, the whole is greater than the sum, and thus wealth is created in a complex economy. For a chaotic system, in contrast, the whole would be less than the sum, and thus wealth is destroyed.

3.4.2 Edge of Chaos

Another way to compare the two concepts is to view complexity as a phase between stable order and unstable chaos (Waldrop, 1992; Flake, 1998; Markose, 2005; compare Miller and Page, 2007, pp. 129–140). At phase transition, complex systems are capable of producing surprising patterns and behaviour for extended periods of time. According to Foley (1998, 2005), a complex system lies on the boundary between stable (point and limit cycle) and chaotic systems, so that structures in their initial conditions can evolve without being destroyed.

Stuart Kauffman (1993, 1995) examines a network of N units, each interacting with K other units in the network. He finds that for large values of K, i.e. when each unit is connected to almost every other unit, the network becomes chaotic. For $K = 0$, the network becomes stagnant. For small values of K, however, the network becomes dynamic but stable, i.e. in the phase of order at the edge of chaos. His findings are supported by data on gene networks from various living species, leading him to hypothesize that 'life exists at the edge of chaos' (Kauffman, 1995, p. 26). Recent research on human brain suggests that the brain functions at a critical point between order and chaos (Kitzbichler *et al.*, 2009).

4. Modelling Complex Systems

Models by design are simplifications of the phenomena under investigation. But CE is not seeking simplification of the world or the emergent behaviour of concerned system; rather, it seeks simplification of the *process* generating the complex phenomena, not the phenomena itself (Brock, 2000, p. 32). As already pointed out, simple local interactions represent an important process for producing rich and complex phenomena. Here we provide a model for such local interactions.

4.1 Specification

Although no single model can characterize all complex systems, a general class could be described based on the following structure.

Let x_i denotes a certain behaviour or property of unit i of a system S, consisting of n units. This could be position, speed or any other behaviour by agent i. The system S is described as complex if agents or units comprising the system are able to self-organize such that the system obtains features that are not achievable at the level of agents. This could be reached when each unit or agent's behaviour is determined by two types of variables: *independent variables* and *relative variables*.

Independent variables are variables determined outside the system, i.e. they are exogenous to all units or agents. Relative variables are variables describing the behaviour of other units or agents within the system. In particular, they describe the behaviour of *local* neighbours of each agent. These variables are obviously endogenous. Thus we can write:

$$x_{i,t} = f(\mathbf{z}_{i,t-1}, \mathbf{x}_{-i,t-1}) \tag{1}$$

where $\mathbf{z}_i$ represents a vector of independent variables affecting agent i, whereas $\mathbf{x}_{-i}$ represents the behaviour of local neighbours of agent i. (If $\mathbf{x}_{-i}$ includes agent's own past behaviour, it combines relative behaviour with habit formation; see Pollak, 1976.) Agents are assumed to follow essentially the same rules in reacting to these variables, up to some degree of variability (e.g. up to an affine transformation of the function f).

This representation is consistent with a wide range of complex systems. For example, for a bird flock, each bird is influenced by weather and regional geography as independent variables. But they are also influenced by nearby birds. For fireflies, the independent variables include the time of the day (day or night; where flashing is restricted to night time), whereas the relative variables include the outside flash received from surrounding flies. And so on.

This characterization allows the system to self-organize, as each unit or agent would adjust its behaviour to independent variables in accordance to the behaviour of its neighbours. As each agent adjusts to its neighbours, the whole group eventually synchronizes its behaviour to the independent variables.

The independent variables are essentially available to all agents collectively, as it is apparent from the above examples. This is necessary for the system to organize and achieve global functioning. However, each unit or agent would be exposed to a subset of these variables. For example, each bird in a flock would look at a certain part of the region, and each fish in a school would sense a different part of the environment. But these different pieces of information integrate each other to form a whole. So we can view the vector $\mathbf{z}_i$ as different realizations of the same process or different locations of the same landscape. Accordingly, we require that there exists a consistent aggregator function F, such that:

$$\mathbf{z}^* = F(\mathbf{z}_1, \ldots, \mathbf{z}_i, \ldots, \mathbf{z}_n) \tag{2}$$

Vector $\mathbf{z}^*$ is a consistent aggregate of $\mathbf{z}_i$ for all i. For example, in case of ants, $\mathbf{z}^*$ could be the coordinates of target food place. Each ant would have a piece of information, $\mathbf{z}_i$, e.g. the direction towards the place from a certain point. However, all these directions collected from different ants, if consistent, would eventually point to the same place, $\mathbf{z}^*$. Agents however need not know either F or $\mathbf{z}^*$. They know only $\mathbf{z}_i$ and act accordingly. But the structure of the system integrates this dispersed knowledge to reach self-organization and emergence. As Friedrich Hayek (1945, p. 530) points out, knowledge used by economic agents never exists in a concentrated or integrated form, but as dispersed pieces of incomplete knowledge owned by different agents. 'The problem is thus in no way solved if we can show that all of the facts, *if* they were known to a single mind ... would uniquely determine the solution; instead, we must show how a solution is produced by the interactions of people, each of whom possesses only partial knowledge'.

We assume agents react basically in the same manner to their neighbours (up to an affine transformation). If each responds fundamentally differently, their adjustment processes may not be coordinated, and thus the system may not self-organize.

4.2 *Positive Feedback*

The structure of relation (1) allows for positive feedback dynamics. The rise of x for any reason will raise the local relative variables for other agents, $\mathbf{x}$, causing x to rise again in response. In social models, this positive feedback is described as 'social multiplier' (Becker and Murphy, 2000, pp. 14–15).

Feedback mechanism is an essential feature of self-organization (Bonabeau *et al.*, 1999), and can explain how the system may coordinate the behaviour of its units without central control. Positive feedback however might lead to instability if not balanced properly. The presence of independent variables represents an essential mechanism for achieving such balance.

4.3 *Edge of Chaos*

It is insightful to examine how behaviour of (1) would change if it did not balance these two types of variables. Consider the case where each agent responds mainly to independent variables, but negligibly to relative ones. Then there will be no emergent behaviour. Because each agent reacts to different (realizations of) independent variables, these realizations will not be integrated, and their behaviour would be unsynchronized. They become a disorganized collection of units.

In contrast, if each agent responds predominantly to relative variables, there will be an emergent structure, but the system may likely be unstable and chaotic. Given positive feedback, shocks to the behaviour of units will make the whole group continuously react, and the reaction may never settle, as the change of the group would feed back the behaviour of the unit. This can explain fads and related information cascades (Bikhchandani *et al.*, 1992). Herd behaviour has been identified as a contributing factor for cycles and instability (Ball, 2004, pp. 215–221; Shiller, 2005, chapter 9; Cassidy, 2009, chapter 14).

Although relative relations are important for adjustment of units to each other, independent variables are required for global order and functioning. In other words, relative adjustment describes the 'self' part of 'self-organization', whereas independent variables are necessary for the 'organization' part.

This discussion is consistent with the view that complexity lies at the 'edge of chaos' discussed earlier. By including independent variables and relative variables, Equation (1) reflects the dual characterization of complex systems.

The above model can be related to Kauffman's *NK* network model, where small values of K makes the network dynamic but stable, i.e. in the phase of order at the edge of chaos (Kauffman 1993, 1995). Accordingly, the number of units in the vector $\mathbf{x}$ has to be relatively small in order to avoid chaotic behaviour.

4.4 *Diversity*

Another way to look at system (1) is through diversity and similarity. Vector z_i reflects the diversity of information of agents regarding the independent variables. This diversity is important as it allows agents to complement the knowledge and skills of each other to reach global optimum (Page, 2007). Several studies have shown that, in principle, the more agents are heterogeneous in an economy, the more the regularity and stability of the *aggregate* economy (cited in Kirman, 1992, pp. 129–131). Further, diversity in networks has been found to be a crucial factor for their stability (Buchanan, 2002, pp. 146–148).

The vector x_{-i} reflects the similarity of each agent to its neighbours. This is required for coordinating their behaviour, as mentioned earlier. A system of pure similarity becomes vulnerable to instability. This arises from the positive feedback loop of the same variable, as pointed out earlier. Thus, a complex system balances diversity and similarity, homogeneity and heterogeneity. In this manner it is able to be rich and innovative, meanwhile organized and stable.

4.5 *Macro versus Micro Behaviour*

For an outside observer, the whole system might appear behaving as a single entity responding to z^*. An observer might therefore infer that:

$$\bar{x}_t = g(\mathbf{z}^*_{t-1}) \tag{3a}$$

That is, collective (or average) agents respond to aggregate independent variables directly. This would be the representative agent approach. But this tells us nothing of *how* did this relationship emerge in the first place. Ignoring the mechanism implies ignoring important ingredients of the aggregate behaviour. Because each unit reacts to its neighbours, and subsequently to its own past, aggregate behaviour therefore would be also dependent on its own past. Thus a more proper specification of the system would be:

$$\bar{x}_t = g(\mathbf{z}^*_{t-1}, \bar{x}_{t-1}) \tag{3b}$$

The system becomes inherently dynamic. Thus collective behaviour of the system cannot be fully explained by z^* alone. For example, no endogenous cycles can arise from (3a). But this arises naturally from (3b). Still however, many distributional issues would appear irrelevant in (3a, b), whereas they have strong implications on aggregate behaviour if (1) is considered instead (see Kirman, 1992). Further, adopting equation (3) assumes availability of full information regarding z^* to each unit, and an unusual ability to figure out the response function g. Both, full information and the ability to calculate g, are obviously unwarranted. A dilemma therefore arises: How agents are able to coordinate in absence of these requirements? The complexity approach resolves this dilemma by looking at relation (1) instead of (3). By taking relative behaviour into account, neither full information nor perfect computational ability is needed. In other words, adopting the complexity approach allows for richer behaviour with fewer requirements.

5. Relative Behaviour

Neoclassical theory assumes impersonal markets, whereby agents interact only through price signals (Kirman, 1997). Theory of complex systems provides mechanisms for self-organization that help us understand how agents in the economy interact in a manner that produces emergent behaviour. One important mechanism is relative behaviour discussed earlier.

Ignoring such mechanisms, and focusing only on the market, does not make the economy collectively bring any interesting properties over its parts. To the contrary, the well-known theorems of Sonnenschein, Mantel and Debreu, show that aggregate demand may lose important economic properties compared to those of individual agents (Mas-Colell *et al.*, 1995, chapter 17). For example, although individual demand functions should be negatively sloped, aggregate demand function under NE may slope in any direction. The system as a whole therefore becomes *less* than the parts! This makes it clear that a system with rich economic properties cannot be derived from individualistic parts (Cassidy, 2009, p. 70). The 'independent-individual model' (Auyang, 1998, chapter 4) is incompatible with the nature of the economy as a complex system.

To allow aggregate demand to be stable and negatively sloped, non-market conditions have to be introduced. One approach, by Hildenbrand and Kirman (1988, chapter 6), among others, is to impose certain restrictions on the distribution of some characteristics of agents, e.g. income or endowments. This not only restores economic properties of aggregate demand, it also makes it acquire new properties absent from individual demands (p. 216). Local interactions provide a mechanism in line with this approach (Blume and Durlauf, 2001, pp. 29–30). As we shall see later, relative behaviour imposes certain restrictions on agents' behaviour and, subsequently, on their distribution, which allows for emergent economic properties.

Despite the important role such interactions play for the economy as a whole, they have no place in neoclassical theory. As Manski (2000, p. 115) points out, NE views non-market interactions as impediments to 'social optimum', and that such externalities should be eliminated, if possible, and replaced by market based arrangements. But the theorems of Sonnenschein, Mantel and Debreu, tell us that, no matter how clever these market arrangements are, individualistic design fails to produce an economy with interesting or realistic properties.

5.1 *Sympathy, Conformity and Imitation*

Relative behaviour can have a variety of forms. An agent would choose, say, his or her consumption based not only on his own income (independent variable), but also on the consumption level of his or her neighbours or peers (relative variables). One prefers to conform to the group, at least in some respects, rather than being oddly different. Preference for conformity is widely reported in psychological studies (e.g.

Aronson, 2007, chapter 2), and supported by research in neuroscience (Goleman, 2006, pp. 30–32, 40–43).

Sympathy to others may also make agents prefer to behave in a manner that brings them closer to their associates. Adam Smith in *Theory of Moral Sentiments* noted that there are some principles in human nature 'which interest him in the fortune of others, and render their happiness necessary to him, though he derives nothing from it except the pleasure of seeing it' (cited in Wilson, 1993, p. 31).

Although neoclassical theory considers only independent variables, an essential assumption of NE, perfect competition, is driven mainly through relative behaviour, particularly imitation. Frank Knight (1935, p. 46), long time ago, has pointed out that the 'motive for business is to such a large extent that of emulation' (cited in Choi, 1993, p. 116). Even markets with very few agents may behave competitively in presence of imitation (Camerer, 2003, p. 296; Alexopoulos and Sapp, 2006). Despite the central role of competition in economic theory, NE is silent on how competition is actually achieved, and what the process behind it is.

Imitation may play an important role in technology transfer and dissemination of innovation, as Baumol (1993, chapter 9) points out. It is also important for learning. Colin Camerer (2003) surveys experimental evidence of imitation learning, and concludes: 'These results ... suggest imitation should be taken seriously as an empirical source of learning' and that 'imitation may also be a heuristic shortcut to more general types of learning' (p. 298). According to Richerson and Boyd (2005, pp. 12–13), a population of purely individual learners would be stuck with what little each can learn by him or herself. But when individual learning is combined with imitation, however, the population is able to adapt in ways that outreach the abilities of any individual genius.

Regardless of the exact motive for individuals' decision to be influenced by that of others, the importance of relative behaviour arises from a completely different angle: self-organization. Relative behaviour, through local interactions, can propagate local behaviour to the rest of the economy, and thus makes the economy behave as a single entity.

5.2 *Types of Relative Behaviour*

Relative behaviour can be generally classified into two broad categories:

1. Similarity-seeking behaviour. This includes various tendencies for imitation, conformity, equity, reciprocity and altruism. These motives are reflected in a behaviour of the decision maker similar in nature to that of a reference group or person.
2. Dissimilarity-seeking behaviour. This includes innovation, differentiation, status games for positional goods, i.e. goods that improve the position or rank of the decision maker compared to the reference group.

Although the two types appear opposite to each other, it can be argued that similarity seeking is central to social behaviour. It is not difficult to see that it is necessary for forming societies in the first place. Further, similarity serves as a 'focal point' on which expectations could easily converge to, thus solving varieties of coordination games (see Schelling, 1960). Dissimilarity obviously cannot play this role.

Seeking dissimilarity on the other hand can be a good source of innovation and discovery. But it assumes a priori a minimum degree of similarity. People enjoy status over those who are close enough in order for the comparison to make sense, as Robert Frank (1985, pp. 28–30) rightly points out. However, status games or conspicuous consumption are zero-sum games and lead to wasting resources (Frank, 1999; Hopkins and Kornienko, 2004).

5.3 *Complexity, Economics and Social Sciences*

Steven Durlauf (2005, p. 240) points out that complex environments are characterized by social interactions and interdependencies. From the previous discussions, it is not difficult to see why. It is surprising how the structure of complex systems is consistent with behavioural and social characteristics. Relative behaviour is a point at which hard sciences and social sciences meet. It is also a point where neoclassical theory is clearly lacking. This would be a promising direction for cross-disciplinary research that would be fruitful to all related fields.

6. Behavioural Complexity[1]

Based on model (1), we can go a step ahead and examine how economic behaviour might change in such an environment. For simplicity, analysis is focused on consumption behaviour. Economic theory requires consumption to be a function of income (and wealth, as accumulated surplus income). But we add a behavioural assumption: consumption is also affected by that of local neighbours. That is, we assume that:

$$c_{i,t} = f(y_{i,t-1}, w_{i,t-1}, \bar{c}_{-i,t-1}) \tag{4}$$

where $c_{i,t}$ is consumption level of agent i at time t; $y_{i,t-1}$ is income at time $t-1$; $w_{i,t-1}$ is wealth; $\bar{c}_{-i}$ is average consumption of surrounding neighbours. This model has the same structure as (1), with relative variables appearing here in the form of a simple average.

In their study of 'social economics', Becker and Murphy (2000, pp. 8–11) consider social influence on agent's behaviour ($\bar{c}_{-i}$ in our model) as a form of 'social capital'. It represents the accumulation of social behaviour that affects and constrains individual's choice. The main assumption is that social capital has a complementary relationship to individual's choice, i.e. positive relationship. According to Becker and Murphy (2000, p. 13), social capital restricts the individual's choice, so that a rise in income may not greatly affect agent's behaviour compared to the pure individual model. In our case, consumption of high-income agents would be restricted by that of their neighbours.

We consider consumption of 'non-positional' goods rather than conspicuous consumption or status. That is, the average of consumption *levels* of neighbours is considered, rather than the *deference* between the agent's consumption and that of its neighbours. Accordingly, the system has no intrinsic tendency towards instability. Unlike the model of Duesenberry (1949) and related models (e.g. Harbaugh, 1996), no assumption is made regarding the shape or structure of the utility function of agents; relative consumption is simply assumed to affect consumption decisions.

6.1 *Emergent Behaviour*

As agents get different incomes, they cannot have equal levels of consumption. Agents with high income will enjoy high consumption, and vice versa. This means that average consumption for any given neighbourhood will exceed available income for some agents. This creates a gap between desired consumption and available income. There are several possibilities for closing this gap:

One is that agents would move to localities with comparable levels of consumption whereby the gap is substantially reduced. This results in the segregation model of Schelling (1978, 2006). This might explain demographic distribution of neighbourhoods in large cities.

Another possibility would be to exchange labour services for additional income. If agents spend some time looking after their properties, say, then high-income agents may hire low-income agents for an agreed upon wage. This would be Pareto optimal, as low-income agents would earn additional income, whereas high-income agents would enjoy more leisure. Generally speaking, seeking similarity in one dimension (in this case, consumption) creates heterogeneity in other dimensions (labour services). This can explain emergence of markets due to relative behaviour.

A yet third possibility would be financing: surplus agents would finance the consumption gap of deficit agents. This would create interesting dynamics, as elaborated in Al-Suwailem (2008). Here we shall assume that the gap is financed through interest-free lending, and examine resulting overall properties of the two models.

6.2 *Simulation*

The model is implemented using an agent-based environment. The one chosen is NetLogo, developed by Uri Wilensky at Northwestern University (Wilensky, 1999).[2]

There are 1225 agents modelled as patches on a landscape. Each agent receives income and decides his or her consumption accordingly. Each period, every agent gets a random draw from his income distribution. Income is exogenous and is distributed normally with mean μ_i and standard deviation σ. The mean, μ_i, is distributed uniformly across agents.

Initial consumption is determined by initial income and initial wealth. Afterwards, each agent sets his or her consumption level as a weighted average of his resources (income and wealth) and average consumption of local neighbours:

$$c_{i,t-1} = \beta_1 y_{i,t-1} + \beta_2 w_{i,t-1}, \quad \text{for} \quad t = 1 \quad \text{and}$$
$$c_{i,t} = (1 - \lambda)(\beta_1 y_{i,t-1} + \beta_2 w_{i,t-1}) + \lambda \bar{c}_{-i,t-1}, \text{ for } t > 1 \qquad (5)$$

β_1 is 'marginal propensity to consume' out of income; β_2 is marginal propensity to consume out of net wealth, and λ is the weight of relative consumption. If $\lambda = 0$, the model reduces to Ando and Modigliani consumption model (e.g. Hall and

Taylor, 1997). Any surplus of income after consumption is determined will be saved. Accumulated savings are added to wealth. Because savings are used to lend other agents, wealth becomes illiquid and therefore cannot be used for consumption. An agent however may borrow to finance his or her consumption gap against his wealth. An agent can be simultaneously a lender and a borrower.

Savings are deposited in a central agency that manages lending and repayments. Although a central agency might not be in the spirit of an agent-based model, in real life financial management is done electronically and therefore can operate to a large extent centrally. This is mainly a simplifying assumption to focus solely on consumption behaviour and its consequences, without transaction costs or frictions.

In the simple NE model, demand for borrowing does not arise from consumption gap, because relative behaviour is absent; rather, it arises from wealth effect. Higher wealth implies higher desired consumption. If current income is not sufficient, then the agent needs to borrow to finance its current consumption.

6.3 *Financing*

The central agency manages channelling funds from surplus units to deficit units. If aggregate savings are less than total demand for loans (total deficit), funds are rationed for each agent based on the proportion of its deficit to total deficit.

Loans are added to agent's debt, which is deducted from accumulated savings to obtain its current net wealth. Loans are scheduled to be repaid in a pre-determined number of periods, set to 60 periods. (A period in this model can represent one month, so 60 periods is equivalent to 5 years, which is quite common in real life.) Collected repayments are distributed to lenders based on their shares in aggregate accumulated surpluses, or wealth.

Payments of principal loans are not added to income of creditors, but reflect a change in the liquidity of wealth. Total funds available for lending equals total principal payments, plus total current surpluses, plus previous funds not lent out. The consumption gap is assumed to be financed using interest-free lending for both models. Further details and discussions of alternative financing mechanisms are presented in Al-Suwailem (2008).

6.4 *Parameters*

Parameters take a range of values instead of a single point. This accommodates the heterogeneity of agents and supports robustness of results.

1. Marginal propensity to consume out of income $\beta_1 \sim$ uni(0.85 ± 15%).
2. Marginal propensity to consume out of net wealth $\beta_2 \sim$ uni(0.01 ± 30%).
3. Weight of relative consumption for the simple NE model: $\lambda = 0$; for the complex model: $\lambda \sim$ uni(0.5 ± 30%).
4. Income distribution $y_i \sim N(\mu_i, 15)$, where $\mu_i \sim$ uni(75 ± 30%).
5. Number of periods = 1500.
6. Number of agents = 1225.
7. Number of neighbours for each agent = 8.

7. Results

The results presented in Tables 2–4 are the averages of 30 runs for each model, each run with a different, randomly generated, seed number. They are taken for the last period of simulation. Table 2 shows summary statistics for major variables of the two models. Net income is the current draw of income minus amount due to repay

Table 2.   Summary Statistics.

	Simple $\lambda = 0$	Complex $\lambda > 0$
Consumption		
Mean, $	74.5	74.3
Median, $	73.4	74.0
Std	0.22	0.19
No. below 0.5 max	354	126
Net income		
Mean, $	72.5	64.7
Median, $	71.2	64.8
Std	0.24	0.29
No. below 0.5 max	435	537
Net wealth		
Mean, $	1316	1855
Median, $	1245	1746
Std	0.55	1.02
No. below 0.5 max	972	1102

Std: Standard deviation across agents; No. below 0.5 max: Number of agents with values below 50% of the maximum value in the population.

Table 3.   Debt and Wealth.

	Simple $\lambda = 0$	Complex $\lambda > 0$
Wealth, $	1439	2446
Debt, $	123	591
Net, $	1316	1855

Table 4.   Flow of Funds.

	Simple $\lambda = 0$	Complex $\lambda > 0$
Acc. surplus, $	1439	2446
Acc. loans, $	1838	10,534
Acc. no. of loans	940	1112
Average loan size, $	1.96	9.48
Turnover	1.28	4.31

the loan. Net wealth is wealth minus debt, where wealth, as mentioned earlier, is accumulated surpluses of income over consumption.

7.1 *Consumption*

Table 2 shows also that the distribution of consumption across agents is smoother, although the average is a little lower, in the complex model than in the simple model. Relative behaviour helps harmonizing consumption levels amongst agents. But this harmonization comes at a price: Net income is clearly lower in the complex model. Agents borrow to smooth their consumption, so they have to pay installments and thus end up with a lower net income.

7.2 *Wealth*

Net wealth is notably higher, and more skewed, in the complex model than the simple model. It seems that high-income agents, because of the constraint of relative behaviour, consumed less, and thus were able to save more than needed to finance low-income agents. To verify this reasoning, Table 3 presents total levels of wealth and debt in the two models.

Although debt in the complex model is about five times that of the simple model, wealth is sufficiently higher, and net wealth (total wealth – total debt) is about 40% higher in the complex model. Note that financing is interest-free in both models, so lenders do not gain by lending. Thus, higher wealth is stemming from conservative consumption. High-income agents were able to avoid excessively high levels of consumption, thus adding substantially to total wealth, with little effect on average consumption. Maximum consumption at the end of simulation for the simple model, on average over the 30 runs, is 127, whereas that for the complex model is 112. However, the relatively small savings from this reduction in consumption gets accumulated overtime, producing significantly higher wealth. This distributional effect is absent from the simple model, as there is no mechanism for harmonizing consumption among agents.

7.3 *Flow of Funds*

Table 4 shows flow of funds for the two models. Surplus is the amount of income in excess of consumption per period. Accumulated surplus thus represents savings for each agent accumulated throughout the life of the model (which is equivalent to wealth). Accumulated loans represent total amount of money borrowed per agent throughout the life of the simulation. Accumulated repayment represents total amount repaid per agent.

Loans in the complex model are much higher than the simple model. The reason is obvious: Consumption gap is much larger than in the simple model. For the simple model, the gap arises not from relative behaviour, but from wealth effect: Relatively higher wealth levels encourage higher consumption levels. But because wealth is illiquid, agents need to borrow to finance desired consumption. So wealth here plays a similar role to 'permanent income'.

What is worth noting is efficiency of utilizing funds, or turnover. This is the ratio of accumulated loans to accumulated surpluses. The complex model allows each dollar of accumulated savings to be lent over 4.3 times, whereas the simple model 1.28 times only. The complex model is able to channel funds to deficit agents through the web of local interdependence of consumption, and achieve higher efficiency of fund utilization.

7.4 *Dynamics*

Figure 1 shows average consumption of a given run over the lifetime of the simulation. Consumption appears smoother over time in the complex model compared to the simple model. Relative behaviour not only distributes consumption more evenly among agents in a given period, but also more smoothly over time. Standard deviation of average consumption for the last 500 periods of the simulation presented in Figure 1 is 0.26 for the simple model, but 0.15 for the complex model. It seems that local interdependence helps stabilize the economy and reduce fluctuations.

7.5 *Summary*

The results above show that a complex model might be more efficient, more productive and more stable, than standard, atomic NE model. This is one example of

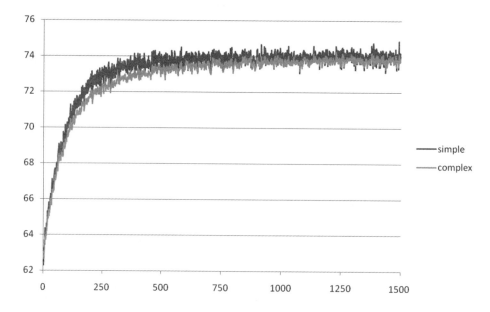

Figure 1. Consumption.

how 'the whole is greater than the sum'. The 'representative agent' model can be misleading in understanding the origins of such properties. Future research may help explore in more detail the emerging properties and behaviour of this sort of complex behaviour.

It might be also worthwhile to examine how the structure of model (1) would apply to other aspects of economic behaviour, for example, production and employment. This would be an intuitive way for extending standard neoclassical relations. From this perspective, CE would be a natural evolution of economic theory beyond NE.

8. Conclusions

Complexity Economics can be characterized as economics of a nonconvex world. In contrast, Neoclassical Economics depends critically on convexity, which makes it exposed to many weaknesses and deficiencies. The absence of these weaknesses from CE is what makes the latter both interesting and more relevant to economic life.

Complex systems are characterized by two main properties: self-organization and emergence. The first relates to the structure of the system, whereas the latter relates to its functions. These two properties can arise only in a nonconvex world, which makes NE inadequate for exploring and studying complex systems.

The paper proposes a modelling framework of complex systems whereby behaviour is determined by exogenous and endogenous variables. The endogenous part, local interdependence and relative behaviour, plays a crucial role in integrating dispersed knowledge conveyed by exogenous variables. This makes the system able to self-organize and thus to show emergent properties.

A practical application of the suggested model in consumption is constructed using agent-based simulation. Results show how unexpected properties may arise from simple local interactions. It also shows how a complex system can in fact be more than the sum of its parts, in contrast to the atomic, NE-based model.

CE is a promising development in the progress of economic studies. The recent global financial crisis has been also a crisis in mainstream economics (Kirman, 2010; Krugman, 2009; Stiglitz, 2010, chapter 9). It is hoped that the growing trends in the profession, along the lines highlighted above, contribute to transforming economics from being 'the dismal science' to being the science of inspiration, creativity and prosperity.

Acknowledgements

This paper is an outgrowth of parts of Al-Suwailem (2008). Special thanks to K. Vela Velupillai and an anonymous referee for insightful and helpful comments. I also thank the participants of the Workshop on Nonlinearity, Complexity and Randomness, held at University of Trento, Italy, 27–28 October, 2009, for lively discussions. The views expressed here do not necessarily represent the views of the organizers of the Workshop or of the Islamic Development Bank Group.

Notes

1. The term 'behavioural complexity' has been used in the literature on managerial leadership to indicate 'the ability to exhibit contrary or opposing behaviours ... while still retaining some measure of integrity' (Denison *et al.*, 1995). Here it means economic behaviour from the perspective of CE.
2. The version used of NetLogo is 3.1.4. The model implemented (RC Model 8.4.5) is a revised and expanded version of that in Al-Suwailem (2008).

References

Abraham, R. (2002) The genesis of complexity. Visual Math Institute. URL: www.ralph-abraham.org (last visited 6 December 2010).

Alexopoulos, M. and Sapp, S. (2006) Exploring the behavior of economic agents: the role of relative preferences. *Economic Bulletin* 12: 1–7.

Al-Suwailem, S. (2008) *Islamic Economics in a Complex World: Explorations in Agent-based Simulation*. Jeddah, Saudi Arabia: Islamic Research and Training Institute, Islamic Development Bank Group.

Aronson, E. (2007) *The Social Animal*. New York, NY: Worth Publishers.

Arrow, K. (1987) Rationality of self and others in an economic system. In R.M. Hogarth and M.W. Reder (eds), *Rational Choice: The Contrast Between Economics and Psychology* (pp. 201–216). Chicago, IL: University of Chicago Press.

Arrow, K. (1988) Workshop on the economy as an evolving complex system: summary. In P.W. Anderson, K.J. Arrow and D. Pines (eds), *The Economy as an Evolving Complex System* (pp. 275–281). Boulder, CO: Westview Press.

Arthur, W.B. (1988) Self-reinforcing mechanisms in economics. In P.W. Anderson, K.J. Arrow and D. Pines (eds), *The Economy as an Evolving Complex System* (pp. 9–31). Boulder, CO: Westview Press.

Auyang, S.Y. (1998) *Foundations of Complex-system Theories in Economics, Evolutionary Biology, and Statistical Physics*. Cambridge, UK: Cambridge University Press.

Baily, M., Litan, R. and Johnson, M. (2008) The origins of the financial crisis. Fixing Finance Series, Paper 3, Washington, DC: Brookings Institution.

Ball, P. (2004) *Critical Mass*. New York, NY: Farrar, Straus and Giroux.

Barabási, A. (2003) *Linked*. New York, NY: Plume, Penguin Group.

Barry, N. (1982) The tradition of spontaneous order. *Literature of Liberty* 5: 7–58. URL: www.econlib.org (last visited 6 December 2010).

Baumol, W.J. (1993) *Entrepreneurship, Management, and the Structure of Payoffs*. Cambridge, MA: MIT Press.

Becker, G. and Murphy, K. (2000) *Social Economics: Market Behavior in a Social Environment*. Cambridge, MA: Belknap Press of Harvard University Press.

Beinhocker, E.D. (2006) *The Origin of Wealth: Evolution, Complexity, and the Radical Remaking of Economics*. Cambridge, MA: Harvard Business School Press.

Ben-Ner, A. and Putterman, L., eds. (1998) *Economics, Values, and Organizations*. Cambridge, UK: Cambridge University Press.

Bikhchandani, S., Hirshleifer, D. and Welch, I. (1992) A theory of fads, fashion, custom, and cultural change as information cascades. *Journal of Political Economy* 100: 992–1026.

Blume, L. and Durlauf, S. (2001) The interactions-based approach to socioeconomic behavior. In S. Durlauf and H.P. Young (eds), *Social Dynamics* (pp. 15–44). Cambridge, MA: MIT Press.

Bonabeau E. and Meyer, C. (2001) Swarm intelligence: a whole new way to think about business. *Harvard Business Review* 79: 107–114.

Bonabeau, E, Dorigo, M. and Theraulaz, G. (1999) *Swarm Intelligence: From Natural to Artificial Systems*. Oxford, UK: Oxford University Press.

Brock, W.A. (2000) Some Santa Fe scenery. In D. Colander (ed.), *The Complexity Vision and the Teaching of Economics* (pp. 29–49). Northampton, MA: Edward Elgar.

Brooks, R. (1991) Intelligence without reason. MIT Artificial Intelligence Laboratory, Memo 1293.

Buchanan, M. (2002) *Nexus: Small Worlds and the Ground Breaking Science of Networks*. New York, NY: W.W. Norton.

Camazine, S., Deneubourg, J.-L., Franks, N.R., Sneyd, J., Theraulaz, G. and Bonabeau, E. (2001) *Self-Organization in Biological Systems*. Princeton, NJ: Princeton University Press.

Camerer, C. (2003) *Behavioral Game Theory*. Princeton, NJ: Princeton University Press.

Camerer, C., Loewenstein, G. and Rabin, M., eds. (2004) *Advances in Behavioral Economics*. Princeton, NJ: Princeton University Press.

Cassidy, J. (2009) *How Markets Fail: The Logic of Economic Calamities*. New York, NY: Farrar, Straus and Giroux.

Choi, Y.B. (1993) *Paradigms and Conventions: Uncertainty, Decision Making, and Entrepreneurship*. Ann Arbor, MI: University of Michigan Press.

David, P. (2005) Path dependence in economic processes: implications for policy analysis in dynamical system context. In K. Dopfer (ed.), *The Evolutionary Foundations of Economics* (pp. 151–194). Cambridge: Cambridge University Press.

Deaton, A. and Muelbauer, J. (1980) *Economics and Consumer Behavior*. Cambridge, UK: Cambridge University Press.

Debreu, G. (1959) *Theory of Value: An Axiomatic Analysis of Equilibrium*. New Haven and London: Yale University Press.

Debreu, G. (1991) The mathematization of economic theory. *American Economic Review* 81: 1–7.

Denison, D.R., Hooijberg, R. and Quinn, R.E. (1995) Paradox and performance: toward a theory of behavioral complexity in managerial leadership. *Organization Science* 6: 524–540.

Duesenberry, J.S. (1949) *Income, Saving, and the Theory of Consumer Behavior*. Cambridge, MA: Harvard University Press.

Durlauf, S. (2005) Complexity and empirical economics. *Economic Journal* 115: F225–F243.

Flake, G. (1998) *The Computational Beauty of Nature: Computer Explorations of Fractals, Chaos, Complex Systems, and Adaptation*. Cambridge, MA: MIT Press.

Foley, D. (1998) Introduction. In P. Albin *Barriers and Bounds to Rationality*, edited with an introduction by D. Foley. Princeton, NJ: Princeton University press.

Foley, D. (2005) The complexity vision in economics. Workshop on Computable Economics, University of Ireland, Galway, March 21–25.

Frank, R. (1985) *Choosing the Right Pond: Human Behavior and the Quest for Status*. Oxford, UK: Oxford University Press.

Frank, R. (1999) *Luxury Fever*. Princeton, NJ: Princeton University Press.

Freeman, C. (1998) Innovation. In J. Eatwell, M. Milgate and P. Newman (eds), *The New Palgrave Dictionary of Economics* (vol. 2, pp. 858–860). Hampshire, UK: Palgrave McMillan Publishers.

Gennotte, G. and Leland, H. (1990) Market liquidity, hedging, and crashes. *American Economic Review* 80: 999–1021.

Gigerenzer, G., Todd, P. and the ABC Research Group (1999) *Simple Heuristics that Make Us Smart*. Oxford, UK: Oxford University Press.

Gintis, H., Bowles, S., Boyd, R. and Fehr, E. (2005) *Moral Sentiments and Material Interests: The Foundations of Cooperation in Economic Life*. Cambridge, MA: MIT Press.

Goleman, D. (2006) *Social Intelligence: The New Science of Social Relationships*. New York, NY: Bantam Books.

Hall, R. and Taylor, J. (1997) *Macroeconomics* (5th edition). New York, NY: W.W. Norton.

Hands, D.W. (2006) Integrability, rationalizability, and path-dependency in the history of demand theory. *History of Political Economy* 38: 153–185.

Harbaugh, R. (1996) Falling behind the Joneses: relative consumption and the growth-saving paradox. *Economics Letters* 53: 297–304.

Hargadon, A. (2003) *How Breakthroughs Happen*. Cambridge, MA: Harvard Business School Press.

Hayek, F. (1945) The use of knowledge in society. *American Economic Review* 35: 519–530.

Heal, G.M. (1999) *The Economics of Increasing Returns*. Northampton, MA: Edward Elgar.

Hildenbrand, W. and Kirman, A. (1988) *Equilibrium Analysis*. Amsterdam: North-Holland.

Holland, J.H. (1988) The global economy as an adaptive process. In P.W. Anderson, K.J. Arrow and D. Pines (eds), *The Economy as an Evolving Complex System* (pp. 117–124). Boulder, CO: Westview Press.

Holland, J.H. (1996) *Hidden Order: How Adaptation Builds Complexity*. Cambridge, MA: Perseus Books.

Holland, J.H. (1999) *Emergence: From Chaos to Order*. Cambridge, MA: Perseus Books.

Hopkins, E. and Kornienko, T. (2004) Running to keep in the same place: consumer choice as a game of status. *American Economic Review* 94: 1085–1107.

Kauffman, S. (1993) *The Origins of Order: Self-organization and Selection in Evolution*. Oxford, UK: Oxford University Press.

Kauffman, S. (1995) *At Home in the Universe: The Search for Laws of Self-Organization and Complexity*. Oxford, UK: Oxford University Press.

Kauffman, S. (2000) *Investigations*. Oxford, UK: Oxford University Press.

Kennedy, J. and Eberhart, R. (2001) *Swarm Intelligence*. San Francisco, CA: Morgan Kaufman Publishers.

Kitzbichler, M.G., Smith, M.L., Christensen, S.R. and Bullmore, E. (2009) Broad-band criticality of human brain network synchronization. *PLoS Computational Biology* 5(3): e1000314. URL: www.ploscompbiol.org (last visited 6 December 2010).

Kirman, A. (1992) Whom or what does the representative individual represent? *Journal of Economic Perspectives* 6: 117–136.

Kirman, A. (1997) The economy as an interactive system. In W.B. Arthur, S. Durlauf and D. Lane (eds), *The Economy as an Evolving Complex System II* (pp. 491–531). Boulder, CO: Westview Press.

Kirman, A. (2010) The Economic Crisis is a Crisis for Economic Theory. *CESifo Economic Studies* 56 (4): 498–535.

Kirman, A. (2011) *Complex Economics: Individual and Collective Rationality*. New York, NY: Routledge.

Knight, F. (1935) *Ethics of Competition*. London: Allen & Unwin.

Krugman, P. (2009) How did economists get it so wrong. *New York Times Magazine* (Sep. 2) URL: www.nytimes.com.

Lee, C. (2005) Emergence and universal computation. In K. Velupillai (ed.), *Computability, Complexity, and Constructivity in Economic Analysis* (pp. 198–217). Oxford, UK: Blackwell Publishing.

Mandelbrot, B. (1997) *Fractals and Scaling in Finance: Discontinuity, Concentration, Risk*. New York, NY: Springer.

Manski, F. (2000) Economic analysis of social interactions. *Journal of Economic Perspectives* 14: 115–136.

Markose, S. (2002) The new evolutionary computational paradigm of complex adaptive systems. In S.-H. Chen (ed.), *Genetic Algorithms and Genetic Programming in Computational Finance* (pp. 443–484). Norwell, MA: Kluwer Academic Publishers.

Markose, S. (2005) Computability and evolutionary complexity: markets as complex adaptive systems (CAS). *Economic Journal* 115: F159–F192.

Martens, B. (2000) Towards a generalized Coase theorem: a theory of the emergence of social and institutional structures under imperfect information. In W.A. Barnett, C. Chiarella, S. Keen, R. Marks and H. Schnabl (eds), *Commerce, Complexity, and Evolution* (pp. 3–20). Cambridge, UK: Cambridge University Press.

Mas-Colell, A., Whinston, M. and Green, J. (1995) *Microeconomic Theory*. Oxford, UK: Oxford University Press.

Miller, J. and Page, S. (2007) *Complex Adaptive Systems: An Introduction to Computational Models of Social Life*. Princeton, NJ: Princeton University Press.

Mirowski, P. (1989) *More Heat than Light: Economics as Social Physics, Physics as Nature's Economics*. Cambridge, UK: Cambridge University Press.

Mitchell, M. (2009) *Complexity: A Guided Tour*. Oxford: Oxford University Press.

Newman, P. (1998) Convexity. In J. Eatwell, M. Milgate and P. Newman (eds), *The New Palgrave Dictionary of Economics* (vol. 1, pp. 645–647). Hampshire, UK: Palgrave McMillan Publishers.

Page, S. (2007) *The Difference: How the Power of Diversity Creates Better Groups, Firms, Schools, and Societies*. Princeton, NJ: Princeton University Press.

Pollak, R. (1976) Interdependent preferences. *American Economic Review* 66: 309–320.

Puffert, D. (2008) Path dependence. In R. Whaples (ed.), *EH.Net Encyclopedia* URL: eh.net/encyclopedia/ (last visited 6 December 2010).

Richerson, P. and Boyd, R. (2005) *Not by Genes Alone: How Culture Transformed Human Evolution*. Chicago, IL: University of Chicago Press.

Romer, P. (1986) Increasing returns and long-run growth. *Journal of Political Economy* 94: 1002–1037.

Romer, P. (1990) Are nonconvexities important for understanding growth? *American Economic Review* 80: 97–103.

Rosser, J.B. (1999) On the complexities of complex economic dynamics. *Journal of Economic Perspectives* 13: 169–192.

Rosser, J.B. (2000) *From Catastrophe to Chaos: A General Theory of Economic Discontinuities* (2nd edition). Norwell, MA: Kluwer Academic Publishers.

Rothschild, M. (2000) Complexity, business, and biological metaphors. In D. Colander (ed.), *The Complexity Vision and the Teaching of Economics* (pp. 285–296). Northampton, MA: Edward Elgar.

Samuelson, P. (1947) *Foundations of Economic Analysis*. Cambridge, MA: Harvard University Press.

Sawyer, R. (2005) *Social Emergence: Societies as Complex Systems*. Cambridge, UK: Cambridge University Press.

Scarf, H. (1981) Production sets with indivisibilities, part I: generalities. *Econometrica* 49: 1–32.

Scarf, H. (1994) The allocation of resources in presence of indivisibilities. *Journal of Economic Perspectives* 8: 118–128.

Schelling, T. (1960) *The Strategy of Conflict*. Cambridge, MA: Harvard University Press.

Schelling, T. (1978) *Micromotives and Macrobehavior*. New York, NY: W.W. Norton.

Schelling, T. (2006) Some fun, thirty-five years ago. In L. Tesfatsion and K. Judd (eds), *Handbook of Computational Economics: Agent-based Computational Economics* (pp. 1639–1644). Amsterdam: North-Holland.

Shiller, R. (2005) *Irrational Exuberance* (2nd edition). Princeton, NJ: Princeton University Press.

Simon, H. (1978) Rationality as process and as product of thought. *American Economic Review* 68: 1–16.

Simon, H. (1997) *Models of Bounded Rationality, Empirically Grounded Economic Reason.* Cambridge, MA: MIT Press.

Smith, V. (2007) *Rationality in Economics: Constructivist and Ecological Forms.* Cambridge: Cambridge University Press.

Stiglitz, J. (2000) The contributions of the economics of information to twentieth century economics. *Quarterly Journal of Economics* 115: 1441–1478.

Stiglitz, J. (2010) *Freefall: America, Free Markets, and the Sinking of the World Economy.* New York, NY: W.W. Norton.

Strogatz, S. (2003) *Sync: The Emerging Science of Spontaneous Order.* New York, NY: Hyperion.

Sugden, R. (1989) Spontaneous order. *Journal of Economic Perspectives* 3: 85–97.

Takayama, A. (1993) *Analytical Methods in Economics.* Ann Arbor, MI: University of Michigan Press.

Varian, H. (1992) *Microeconomic Analysis* (3rd edition). New York, NY: W.W. Norton.

Velupillai, K. (2005a) A primer on the tools and concepts of computable economics. In K. Velupillai (ed.), *Computability, Complexity, and Constructivity in Economic Analysis* (pp. 148–197). Oxford, UK: Blackwell Publishing.

Velupillai, K. (2005b) The unreasonable ineffectiveness of mathematics in economics. *Cambridge Journal of Economics* 29: 849–872.

Velupillai, K., ed. (2005c) Introduction. In K. Velupillai (ed.), *Computability, Complexity, and Constructivity in Economic Analysis* (pp. 1–14). Oxford, UK: Blackwell Publishing.

Velupillai, K. (2007) Variations on the theme of conning in mathematical economics. *Journal of Economic Surveys* 21: 466–505.

Velupillai, K. (2010) *Computable Foundations for Economics.* New York, NY: Routledge.

Waldrop, M. (1992) *Complexity: The Emerging Science at the Edge of Order and Chaos.* New York, NY: Simon and Schuster.

Wilensky, U. (1999) *NetLogo*, URL: ccl.northwestern.edu/netlogo/. Center for Connected Learning and Computer-Based Modeling, Northwestern University, Evanston, IL (last visited 9 December 2010).

Williams, G.P. (1997) *Chaos Theory Tamed.* Washington, DC: Joseph Henry Press.

Wilson, J.Q. (1993) *The Moral Sense.* New York, NY: Free Press.

6

BOUNDED RATIONALITY AND THE EMERGENCE OF SIMPLICITY AMIDST COMPLEXITY

Cassey Lee

'You cannot successfully use your technical knowledge unless you are a fairly educated person, and, in particular, have some knowledge of the whole field of the social sciences as well as some knowledge of history and philosophy. Of course real competence in some particular field comes first. Unless you really know your economics or whatever your special field is, you will be simply a fraud. But if you know economics and nothing else, you will be a bane to mankind, good, perhaps, for writing articles for other economists to read, but for nothing else'. (Hayek, 1991, p. 38)

'We feel clearly that we are only now beginning to acquire reliable material for welding together the sum total of all that is known into a whole; but on the other hand, it has become next to impossible for a single mind fully to command more than a small specialized portion of it . . . I can see no other escape from this dilemma than that some of us should venture to embark on a synthesis of facts and theories, albeit with second-hand and incomplete knowledge of some of them – and at the risk of making fools of ourselves'. (Schrödinger, 1967, p. 1)

1. Introduction

The notion of rationality and the way in which it is assumed and applied in economics is a much debated topic within the discipline itself and beyond. The vast body of literature under the headings of 'behavioural economics' and 'economics and psychology' have attempted to make sense of the extent to which and the manner in which rationality in reality differs from rationality as it is assumed in economics. The

Nonlinearity, Complexity and Randomness in Economics, First Edition.
Stefano Zambelli and Donald A.R. George.
© 2012 John Wiley & Sons. Published 2012 by John Wiley & Sons, Ltd.

term 'bounded rationality', which can be traced back to Herbert Simon's influential contributions in the 1950s, has been used by many when referring to departures from the conceptualization of rationality as consistency or rationality as maximization in mainstream economic theory. Today, the notion of bounded rationality has a permanent place in economics. Its impact has been profound in terms of our theoretical and empirical understanding of decision making and judgement, markets, organizations and institutions.

Parallel to the current research in mapping the boundaries of bounded rationality (to paraphrase Kahneman's Nobel lecture title) is an increasingly influential line of research that attempts to transform economics, this time into a social science that embraces complexity theory. A core element within this research programme is its focus on the emergence of complex structures from micro-level interactions between relatively simple parts/elements/agents. An analysis of how bounded rationality and complexity is related should be of great interest to economists. Most economists are likely to agree on the bounded rational nature of the human species as well as the complex nature of the economy. Yet, these two aspects have often been considered and researched separately with a few exceptions even though both are inextricably linked. This is a key aspect of Herbert Simon's ideas.

The purpose of this essay is to explore the relationship between the simple and the complex in economics by anchoring our analysis on bounded rationality. The point of view taken in this essay is that bounded rationality and the complexity of environment are both inextricably linked – that the emergence of complex social structures would not possible without interactions between bounded rational agents and vice-versa. Furthermore, the bounded rational nature of agents is in itself a consequence of a complex environment. What this implies in terms of a broader vision of economics is a topic worth exploring.

2. Rationality

The notion of rationality occupies a central position in modern economic theory. Blaug (1992, p. 230) opines that neoclassical economists regard the rationality postulate as part of the Lakatosian 'hard core' in their research programme. Within choice theory, many have characterized rationality in terms of preferences conforming to a set of axioms such as completeness, reflexivity, transitivity and continuity.[1] Walsh (1996) has labelled this approach as 'rationality as consistency'. Others have argued that the predominant view of rationality is that of 'rationality as maximization', for example, utility (or profit) maximization.[2] The two are related, that is, a 'perfectly' rational agent is one exhibiting 'consistent maximization of a well-ordered function' (Becker, 1962, p. 1) or alternatively (and more generally), one who 'makes decisions consistently in pursuit of his own objectives' (Myerson, 1991, p. 2). To scholars from other disciplines, such views may seem to be a very narrow view of human rationality. For the purpose of exploring the nature and implications of departures from perfect rationality, it is perhaps useful to note that such views were not always the predominant ones in economics.

In terms of ancestral views and visions, scholars point to a more 'pragmatic' notion of rationality adopted by Adam Smith in terms of 'preferring more to less' (Arrow, 1986, p. S388) and satisficing behaviour described as 'practical behavior of reasonable persons' (Simon, 2000, p. 27). Elsewhere, Simon (1997, p. 6) suggests that rationality, in so far as it can be inferred from Adam Smith's works, can be interpreted to mean 'having reasons for what you do'. An interesting and related issue in discussions on rationality is the role of self-interest. Simon (1997, p. 7) provides such an interpretation: '... the economic actors are certainly behaving rationally – that is, pursing what is they suppose to be their self-interest'. In this regard, Sen (1977) has argued for a need to go beyond this conceptualization of rationality as self-interest. This brings in the question of ethics and morality and their relationship to rationality. Walsh (1996), for example, cites Hilary Putnam's observation that 'our values of equality, intellectual freedom, and rationality, are deeply connected'.[3]

Beyond the classical economics period or rather at the tail end of it, it can perhaps be argued that the notion of rationality underwent further narrowing in the form of utilitarianism in the 1850s and 1860s and later in the form of the marginal utility doctrine via the works of Stanley Jevons, Carl Menger and Leon Walras in the 1870s.[4] The next significant development was the formulation of demand/preference theory based upon an ordinal interpretation of utility – indifference curves via Fisher and Pareto in the 1890s, consumer behaviour based on ordinal utility via Hicks and Allen in 1934 and Samuelson's weak axiom of revealed preference in the late 1930s.[5] These developments were crucial in establishing the basic axioms underlying the rationality-as-consistency approach in choice theory.

The 1930s also saw the beginnings of a dramatic transformation of economics of a different sort, namely the axiomatization of economic theory via the works of John von Neumann, Oskar Morgenstern and Abraham Wald. After the Second World War, the axiomatic method gained a permanent foothold in economic theory through general equilibrium analysis and social choice theory in the 1950s.[6] One interpretation of these developments (hopefully not a too naive one), is that the sanctity or unassailability of the rationality-as-consistency view in economics was further entrenched by the axiomatization of economic theory.

Apart from these developments, two other developments that are usually mentioned in discussing rationality in modern economics, namely, game theory and rational expectations. Formal treatments of game theory dates as far back as 1912 in the form of Ernst Zermelo's work followed by the 'subjective' approach by von Neumann and Nash in the 1940s–1950s (Vellupilai, 2009, p. 1411). Rational expectations was first proposed by John Muth in 1961 and developed later by Robert Lucas and Thomas Sargent in the 1970s. What are the notions of rationality associated with these developments?

The discussions on the notion of rationality in game theory have centred around a number of issues. These relate to whether the axioms underlying a given game characterize a rational person, for example, agents maximize or minimize payoffs and the efficient division of the game's surplus (Simon, 1991a, p. 2; Samuelson, 1996, p. 19). Rationality in game theory has also been related to the ability of agents to undertake long backward-induction calculations in extensive form games (Simon, 1991a, p. 24).

Not only are agents (players) in game theory usually assumed to be perfectly rational, such rationality is assumed to be common knowledge (known to all players).[7] In contrast, evolutionary game theory does away with any assumption of maximizing but this problem is not really addressed as the players in such theories do not correspond to individual players (Aumann, 1997, p. 5). Overall, the notion of rationality remains an open problem within game theory. Many scholars have advocated the usefulness of incorporating bounded rationality in game theory albeit there are disagreements about how this should be accomplished. For example, commenting on a preliminary draft of Ariel Rubinstein's book on modelling bounded rationality, Herbert Simon advocates an approach anchored 'careful observation and experimentation' rather than 'casual observations' (Rubinstein, 1998, p. 188).

In rational expectations, discussions on the notion of rationality center around how agents confront uncertainty about the future. In this regard, the standard assumptions are ones in which 'people behave in ways that maximize their utility (their enjoyment of life) or profits' and 'outcomes do not differ systematically (i.e. regularly or predictably) from what people expected them to be'.[8] The former suggests that agents in rational expectations are fully rational in the sense of maximizing. The latter implies that uncertainty is removed from agents by assuming that all of them know the correct model of the economy (Simon, 1991a, p. 8).[9] The consequence of this is that agents are able to predict the future with accuracy, thus enabling them to behave in a substantively rational manner (Simon, 1976, p. 79).

3. Bounded Rationality

3.1 *Bounded Rationality: Origins*

Within economics, there have been some interests in departing from the notion of 'perfect rationality' (either in the form of rationality as consistency or rationality as maximization). To date, there is no consensus on the form in which such departures *should* assume in theoretical models (a normative issue). This is encapsulated by Frank Hahn remarks that 'there is only one way to be perfectly rational, while there are an infinity of ways to be partially rational . . . where do you set the dial of rationality?'.[10] To further muddle this debate, the theoretical and empirical responses to this challenge in terms of departures from rationality have been variously labelled as non-rational, irrational and bounded rational.[11] Among these terms, the most often used one is that of bounded rationality.

The notion of 'bounded rationality' can be traced back to the pioneering work of Herbert Simon beginning in the 1950s. In an early work, Simon (1955) embarked on an attempt to drastically revise the concept of economic man by paying attention to the limits in the information and computational capacities of an economic man:

> 'Broadly stated, the task is to replace the global rationality of economic man with a kind of rational behavior that is compatible with the access to information and the computational capacities that are actually possessed by organisms, including man, in the kinds of environments in which such organisms exist'. (Simon, 1955, p. 99)

Thus, the term 'bounded rationality' can be interpreted to mean rational choice under computational constraints (Simon, 1955, p. 101). Within this interpretation, satisficing, in Simon's words, are 'approximating procedures' or 'simplifications the choosing organism may deliberately introduce into its model of the situation in order to bring the model within the range of its computing capacity' (Simon, 1955, p. 100). In the paper, in addition to the incorporation of simpler (discrete) pay-off functions, Simon introduced information gathering which improves the precision of behaviour-outcome mapping. The notion of 'aspiration level' was also introduced with the view that this can change depending on the ease of discovering satisfactory alternatives (Simon, 1955, p. 111).[12]

Simon's emphasis on the computational foundations of decision making were probably further reinforced after 1955 when he became more involved in research on problem-solving in cognitive psychology and computer science (artificial intelligence).[13] By the 1970s, the term 'procedural rationality' was used to denote a concept of rationality which focused on 'the effectiveness of the procedures used to choose actions' (Simon, 1978, p. 9) where the process of choice is important (Simon, 1978, p. 2; Simon, 1976, p. 131). This is different from the notion of 'substantive rationality' found in concepts such as 'rationality as maximization' or 'rationality as consistency' where choice is entirely determined by the agent's goals subject to constraints (and consistency requirements). Since the goals of agents are either assumed (maximizing utility) or are embedded in the axioms of preferences, the focus of substantive rationality lies in the results of rational choice. In discussing the concept of procedural rationality, Simon (1976, pp. 72–73) also highlighted the importance of using heuristics as means of selectively searching the 'immense tree of move possibilities'. Furthermore, Simon (1978, p. 12) attempted to relate the two concepts of satisficing and heuristics to the theories of computational complexity (which emerged in the 1960s) and heuristic search:

'One interesting and important direction of research in computational complexity lies in showing how the complexity of problems might be decreased by weakening the requirements for solution – by requiring solutions only to approximate the optimum, or by replacing an optimality criterion by a satisficing criterion'.

'The theory of heuristic search is concerned with devising or identifying search procedures that will permit systems of limited computational capacity to make complex decisions and solve difficult problems. When a task environment has patterned structure, so that solutions are not scattered randomly throughout it, but are located in ways related to the structure, then an intelligent system capable of detecting the pattern can exploit it in order to search for solutions in a highly selective way'.

3.2 Bounded Rationality: Empirical and Theoretical Developments

The rich ideas of Simon not withstanding, it took another decade, namely in the late 1980s, before bounded rationality received significant attention within economics (Klaes and Sent, 2005, p. 45). Even so, not all researchers whether they are empiricists (which includes experimentalists) or theoreticians used the term 'bounded rationality' in the same manner. Within the empiricists/experimentalists camp, which originated from the field of psychology, the early work on heuristics and biases by Tversky and Kahneman (1974) made no reference to Simon's work. This could be due to the distinction that they make between reasoning and intuitive thoughts, the latter being more important to judgements and choices (Kahneman 2003, p. 1450). Simon does not seem to have made this distinction even though he did acknowledge the importance of the unconscious: '... we cannot rule out the possibility that the unconscious is a better decision-maker than the conscious' (Simon, 1955, p. 104). In Kahneman's Nobel lecture, he describes his work with Tversky as an exploration of the psychology of intuitive beliefs and choices and an examination of their bounded rationality (Kahneman, 2003, p. 1449). However, in their seminal works, explicit references to bounded rationality were only made in discussing framing effects (Tversky and Kahneman, 1981, p. 458). Much of the body of research carried out under the banner of 'Behavioral Economics' or 'Economics and Psychology' were devoted to testing departures from elements of substantive rationality such as complete preferences, expected utility, Bayesian updating and exponential discounting, among others (see Camerer, 1998; Rabin, 1998). This can also be inferred in the following remarks in Rabin (1998, fn. 1) which could be interpreted as a reference to Simon's approach:

> 'Another topic I have omitted is "non-psychological" models of bounded rationality. Researchers have formulated models of bounded rationality (based on intuition, computer science, or artificial intelligence) meant to capture cognitive limits of economic actors, but which do not invoke research on the specific patterns of errors that human beings make'.

On the theoretical front, a number of different approaches to modelling bounded rationality have been adopted since the 1980s. To make sense of the literature, it is perhaps useful to try to classify the diverse models and methods that have been used to theorize some of the implications of bounded rationality.

One approach originates from the efforts by mathematicians and computer scientists to understand the foundation of mathematics as well as the nature and limits of computation. The origins of computability theory can be traced back to two monumental works in the 1930s. In 1931, Kurt Gödel shattered the Hilbertian program of attempting to derive all mathematics from a complete and consistent set of axioms. Gödel showed that there are true statements within such systems that are not provable. For the theory of computation, this result implies that 'there are some functions on the integers that cannot be represented by an algorithm – that is, cannot be computed' (Russell and Norvig, 1995, p. 11). This was to be followed by Alan Turing's proof that there are some functions that even powerful computing devices (such as the Universal Turing Machine) cannot compute.

The body of literature known as 'computable economics' and 'algorithmic economics' associated with the works of K. Vela Velupillai represent, perhaps, the most sustained application of computability theory to economics.[14] Surprisingly, there have been very little discussions on bounded rationality within a computability framework. Exceptions include Velupillai (2000) and Vellupilai (2010). Both works advanced several important points. The modelling of bounded rationality algorithmically (e.g. via the use of Turing machines) implies that choice and decision making are intrinsically dynamical processes. Equally important, bounded rationality is not a constrained version (or a special case) of rationality in the so-called 'Olympian models' (in our parlance, models where agents are fully rational). Rather, bounded rationality should be perhaps considered as the general case and full rationality a special case.

Another line of theoretical approach to bounded rationality that is related to computational theory but is different from the computability approach discussed above, involves the use of finite state automata to model limits to strategies that players can employ in games.[15] Early pioneers include Neyman (1985) and Rubinstein (1986). In these works, each player is assumed to employ an automaton (often a Moore machine) to play the game. Here, 'bounded rationality' can be interpreted in terms of limits to the number of states of the automaton. Such limits can either be exogenously determined (as in Neyman) or endogenously determined (as in Rubinstein). In the latter case, the number of states in the automaton is determined by a trade-off between the cost of maintaining such states and payoffs from a repeated game.

Another automata-based approach which is closer to 'applied' computational theory or computational complexity theory is that of Gilboa (1988) and Ben-Porath (1990). In contrast to the works of Neyman and Rubinstein, which look at complexity of implementation, these works consider the complexity of computation involved in selecting strategies. Here, the analysis of the complexity of computation involves assessing the amount of resources (such as time and memory) required to solve computational problems. This is analysed in terms of whether a polynomial time algorithm exists to solve a given computation problem such as Nash equilibrium. Overall, the results obtained suggest that Nash equilibria can be hard to compute (i.e. requires non-polynomial time) except for restricted cases (e.g. anonymous opponents and graphical structures).[16] What of bounded rationality within a computational complexity context? Roughgarden (2010, p. 231) argues that:

> 'For equilibrium computation problems, polynomial-time solvability correlates well with efficient learnability and has an appealing interpretation in terms of boundedly rational participants. While the exact definition of "hard" varies with the nature of the problem, all such hardness results suggest that no fast and general algorithm will be discovered, motivating the study of heuristics, distributional analyses, domain-specific special cases, and alternative, more tractable equilibrium concepts'.

The above remarks suggest that questions pertaining to the hardness of solving a problem, ways of reducing this hardness and the nature of the problem to be solved are inextricably linked. This insight is not entirely new and can be found in some of Herbert Simon's earliest published works. It provides a call for a reconsideration of how bounded rationality should be framed.

4. Bounded Rationality and the Complexity of Environment

4.1 *Some Early Views From Simon*

Herbert Simon's seminal 1955 paper that contained his early ideas of bounded rationality was followed by an equally interesting paper that was published a year later.

In the paper, Simon (1956, p. 120) articulated the importance of considering the environment within which bounded rational agents operate:

'A great deal can be learned about rational decision making by taking into account, at the outset, the limitations upon the capacities and complexity of the organism, and by taking into account of the fact that the environments to which it must adapt possesses properties that permit further simplification of its choice mechanisms'.

This line of thinking continued to pre-occupy Simon and his collaborator, Allen Newell, in their subsequent work. For example, an entire chapter (three) in Newell and Simon (1972) was devoted to the 'task environment' defined as 'an environment coupled with a goal, problem, or task'. The centrality of the interdependence between bounded rationality and the task environment is clearly articulated in the book using a scissors metaphor reminiscence of Marshall's use of the same metaphor for demand and supply:

'Just as a scissors cannot cut without two blades, a theory of thinking and problem solving cannot predict behavior unless it encompasses both an analysis of the structure of task environments and an analysis of the limits of rational adaptation to task requirements'. (Newell and Simon, 1972, p. 55)

In their theory, the locus of the links and interactions between the external environment and bounded rationality is the 'problem space' which is described as 'the space in which his problem solving activities takes place' (Newell and Simon, 1972, p. 59) This problem space is not exogenously given but is something that is derived internally (within the agent's mind) via the construction of an internal representation of the task environment (Newell and Simon, 1972, p. 59).

Another interesting point that Newell and Simon make is the possibility of shifting the boundary between the problem solver (as an information processing system or IPS) and the environment (Newell and Simon, 1972, p. 81) – which is accompanied by the need for another parameter, namely the intelligence of the problem solver (Newell and Simon, 1972, p. 82). A reading of (Newell and Simon, 1972, pp. 81–82) suggests that intelligence is related to the predictive abilities of a problem solver, which in turn can only be defined in terms of the type (or classes) of environment in which such abilities are valid. In an intriguing discussion of an extreme case of shifting such boundaries, Newell and Simon suggest that:

'We must exercise caution, however, in shifting the boundary between problem solver and environment. If we move particular operators and classify them with the task environment, there is a danger that a problem solver will disappear entirely, and that there will be no room at all for a theory of him'. (Newell and Simon, 1972, p. 81)

This is indeed what the literature on situated or embodied cognition seems to imply (Anderson, 2003). The other extreme would be of course, to shift the boundary entirely away from the environment which perhaps has an equally disturbing implication that there is actually no problem to be solved except for that which exists in the mind of the problem solver! Another interesting point that (Newell and Simon, 1972, pp. 93–94) make is the possibility of employing methods to reduce the problem space that needs to be explored to find a solution. After employing such methods, the agent will be left with an irreducible problem space that has to be examined in its entirety.

4.2 Some Recent Developments

The vision on the interdependence between bounded rationality and the environment within which decisions are made continues to find resonance in contemporary views:

> 'Models of bounded rationality describe how a judgement or decision is reached (that is, the heuristic processes or proximal mechanisms) rather than merely the outcome of the decision, and they describe the class of environments in which these heuristics will succeed or fail'. (Gigerenzer and Selten, 2001, p. 4)

The emphasis on context/environment suggests that there has to be a matching between the decision/judgement processes that are used and the structure/complexity of the environment (problems) to which they are applied. The term 'ecological rationality' has been used by Vernon Smith to denote this heuristic-environment matching. This can be contrasted with the term 'constructivist rationality' in which social institutions are created 'top-down' by what (Smith, 2003, p. 467) describes as 'conscious deductive processes of human reason'.

What are the sources of ecological rationality and how do they come about? Smith (2003, p. 469) suggests that such order 'emerges out of cultural and biological evolutionary processes'. The diverse views on the subject matter seem to suggest that our current state of knowledge in this area is far from complete and definitive. For example, there are at least five different views/theories on this subject, namely sociobiology, human behavioural ecology, evolutionary psychology, memetics and gene-culture co-evolution (Laland and Brown, 2002).

Following a co-evolutionary line of argument and perhaps inspired by similar views advanced by Simon (1956) and Newell and Simon (1972), it can be perhaps be further argued that the bounded rational nature of the human species is inextricably linked to the complexity of the environment. This is put forward succinctly by Gigerenzer (2001, p. 5):

> 'Simple heuristics can succeed by exploiting the structure of information in an environment. In other words, the environment can do part of the work for the heuristic'.

A similar view is advanced by Rubinstein (1998, p. 3) on the relationship between formal social institutions and decision making:

> 'Many social institutions, like standard contracts and legal procedures, exist, or are structured as they are, in order to simplify decision making'.

Furthermore, the bounded rational nature of humans also leads to the formation of formal and non-formal social structures and relationships (e.g. markets, non-markets, organizations, institutions, norms and conventions) that not only affect the choice and efficacy of 'approximating procedures' (to use Simon's terminology) but are themselves outcomes of such procedures:

> 'Rules emerge as a spontaneous order – they are found – not deliberately designed by one calculating mind. Initially constructivist institutions undergo evolutionary change adapting beyond the circumstances that gave them birth. What emerges is a form of "social mind" that solves complex organization problems without conscious cognition. This "social mind" is born of the interaction among all individuals through the rules of institutions that have to date survived cultural selection processes'. (Smith, 2003, p. 500)

Thus, what emerges is a social structure that acts as a collective problem-solving mechanism that sometimes complements and substitutes the judgement and decision processes at the individual level. Here, we recognize the ability of bounded rational agents to partake in some rational constructions that can further adapt and evolve, sometimes in unpredictable directions (this is a view articulated by Vernon Smith). This also extends to more tacit social constructions/relations such as norms and conventions. For example, Conlisk (1996, p. 677) suggests that:

> 'Norms might be the cause of bounds on individualistic rationality. Or norms might be the effect of bounded rationality . . . docility to social norms improves economic fitness by inducing people to augment their limited rationality with the collective wisdom of their social group'.

Such ideas also seem to be related to what Arrow (1986) considers to be Adam Smith's profound insight captured in the invisible hand metaphor:

> 'Actually, the classical view had much to say about the role of knowledge, but in a very specific way. It emphasized how a complete price system would require individuals to know very little about the economy other than their own private domain of production and consumption. The profoundest observation of Smith was that the system works behind the backs of the participants; the directing "hand" is "invisible." Implicitly, the acquisition of knowledge was taken to be costly'. (Arrow, 1986, p. S391)

The invisible hand metaphor has been the subject of market experiments for some time. An early example is Smith (1962), who provided experimental evidence that price adjustments were not consistent with that associated with a Walrasian tântonnement and that a decentralized trading system could bring about economic equilibrium. Perhaps, even more startling, Gode and Sunder (1993) showed that allocative efficiency can be achieved in markets populated by traders with zero intelligence. Aside from these works, there have been other attempts by economists to discuss and model decentralized (micro-level) interactions, often incorporating some form of departures from full rationality. Kirman (2003, p. 22) emphasizes the importance of decentralized market interactions involving individuals with 'limited reasoning and calculating capacities'. Both Kirman (1997) and Axtell (2007) argue that a fruitful way forward is to model decentralized interactions within networks. In a later paper, Kirman *et al.* (2007) modelled the self-organization of social networks via the assumption of bounded rational agents in a 'spatially myopic sense' (i.e. capable of interacting with only a subset of neighbours).

An issue that arises in virtually all these works is the the emergence of patterns arising from local interactions albeit without sufficient attention paid to the computational aspects whether from a computability or a computational complexity point of view. On this issue, it is perhaps useful to note recent attempts to deal with some of the computational theoretical problems associated with general equilibrium theory. While Axtell (2005) argued that the Walrasian general equilibrium is an implausible conception given the difficulty (NP hard) to compute it. In an even more devastating critique of the theory, Velupillai (2006) argued that the standard computable general equilibrium (CGE) model is not computable. In other words, since the equilibrium in a general equilibrium (GE) model cannot even be computed (solved algorithmically without any resource constraints) – there is not much point in even discussing the computational complexity of the problem (or computation under resource constraints). This is a distinction between what is solvable in principle (computable) and what is solvable in practice (tractable). A non-computable problem cannot be solved at all while a computable problem may not be solvable in practice, that is, intractable. (see Davis *et al.*, 1994, p. 444).

Clearly, the topic on the relationship between bounded rationality and the environment requires further research especially from more empirical evidence (anchored within an information-processing and computational framework) as well as theoretical explorations along the lines of computability and computational complexity. The full richness and relevance of Simon and Newell's vision on the subject can be seen from other disciplines. A particularly fruitful area of research involves the study of decision making in social insects. Interesting results include ant colonies that exhibits optimal decision making (e.g. Edwards and Pratt, 2009) and that can even solve NP-hard problems such as the Travelling Salesman Problem (Dorigo and Gambardella, 1997). Even more intriguing are perhaps studies on colony-level cognition where internal representation of cognition are found in individual insects and their interactions with each other (Marshall and Franks, 2009). Within social insect colonies, mutually interacting populations must reach an activation threshold before a decision takes place. Similar to the role played by Simon's satificing concept, the decision threshold 'can be varied to achieve either quick but inaccurate, or accurate but slow decisions' (Marshall and Franks, 2009, p. R395). Empirical observations in this area have been accompanied by computational complexity-based modelling (of the Crutchfield statistical complexity variety), for example, Delgado and Sole (1997).

There has been little interest in drawing lessons from such studies for economics, perhaps because many economists would consider ants are way too different ('less intelligent' or complex?) than humans. Kirman (1993) is a rare exception. In his paper, Alan Kirman emphasizes on how asymmetric outcomes (e.g. herding) can 'emerge' from stochastic interactions between symmetric (identical) and simple agents (ants). Another interesting feature of Kirman's model is the analysis of equilibrium as a process where the only meaningful characterization would be in terms of the 'equilibrium distribution of the process'. One interesting question that comes to mind is whether the shifting of the boundaries between the problem solver and environment might entail a trade-off between centralization and decentralization in a parallel information processing system. How then would a shift change computational complexity of the colony? A question of a similar spirit can also be to ask about the computability of such a system. Finally, such discussions also compel us to ponder another question – whether it might be useful to consider how 'simplicity' as in bounded rationality can emerge and co-evolve with a changing complex environment.

5. The Emergence of Simplicity Amidst Complexity

5.1 *The Complexity of Organisms and Environment*

Complexity and complex system are issues that have preoccupied scholars for a long time including Herbert Simon. After publishing two seminal papers that articulated the idea and importance of bounded rationality and how they relate to the environment (Simon, 1955, 1956), Herbert Simon went on to publish a paper titled 'The Architecture of Complexity' in 1962 (Simon, 1962). In a sense, Simon's interests in complexity and complex systems is a natural extension of his earlier works published since the mid-1950s. In Simon (1955, p. 101), the 'levels of computational complexity' was an issue raised in relation to bounded rationality (in terms of the employment of 'schemes of approximation'). Furthermore, not only is an organism complex (Simon, 1956, p. 129), the choice process associated with bounded rationality can differ in terms of different degree of rationality (Simon, 1956, p. 133). In addition, the 'complexity' of the environment also matters. In Simon's example involving the case of an organism seeking food, the 'complexity' of the environment matters. This was discussed in terms of the richness of randomly distributed food points and the density of paths (leading to them) (Simon, 1956, p. 131). In addition, Simon also noted that learning could enhance an organism's survival if food points are not randomly distributed such that clues to their location exist along paths leading to them (Simon, 1956, p. 135).

To discuss the issue of the complexity (or simplicity) of an organism and its environment, a more precise way to defining complexity is needed. One such approach would be to use Kolgomorov Complexity (or algorithmic information content) to measure complexity. The Kolgomorov Complexity K of an object is measured by the smallest program that can be used to compute it. A random object of length n would have a maximum K number equal to n. In contrast, an object comprising a string of n ones has a K approximately equal to $\log n$. The next challenge is to decide what to measure – the physical/biological or behavioural aspects of an organism. It is a difficult question to address as it leads to deep questions such as those relating to the roles of biological and cultural evolution. Both are related as an organism's capacity to learn, produce and transmit knowledge is likely to be biologically constrained to some extent.

5.2 *Bounded Rationality and the Environment*

In the model used in Simon (1956), the organism is assumed to have a fixed aspiration level (in terms of maintaining average food intake rather than maximizing) and an ability to see a finite number of moves ahead. When food points are randomly distributed, these two characteristics of the organism are sufficient to ensure a higher survival probability for the organism than when it behaves randomly. This example suggests that when the environment is maximally Kolgomorov complex (randomly distributed food points), the organism is likely to be found to be using decision procedures that are less than maximal Kolgomorov complex.[17]

What if food points are not randomly distributed and, in addition, clues on the distribution of food points can be detected by the organism? In such a case, Simon argued that the adoption of a systematic exploration strategy (i.e. heuristics) is associated with a higher survival probability than a completely random behaviour. This suggests that it pays (in terms of survival probability) for organisms to be less than maximal Kolgomorov complex when the environment is also less than maximal Kolgomorov complex (i.e. food points are not randomly distributed). An important issue to consider is whether some degree of randomness must be present in to ensure survivability especially in a changing environment.

The above discussions suggest that not only is bounded rationality (as in less than maximal Kolgomorov complex) more prevalent, the form in which it takes (satisficing, heuristics or both) depends on the nature of the environment, that is, heuristics involving learning to exploit some systematic feature of the environment. The prevalence of bounded rationality could also be interpreted to mean that the type of 'Olympian rationality' commonly assumed in many mainstream economics models is indeed a special case (as Vellupilai, 2010 has argued), that is, precisely because the spectrum encompassing the collection of choice procedures are obviously less than that associated with maximal Kolgomorov complexity. It is a special case where the organism has no constraints in terms of its ability to look forward (full knowledge of how food points are distributed) and/or is a maximizer (searching the entire problem space).

Would such interpretations differ in the case of organisms undertaking parallel information processing such as social insects? Going back to the earlier example, the employment of random foraging strategies (high K) under parallel information processing conditions (and in an environment where food points are randomly distributed) could be enough to ensure survivability of the colony. Does this mean that less complex choice procedures under parallel information processing work as well as complex choice procedures under serial information processing?[18] This may be a wrong comparison (question) as random foraging behaviour within social insect colonies may not necessarily be less complex. Why? The collective computations undertaken by social insects, even though based on simple choice procedures (e.g. randomizing) at the individual level, may be interpreted (as many have done) as an emergent property. That is, if it can be shown that the Kolgomorov complexity measure of the resulting 'collective choice procedures' (K') is actually lower. Can this be true? Can a collective choice procedure, comprising of individual choice procedure with high Ks, have a lower K'? It is possible that the Kolgomorov complexity of parallel information processing systems may be lower even without any emergent properties. For example, the average lower bound Kolgomorov complexity of a sequential sorting of n elements is in the order of $\frac{1}{2}\log n$ whereas that of a parallel stacks is $\sqrt{n}$

(Vitanyi, 2007). However, could emergent properties in such systems (provided they exist) drive the Kolgomorov complexity even lower?

5.3 *Emergence and Hierarchies*

There is currently no definition of the term 'emergence' that is universally accepted in the academic research community across different disciplines. Some refer to emergence as a '*property* of a system not reducible to, nor readily predictable from the properties of individual system components' (Halley and Winkler, 2008, p. 10). Some have emphasized emergence as a '*process* that leads to the appearance of a structure not directly described by the defining constraints and instantaneous forces that control a system' (Crutchfield, 1994, p. 12). Others consider emergence as involving the *detection* of 'some new feature that makes the overall description of the system simpler than it was before' (Deguet *et al.*, 2006, p. 24).

Instead of trying to reconcile these definitions, it might be perhaps more useful to discuss theoretically how emergence might occur. To begin with, emergence is an outcome of local interactions between large number of components of the system. Such local or micro-level interactions lead to the formation of spatio-temporal patterns or properties at the global or macro-level. Obviously, not all local-level interactions lead to emergence. In system with emergent properties, local interactions have been described as 'non-trivial' in the sense that they result in a reduction in the degrees of freedom (Prokopenko *et al.*, 2008, p. 11). This is similar to Simon's (Simon, 1962, p. 476) description of 'strong interactions' which not only reduces the capacity of the components to interact further but leads to the formation of sub-systems that interact weakly among themselves. Thus, systems with emergent properties are hierarchic systems (in the sense of being 'composed of interrelated sub-systems') with the property of 'near-decomposability' (where the system can be described at the aggregate or macro-level in terms of the weak interactions between the sub-systems (Simon, 1962, p. 468 and p. 478). Furthermore, 'only the aggregate properties of their parts enter into the description of the interactions of those part' (Simon, 1962, p. 478). This would also imply that the Kolgomorov complexity of the system at the macro-level is actually lower (as argued earlier). It should also be noted that Simon has attempted to operationalize the strength of interactions in terms of frequency interactions, an idea which has some resonance in institutional economics (Williamson, 2000).

What are implications of such views on bounded rationality? First, bounded rationality relates to micro-level interactions in complex social systems. Since there is diversity in the degree of complexity of social systems across time and space, the complexity of any (social) system may be found in the nature of bounded rationality of organisms/agents in that system. This in turn affects the type of interactions in the system – whether they are non-trivial or not – with consequence on the formation or non-formation of hierarchies. For example, the response threshold to stimuli (read bounded rationality, satisficing) of each individual will affect the emergence of collective phenomena in social insects. An even more challenging question is what drives bounded rationality. From an evolutionary point of view, the prevailing form of bounded rationality would have been subject to selection within a given environment.

Thus the degree of 'simplicity' that is associated with bounded rationality would be inextricably linked to the environment. This has led some scholars to identify 'genomic complexity with the the amount of information a sequence stores about its environment' (Adami *et al.*, 2000, p. 4463).

6. Concluding Remarks

The predominant view of rationality in economics today is one of 'rationality as consistency' or 'rationality as maximizing'. While departures from such notions of Olympian rationality (to paraphrase Professor Velupillai) do get some attention in the research community in the form of bounded rationality, the resulting body of research is one that mostly either treats bounded rationality as a constrained form of rationality (therefore a special case) or is devoid of the rich computational impli-cations suggested in Herbert Simon's original works. Furthermore, a key insight of Simon's work is missing – that of the inter-dependence between the problem solver and his/her environment.

On this, several important insights can be derived from Simon's work as well as other recent contributions from outside economics. The boundaries between bounded rationality and its environment can shift. The form and degree of complexity of bounded rationality is dependent on the structure (and hence the complexity of) the environment. Collective decision-making processes involving multiple local interac-tions can result in the emergence of hierarchies. This reduces the Kolgomorov com-plexity of the system. Thus, the 'simplicity' that we associate with bounded rationality in the form of simplifying mechanisms such as satisficing is in fact crucial for the emergence of complex systems.

A minority of economists have already begun incorporating some of these insights in their work, for example, North (2005). The road ahead for those interested to pursue their research along such lines will not be an easy one due the number of disciplines outside economics that are involved, most of which are unfamiliar to the average economist. However, the returns from learning from these other disciplines are likely to be very large indeed.

Acknowledgements

The author would like to thank K. Vela Velupillai and Stefano Zambelli for useful com-ments and suggestions. The usual caveat applies.

Notes

1. See for example, the formal exposition in Varian (1992, pp. 94–95).
2. See Arrow (1986, pp. S388–S390) and Simon (1976, p. 67).
3. The discussions in Smith (2003) seem to hint at the possible gains from further examining, first the broad views held by Scottish philosophers such as David Hume and Adam Smith, and second, more specifically, an integrated view of Smith's visions on rationality inferred from the *Wealth of Nations* and the *Moral Sentiments*.

4. We rely on Blaug (1985) for this and the following narrative.
5. See Blaug (1985, Ch. 9) and Blume and Easley (2008, p. 2).
6. See Ingrao and Israel (1990) and Giocoli (2003).
7. A number of paradoxes arise out of the common knowledge assumption, the solution to which lies in distinguishing between outcome of a game and the assumptions on agents' behaviour. See Dekel and Gul (1997) and the Autumn issue of the Journal of Economic Perspectives, 1992.
8. Thomas J. Sargent. 'Rational Expectations'. The Concise Encyclopedia of Economics. 2008. Library of Economics and Liberty. Retrieved October 4, 2010 from the World Wide Web: http://www.econlib.org/library/Enc/RationalExpectations.html
9. This is similar to the common knowledge assumption in game theory. The correct model of the economy is 'common knowledge' among agents in the macroeconomy.
10. See Waldrop (1992, p. 92).
11. Do these terms refer to different things? Gigerenzer and Selten (2001) defines irrationality in terms of discrepancies between a norm and human judgement (e.g. in terms of optimization, probability and utilities – elements of what is known as substantive rationality). In contrasts with irrationality, models of bounded rationality dispenses with these types of human judgement. In fact, bounded rationality is considered to be related to non-rationality.
12. It is interesting to note that at this juncture Simon used the term 'approximate rationality' in his concluding remarks. Klaes and Sent (2005, p. 37) suggests that the term 'bounded rationality' is likely to have been first used in Simon (1957).
13. This change in Simon's research focus is discussed in Simon (1982, p. 401) and Simon (1991b, p. 189).
14. These terms were coined by K.Vela Velupillai. Early contributors who have applied computability theory to decision-making problems include Michael Rabin, Alain Lewis and Preston McAfee (see, Velupillai, 2000, p. 17). Other contributors in the 1980s include Luca Anderlini and Kislaya Prasad.
15. See Aumann (1997) for a good summary and Chatterjee and Sabourian (2008) for a more extensive survey.
16. For a recent summary of the state-of-art research in this area, see Daskalakis *et al.* (2009) and Kalai (2009). The fact that both tend to be mutually exclusively applied in economic theory reflects the difficulties encountered in reconciling both within a single modelling exercise, as Roughgarden (2010, p. 210) has argued.
17. In the paper, the food points appear to be distributed over a graph-theoretic (regular) tree (in Simon's words, 'branching system of paths', Simon, 1956, p. 131). There is a need to differentiate between the Kolgomorov complexity measure K of a regular graph tree (which is low) and the Kolgomorov complexity of the randomly distributed food points (which is high). The latter suggests that the Kolgomorov complexity of the environment facing the organism is high.
18. Perhaps even better given that social insects have been around and may be around longer than humans!

References

Adami, C., Ofria, C. and Collier, T. (2000) Evolution of biological complexity. *Proceedings of the National Academy of Sciences of the United States of America* 97(9): 4463–4468.

Anderson, M. (2003) Embodied cognition. *Artificial Intelligence* 149: 91–130.

Arrow, K. (1986) Rationality of self and others in an economic system. *Journal of Business* 59(4): S385–S399.

Aumann, R.J. (1997) Rationality and bounded rationality. *Games and Economic Behavior* 21: 2–14.

Axtell, R. (2005) Complexity of exchange. *Economic Journal* 115: F193–F210.

Axtell, R. (2007) What economic agents do: how cognition and interaction lead to emergence and complexity. *Review of Austrian Economics* 20: 105–122.

Becker, G. (1962) Irrational behavior and economic theory. *Journal of Political Economy* 70(1): 1–13.

Ben-Porath, E. (1990) The complexity of computing a best response automaton in repeated games with mixed strategies. *Games and Economic Behavior* 2(1): 1–12.

Blaug, M. (1985) *Economic Theory in Retrospect*, 3rd edn. Cambridge: Cambridge University Press.

Blaug, M. (1992) *The Methodology of Economics*. Cambridge: Cambridge University Press.

Blume, L. and Easley, D. (2008) Rationality. In S. Durlauf and L. Blume (eds), *The New Palgrave Dictionary of Economics*, 2nd edn. London: Palgrave Macmillan.

Camerer, C. (1998) Bounded rationality in individual rationality decision making. *Experimental Economics* 1(2): 163–183.

Chatterjee, K. and Sabourian, H. (2008) Game theory and strategic complexity. Mimeo, Technical report.

Conlisk, J. (1996) Why bounded rationality? *Journal of Economic Literature* 34(2): 669–700.

Crutchfield, J. (1994) The calculi of emergence: computation, dynamics and induction. *Physica D* 75: 11–54.

Daskalakis, C., Goldberg, P.W. and Papadimitriou, C.H. (2009) The complexity of computing a Nash equilibrium. *Communications of the ACM* 52(2): 89–97.

Davis, M., Sigal, R. and Weyuker, E. (1994) *Computability, Complexity and Languages*. San Diego: Academic Press.

Deguet, J., Demazeau, Y. and Magnin, L. (2006) Elements of the emergence issue: a survey of emergence definitions. *Complexus* 3: 24–31.

Dekel, E. and Gul, F. (1997) Rationality and knowledge in game theory. In D. Kreps and K. Wallis (eds), *Advances in Economics and Econometrics: Theory and Applications*. Cambridge: Cambridge University Press.

Delgado, J. and Sole, R. (1997) Collective-induced computation. *Physical Review E* 1997(55): 2338–2344.

Dorigo, M. and Gambardella, L.M. (1997) Ant colonies for the travelling salesman problem. *BioSystems* 43: 73–81.

Edwards, S. and Pratt, S. (2009) Rationality in collective decision-making by ant colonies. *Proceedings of the Royal Society*, pages 1–7.

Gigerenzer, G. (2001) Decision making: nonrational theories. *International Encyclopedia of the Social and Behavioral Sciences* 5: 3304–3309.

Gigerenzer, G. and Selten, R., editors (2001) *Bounded Rationality: The Adaptive Toolbox*. Cambridge, MA: MIT Press.

Gilboa, I. (1988) The complexity of computing best-response automata in repeated games. *Journal of Economic Theory* 45: 342–352.

Giocoli, N. (2003) *Modeling Rational Agents*. Cheltenham: Edward Elgar.

Gode, D. and Sunder, S. (1993) Allocative efficiency of markets with zero-intelligence traders: market as a partial substitute for individual rationality. *Journal of Political Economy* 101(1): 119–137.

Halley, J. and Winkler, D. (2008) Classification of emergence and its relation to self-organization. *Complexity* 13(5): 10–15.

Hayek, F. (1991) On being an economist. In W.W. Bartley and S. Kresge (eds), *The Trend of Economic Thinking; Essays on Political Economists and Economic History*, Vol. III. London: Routledge.

Ingrao, B. and Israel, G. (1990) *The Invisible Hand: Economic Equilibrium in the History of Science*. Cambridge, MA: MIT Press.

Kahneman, D. (2003) Maps of bounded rationality: psychology for behavioral economics. *American Economic Review* 93(5): 1449–1475.

Kalai, E. (2009) The complexity of computing Nash equilibrium. *Commun. ACM* 52(2): 88–88.

Kirman, A. (1993) Ants, rationality and recruitment. *Quarterly Journal of Economics* 108(1): 137–156.

Kirman, A. (1997) The economy as an evolving network. *Journal of Evolutionary Economics* 7: 339–353.

Kirman, A. (2003) The structure of economic interaction: individual and collective rationality. Mimeo.

Kirman, A., Markose, S., Giansante, S. and Pin, P. (2007) Marginal contribution, reciprocity and equity in segregated groups: bounded rationality and self-organization in social networks. *Journal of Economic Dynamics and Control* 31: 2085–2107.

Klaes, M. and Sent, E.-M. (2005) A conceptual history of the emergence of bounded rationality. *History of Political Economy* 37(1): 27–59.

Laland, K. and Brown, G., eds (2002) *Sense and Nonsense: Ecolutionary Perspectives on Human Behavior*. Oxford: Oxford Press.

Marshall, J. and Franks, N. (2009) Colony-level cognition. *Current Biology* 2009(19): R395–R396.

Myerson, R. (1991) *Game Theory*. Cambridge, MA: Harvard University Press.

Newell, A. and Simon, H. (1972) *Human Problem Solving*. Englewood Cliffs, NJ: Prentice-Hall.

Neyman, A. (1985) Bounded complexity justifies cooperation in finitely repeated prisoners' dilemma. *Economic Letters* 19(1): 227–229.

North, D. (2005) *Understanding the Process of Economic Change*. Princeton: Princeton University Press.

Prokopenko, M., Boschetti, F., and Ryan, A. (2008) An information-theoretic primer on complexity, self-organization, and emergence. *Complexity* 15(1): 11–28.

Rabin, M. (1998) Psychology and economics. *Journal of Economic Literature* 36(1): 11–46.

Roughgarden, T. (2010) Computing equilibria: a computational complexity perspective. *Economic Theory* 42: 193–236.

Rubinstein, A. (1986) Finite automata play the repeated prisoners' dilemma. *Journal of Economic Theory* 39: 83–96.

Rubinstein, A. (1998) *Modeling Bounded Rationality*. Cambridge, MA: MIT Press.

Russell, S. and Norvig, P. (1995) *Artificial Intelligence: A Modern Approach*. Englewood Cliffs, NJ: Prentice Hall.

Samuelson, L. (1996) Bounded rationality and game theory. *Quarterly Review of Economics and Finance* 1996(36): 17–35.

Schrödinger, E. (1967) *What is Life?* Cambridge: Cambridge University Press.

Sen, A. (1977) Rational fools: a critique of the behavioral foundations of economic theory. *Philosophy and Public Affairs* 6(4): 317–344.

Simon, H. (1955) A behavioral model of rational choice. *Quarterly Journal of Economics* 69: 99–118.

Simon, H. (1956) Rational choice and the structure of the environment. *Psychological Review* 63(2): 129–138.

Simon, H. (1957) *Models of Man*. New York: Wiley.

Simon, H. (1962) The architecture of complexity. *Proceedings of the American Philosophical Society* 106(6): 467–482.

Simon, H. (1976) From substantive to procedural rationality. In S. Latsis (ed.), *Method and Appraisal in Economics*. Cambridge: Cambridge University Press.

Simon, H. (1978) Rationality as process and as product of thought. *American Economic Review* 68(2): 1–16.

Simon, H. (1982) *Models of Bounded Rationality*. Cambridge, MA: MIT Press.

Simon, H. (1991a) Game theory and the concept of rationality. Mimeo, Paper No. 493 in the Herbert Simon Collection.

Simon, H. (1991b) *Models of My Life*. New York: Basic Books.

Simon, H. (1997) *An Empirically Based Microeconomics*. Cambridge: Cambridge University Press.

Simon, H. (2000) Bounded rationality in social science: today and tomorrow. *Mind & Society* 1(1): 25–39.

Smith, V. (2003) Constructivist and ecological rationality in economics. *American Economic Review* 93(3): 465–508.

Smith, V.L. (1962) An experimental study of competitive market behavior. *The Journal of Political Economy* 70(2): 111–137.

Tversky, A. and Kahneman, D. (1974) Judgement under uncertainty: heuristics and biases. *Science* 185(4157): 1124–1131.

Tversky, A. and Kahneman, D. (1981) The framing of decisions and the psychology of choice. *Science* 211(4481): 453–458.

Varian, H. (1992) *Microeconomic Analysis*. 3rd edn. New York: Norton.

Velupillai, K. (2000) *Computable Economics*. Oxford: Oxford University Press.

Velupillai, K.V. (2006) Algorithmic foundations of computable general equilibrium theory. *Applied Mathematics and Computation* 179(1): 360–369.

Vellupilai, K. (2009) Uncomputability and undecidability in economic theory. *Applied Mathematics and Computation* 215(4): 1404–1416.

Vellupilai, K. (2010) Foundations of boundedly rational choice and satisficing decisions. *Advances in Decision Sciences* 2010: 1–16.

Vitanyi, P. (2007) Analysis of sorting algorithms by kolmogorov complexity (a survey). In I. Csiszar, G. Katona and G. Tardos (eds), *Entropy, Search, Complexity, Bolyai Society Mathematical Studies*, 16. New York: Springer-Verlag.

Waldrop, M. (1992) *Complexity: the Emerging Science at the Edge of Order and Chaos*. New York: Simon & Schuster.

Walsh, V. (1996) *Rationality, Allocation and Reproduction*. Oxford: Clarendon Press.

Williamson, O.E. (2000) The new institutional economics: taking stock, looking ahead. *Journal of Economic Literature* 38(3): 595–613.

7

EMERGENT COMPLEXITY IN AGENT-BASED COMPUTATIONAL ECONOMICS

Shu-Heng Chen and Shu G. Wang

1. Motivation and Introduction

1.1 Emergence in an Integrated Framework

If we were to regard economics as being studied in an interdisciplinary scientific context, then it would be amazing to perceive how economics has constantly expanded and become intertwined with other old and new disciplines. The expansion does not just refer to the enlargement of the application domains, as Gary Becker already pointed out a long while ago (Becker, 1981, 1996), but it also denotes the consolidation of the foundations of economics via the enrichment contributed by other disciplines. Many of these kinds of interdisciplinary studies have been conducted so superbly that they have led to the award of a Nobel Prize. Among them, the three which concern us the most are Herbert Simon's and Daniel Kahneman's contributions on the *behavioural, cognitive and psychological foundations* of economics (Simon, 1997; Kahneman, 2003), Thomas Schelling's pioneering piece on the *agent-based foundation* of economics (Schelling, 1978), and Vernon Smith's *experimental foundation* of economics (Smith, 2006).

This enduring interdisciplinary trend has to some extent changed our own perception of the status of economics in the social sciences. Economics, which used to be regarded as having a very prestigious position or even being the Queen in the social sciences, has now become a much more friendly civilian who also humbly learns from and interacts with other members of the social sciences. Nonetheless, this humble position does not lead to a deterioration in the substance of this discipline as a science; quite on the contrary, it enhances this substance. One of the best manifestations of this is the recent integration of the following four branches of economics: *behavioural*

Nonlinearity, Complexity and Randomness in Economics, First Edition.
Stefano Zambelli and Donald A.R. George.
© 2012 John Wiley & Sons. Published 2012 by John Wiley & Sons, Ltd.

economics, neuroeconomics, experimental economics and *agent-based computational economics (ACE).*[1] The essence of the research network of the four is an integration of *human agents* and *software agents* in economics research, and this integration becomes increasingly active when it has elements and ideas that are constantly being imported from psychology, cognitive science, physics and neural science.

This augmented integration not only makes us better equipped to look into how human beings actually behave and why they behave in that way, but it also advances our understanding and predictions of the possible social consequences arising from these behavioural elements. For the latter, we are inquiring into how these behavioural elements can contribute to the *emergent complexity* that appears at a higher or aggregate level. The *sum* of these four pillars makes such emergent complexity differ from each of the four with some promising synergy effects.

First, although behavioural economics and neuroeconomics enable us to know the cognitive biases and possible neural mechanisms of these behavioural constraints, they normally do not move further to see whether these biases can have non-trivial aggregate effects.[2] This so-called *emergent phenomenon argument* is one major argument against neuroeconomics as well as behavioural economics (Clithero, Tankersley, and Huettel, 2008). Second, although experimental economics can help us observe the aggregate outcomes or policy/design effectiveness directly from human behaviour, it normally downplays the possible influences of the cognitive and psychological attributes of subjects, and may even assume these effects to be noises crossing different experiments (Frederick, 2005). This ignorance is partially due to the fact that cognitive, psychological or even cultural attributes of human subjects are costly to know and are difficult to control. As for the last restriction, ACE can provide a relaxation by using *software agents* and can generate the emergent complexity from these software agents (Duffy, 2006). However, it must work with the other three pillars to ensure that the design of the software agents is appropriate via some formal procedure, such as the *Turing test* (Arifovic, McKelvey, and Pevnitskaya, 2006). Therefore, by putting the four together, we can move further to explore the emergent complexity of the cognitive, psychological and cultural characteristics of economic agents.

1.2 *Organization of the Paper*

The remainder of this paper is organized as follow. In Section 2, we provide a brief review of the complex system which gained its popularity in the 1980s in both physics and economics. Its extensive applications to agent-based economic and financial models in the 1990s has generated a major class of ACE models called the *N*-type models (Chen, 2008). This complex system, however, is composed of only *simple and homogeneous agents*, which means that this system is not far away from the *particle system* in physics, and in many regards cannot accommodate the needs of the integrated framework mentioned above. We, therefore, starting from Section 3, review the other class of complex systems, which is also known as the class of *complex adaptive systems* (CAS) (Arthur, Surlauf, and Lane, 1997; Miller and Page, 2007). One essential ingredient of the CAS is the *autonomous agent*.

The second part of the paper introduces two new elements which have recently been introduced to ACE. The first element concerns the human nature (neurocognitive aspect) of the *autonomous agents*. The role of intelligence or cognitive capacity has been recently studied in the context of experimental economics. Section 4 provides a review of the development of this literature. Nevertheless, the counterpart work in ACE is rather lacking, and so Section 5 highlights some initial progress, pointing out possible avenues for future research. Section 6 introduces the second new element, namely, *modularity*, and is followed by the concluding remarks which are given in Section 7.

2. Agent-based Models with Simple Agents

The conventional complex systems are readily demonstrated by Thomas Schelling's segregation model (Schelling, 1978), John Conway's *Game of Life* (Gardner, 1970) and Stephen Wolfram's Cellular Automata (Wolfram, 1986). As simplifications of the more complex von Neumann's self replicating automata (von Neumann, 1966), these agent-based systems nicely demonstrate what the *emergent properties* are, in particular, in the spirit of *unpredictability*.[3] The essence of these complex systems is simply to show how agents with simple and even homogeneous rules can together generate very complex patterns which are difficult to predict. However, not all behavioural rules will lead to emergent complexity. Therefore, one has to carefully choose the behavioural rules that lead to complex and unpredictable patterns.[4]

Given its brevity, this complex system paradigm has been powerfully applied to a number of economic systems, and the most successful and attractive one is probably the *agent-based financial market*. If simple behavioural rules can generate complex patterns, then it is not implausible that the entire financial market complexity can be generated by very simple and almost homogeneous financial agents. Li and Rosser (2004) and many others adopted this approach in modelling financial markets. In these kinds of models, the behavioural rules of financial agents are governed by very simple discrete choice models with only a few alternatives, say, two or three, which are also known as N-type models. It has been shown that this simple setting is already sufficient for generating various complex financial dynamics, such as volatility clustering, fat tails, long memory, bubbles and crashes.[5]

However, the main issue is that the agents in these systems are all simple. There is no feedback from the systems to the agents. The emergent complexity is only demonstrated for outside observers of the systems. The agents within the systems are, however, not conscious of the emergent complexity. Neither will they do anything about it, not to mention learning, adapting or discovering. By taking the familiar *fundamentalist–chartist model* as an example, regardless of what kinds of patterns appear in the aggregate dynamics, what our fundamentalists or chartists can do is simply follow a very static reverting or extrapolating form of behaviour. The only allowed learning or adaptive behaviour is manifested through their discrete choice model which generates the switching behaviour between the two possible behavioural alternatives. Therefore, agents are very passive or even idle.

3. Agent-based Models with Autonomous Agents

3.1 *Autonomous Agents*

In contrast to the agent-based models with simple agents, the other class of agent-based models replaces the simple agents with *autonomous agents*. The autonomous agent is the agent who is able to behave (to think, to learn, to adapt and to make strategic plans) with a set of specifications and rules which are given initially, and are fixed with no further intervention. The use of autonomous agents is, in one way or the other, connected to the notion of *bounded rationality*, initiated by Herbert Simon.

To build autonomous agents, agent-based computational economists need to employ existing algorithms or develop new algorithms which can enable agents to behave with a certain degree of autonomy. For example, among many alternatives, genetic algorithms and genetic programming (GP) are two of the most popular. The distinguishing feature delivered by these tools is that it allows the agents to learn and to discover on their own, and hence it enriches our study of the emergent complexity not only at the macro level, but also at the micro level. Moreover, it provides us with a more vivid demonstration of the macro–micro relationship.

3.2 *Emergent Novelties*

To illustrate the kind of emergent complexities addressed in the agent-based models with autonomous agents, we shall compare the evolution of their micro-structure with that of the models with simple agents. We shall in particular provide this illustration using examples from agent-based financial markets, namely, the *market fraction hypothesis* versus the *dinosaur hypothesis*.

The *market fraction hypothesis* (MFH) is associated with agent-based financial models with *simple agents*, in particular, the famous fundamentalist–chartist model (Kirman, 1993; Brock and Hommes, 1998; He and Li, 2008). The market fraction refers to the fraction of each type of agent at a certain time. Market fractions co-evolve with the asset price dynamics. The MFH is then composed of two parts, namely, the short-run one and the long-run one. The short-run one basically says that most of the time the market fraction is distant from the equal share, say, 50% in the case of fundamentalists and chartists, or 33% if contrarians are also included. Between zero and one, the market fraction can exhibit large fluctuations. In other words, the entropy of the market fraction rarely comes close to its maximum. The long-term MFH, however, says that, if we take lone enough, the fractions of each type of trader are approximately equal. Hence, in the long-run, the performances of fundamentalists and chartists are equally good; neither can drive the other out of the market.

Although the MFH is an interesting abstraction of the complex dynamic market microstructure and can even be tested econometrically, it fails to capture one essential dimension of markets, namely, *novelty*. From time to time, only a fixed number of rulcs is available. The aggregate dynamics will not generated new rules or behaviours, hence the further feedback cycling between micro and macro is limited.

The *dinosaur hypothesis* is associated with agent-based financial models with *autonomous agents* (Arthur, 1992; Chen and Yeh, 2001). The use of the metaphor 'dinosaur' implies that each rule, no matter how powerful or how popular it has been, will eventually be driven out by the market. This kind of emergent complexity is not shared by the former models with simple agents.

These two classes of agent-based models are simultaneously used by economists, and their advantages and disadvantages are also well discussed in the literature (Tesfatsion and Judd, 2006). We do not intend to defend either of them except to indicate that autonomous agents can be more useful when agent-based models are placed in the interdisciplinary framework that we outlined in Section 1.1, in particular, in terms of its integration with modern behavioural and neural experiments in economics. We shall come to this point in the next few sections.

4. Intelligence in Experimental Economics

It is probably only very recently that experimental economists started to realize that traditional experiments with human subjects are not as tightly controlled as we might think. Figure 1 indicates a deliberate selection process of experimental subjects based on their heterogeneity in terms of intelligence, personality and cultural backgrounds. These three dimensions of human factors have recently received increasing treatment among experimental economists.

In this section, we shall briefly review the literature which connects *parameterized intelligence* to behavioural experiments in economics. We shall categorize the literature based on how intelligence is introduced as a key parameter in the respective experiments, or, alternatively, which aspect of intelligence is involved in the decisions of the associated experiments. A number of cognitive tasks stand out, namely, the *depth of reasoning*, *judgements* and *cooperation*.

Before we proceed further, maybe it is necessary to make one point clear. Measuring personal traits, including cognitive ability, personality and culture, is not a straightforward job. Various measures have been developed over time and they were and are under constantly reviewed. Criticisms, debates and some associated controversial issues are extensively available.[6] Taking them into account will be beyond the scope of the paper. Here, we simply acknowledge these possible limitations or constraints to which this section may be subject to. This section is simply to point out the recent trend and attempt to bring the dimensions of intelligence into the studies of experimental economics, which is more generally sketched in Figure 1. Given the complexities of the associated measure, this attempt is naturally facing several potential challenges and fundamental questions.

4.1 *Depth of Reasoning*

Among all aspects of decision making, *complexity* seems to be the most natural connection to human intelligence. Obviously, complex problem solving requires intelligence. However, not all experiments can give rise to a natural measure of the complexity with regard to the elicited decision making. Exceptions exist only in a

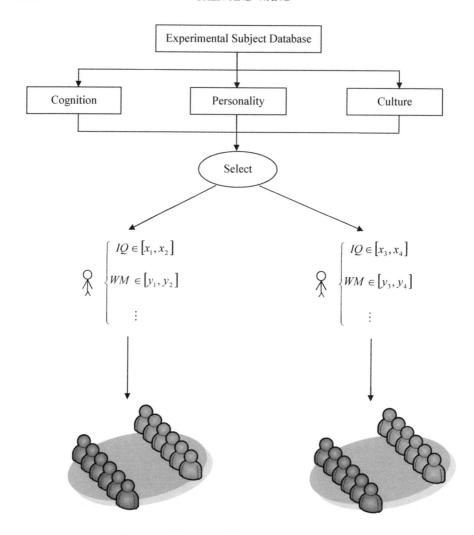

Figure 1. Behavioural Experimental Economics.

Notes: A database storing experimental subjects' cognitive, personality and cultural
attributes is established. Designers can then select subjects based on their needs. For
example, as indicated above, two experiments are conducted to test the significance of
intelligence effects. Experimental subjects are selected based on the required range of IQ,
working memory, etc.

few experiments, particularly those based on the notion of *iterated dominance*, such
as the dirty face game (Littlewood, 1953), and Keynes' beauty context game (Nagel,
1998), etc. The interesting feature of these games is that it allows us to develop a
step-by-step computation in the acquisition of a dominant strategy, and hence develop
a complexity measure in the spirit of computational theory.

In the iterated dominance game, the number of steps required to eliminate all dominated strategies is also called the *depth of reasoning*. How deliberate a strategic behaviour is can then be connected to this depth. Differentiating the complexity of games based on the depth of reasoning or steps of iterated reasoning is not new (Camerer, 2003); however, the involvement of the intelligence variable in experimental games was absent until very recent. For example, in a *beauty contest game* (Nagel, 1998), Ohtsubo and Rapoport (2006) found a positive relationship between the depth of reasoning and the intelligence measure known as the imposing memory task.

4.2 *Judgements and Learning*

Of course, not all games have an iterated-dominance structure, yet intelligence remains important in other contexts. *Judgemental forecasting* can be an example. Whether the ability to make a good judgement can be related to subjects' cognitive capacity becomes another issue of interest for experimental economists. Casari, Ham, and Kagel (2007) introduced intelligence variables into the *common value auction* experiment (Kagel and Levin, 2002), and found that cognitive ability as measured by SAT (Scholastic Aptitude Test)/ACT (American College Testing) scores matters in terms of avoiding the *winner's curse* (Kagel and Levin, 1986). It is also found that bidders with below median composite SAT/ACT scores, on average, suffer from a winner's curse even as experienced bidders.

4.3 *Cooperation, Generosity and Fairness*

Intelligence involved in the depth of reasoning or judgemental forecasting mainly concerns the correlation between intelligence and *individual performance*. What may be equally, or even more, important is the correlation between intelligence and *social performance*. The study of this correlation is important because there is already a pile of studies indicating the positive impact of intelligence on a country's economic performance, and another pile of studies showing that trust and social capital are essential elements of economic development (Landes, 2000; Francois and Zabojnik, 2005). Therefore, to connect these two piles of empirical studies, it is natural to ask: would intelligence facilitate the formation of cooperation, social capital and trust? Alternatively, as posed by Jones (2008), *are smart groups more cooperative?*

Segal and Hershberger (1999) is the first study which examines how intelligence quotient (IQ) can affect cooperation. They report how pairs of identical and fraternal twins play a repeated prisoner's dilemma game. Their results indicate that pairs scoring higher in terms of IQ were more likely to be *mutually cooperative* than pairs scoring lower in terms of IQ. Jones (2008) corroborates this result using university students as experimental subjects. It is found that students cooperate 5–8% more often for every 100-point increase in the school's average SAT score. Following Axelrod (1984), he argued that *patience* and *perceptiveness* are two important personal traits which promote cooperation, and smarter people, as many other empirical studies have verified, are more patient and more perceptive (Benjamin and Shapiro, 2005; Frederick, 2005).

In addition to the test based on parametric intelligence, there are a number of studies that examine the effects of intelligence by manipulating cognitive loading through taxing short-term memory capacity. In a *dictator game*, Cornelissen, Dewitte, and Warlop (2007) found that under a higher cognitive load 'dictator' tends to offer more. In their study, short-term memory is manipulated by asking the subjects to memorize a string of eight numbers.

5. Intelligence in Agent-based Computational Economics

Despite the increasing tendency to make intelligence an explicit control variable in experimental economics and to explore its emergent outcomes, agent-based computational economics, which is normally claimed as the software counterpart of experimental economics, has paid almost no attention to this development. On the contrary, from a pure engineering viewpoint, there is a tendency to make software agents as smart as possible, and usually *equally smart*. This design principle, therefore, obviously contradicts our understanding of human agents. If the society of software agents cannot reasonably reflect the dispersion of human intelligence, then any resultant social simulation would be of little help to us in gaining insights into the emergent complexities, such as the perplexing relationship between IQ and social development (Lynn and Vanhanen, 2002; Lynn, 2006). Therefore, designing software agents with heterogeneous intelligence is the next step in exploring the emergent complexities of ACE.

5.1 *Agent-based Models with Heterogeneous Working Memories*

Chen, Zeng, and Yu (2008) have probably developed the first agent-based model to tackle this issue. In the context of the agent-based double auction market, they used GP to model agents' adaptive behaviour. This way of modelling is not new; however, they no longer assume that agents are equally smart; instead, following the series of experiments which provided evidence of the importance of heterogeneity in subjects' short-term memory capacity (Cornelissen, Dewitte, and Warlop, 2007), they manipulated one control parameter of GP so that the agents' 'working memory capacity' can be 'born' differently. The parameter which they manipulated was the *population size*.

GP is a population-based algorithm, which can implement parallel processing. Hence, the size of the population will directly determine the capability of parallel processing. On the other hand, the human's short-term memory capacity is frequently tested based on the number of the cognitive tasks which human beings can simultaneously process. Dual tasks have been used in hundreds of psychological experiments to measure the attentional demands of different mental activities (Pashler, 1998). Hence, the population size seems to be an appropriate choice with regard to mimicking the working memory capacity of human agents.[7] A smaller population size, therefore, corresponds to a smaller working memory capacity, whereas a larger population size corresponds to a larger working memory capacity. In this way, a market composed of agents with different working memory capacity is introduced.

Chen, Zeng, and Yu (2008) then simulated this agent-based double auction market, and examined the emergent properties at both the macro level (the market performance) and the micro level (the individual performance). At the macro level, they run a regression of market efficiency on the population size (a proxy for the working memory capacity). It is found that working memory capacity has a positive and significant impact on the market efficiency, which is measured by the sum of the realized consumer's and producer's surpluses. Hence, the same institutional arrangement when applied to a population of agents with different intelligence may have different results in terms of market efficiency. The more intelligent group will perform better than the less intelligent one. Of course, this result can still be crude, and require more extensive tests, but the point here is how agent-based simulation by incorporating the intelligence variable can be more communicative with field data (Weede and Kampf, 2002; Jones and Schneider, 2006; Ram, 2007).

In addition to the aggregate outcome, they also compared the strategies learned from agents with different working memory capacity. Because all the strategies learned from GP have their LISP (list programming) structure, they can be depicted as a parse tree. This tree structure gives us a simple measure of the complexity for any acquired strategies based on the sizes of the trees. Chen, Zeng, and Yu (2008) then analyse the relation between the complexity of profitable strategies learned by the agents and their associated working memory capacity. They find that some strategies which are more complex but also more profitable had never been found by agents with a capacity of 10, but could quite frequently be found by agents with a capacity of 50. Further analysis of these strategies shows that additional capacity facilitates the combinatorial operation which agents need to cook up with more complex and profitable strategies. In a sense, this result extends the findings of Ohtsubo and Rapoport (2006) to a more complex situation, namely, a double auction game.

A more challenging part of their work is to examine the co-evolutionary dynamics when competing agents become equally smarter. This brings us closer to the situation discussed in Section 4.3. Chen, Zeng, and Yu (2008) show that, even in a competing situation like the double auction game, pairs of smarter agents can figure out a way to cooperate so as to create a win-win situation, whereas this collaboration is not shared by pairs of less smarter agents.

Altogether, agent-based modelling with proper incorporation of the essential characteristics of human agents can make itself a proper toolbox to enhance our understanding of the emergent outcomes from human experiments or from field data. The entire picture is provided in Figure 2.

5.2 Intelligence and Learning Algorithms

We have mentioned the recent experimental economics that has focused on the intelligence effect. By parameterizing intelligence using short-term memory, Casari, Ham, and Kagel (2007) introduced intelligence variables into the *common value auction* experiment (Kagel and Levin, 2002), and found that cognitive ability as measured by SAT/ACT scores matters in terms of avoiding the *winner's curse* (Kagel and Levin, 1986). Casari, Ham, and Kagel (2007)'s result has important implications for

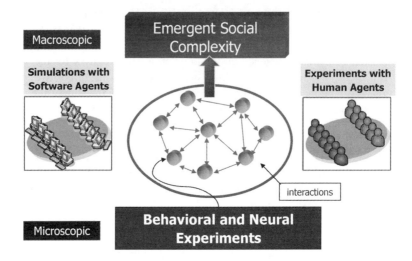

Figure 2. ACE and Experimental Economics: Building a Bridge by Human-Like Designs of Software Agents.

agent-based economic modelling and agent engineering, because they show that intelligence not only influences agents' static performance, but also their *learning dynamics*. So, even though the experiments are repeatedly conducted with the same subjects, their performance may not converge or may only converge at a slow rate.

In agent-based modelling, this phenomenon was first addressed in Feltovich (2005). Feltovich (2005) shows that if decision makers learn via a specific version of reinforcement learning, their behaviour typically changes only *very slowly*, and persistent mistakes are likely. Feltovich (2005) pointed out the difference between slow learning and no learning. Although Feltovich (2005) did not make explicit reference to short-term memory capacity, his manipulation of reinforcement learning can, in a sense, be interpreted as a search for software agents with lower short-term memory capacity.

In Feltovich (2005)'s case, the cognitive capacity of software agents is manipulated with the same learning algorithm, namely, reinforcement learning. Nevertheless, reinforcement learning has been frequently compared with other learning algorithms in the agent-based modelling of games, for example, belief-based learning and genetic algorithms (Duffy, 2006). Therefore, here comes another issue, i.e. instead of manipulating the control parameters of the same algorithm, be it GP (Chen, Zeng, and Yu, 2008) or reinforcement learning (Feltovich, 2005), *how can one choose or compare different learning algorithms in light of the heterogeneity of various forms of parameterized intelligence?* This is the second kind of issue facing agent-based economic modelling, and is slightly different and more advanced than the one discussed in Section 5.1. To make this clear, we shall use Charness and Levin (2009) as an illustration.

Charness and Levin (2009) further pursued the issue between intelligence and learning behaviour. Their finding shows that the failure to perform Bayesian updating can be a cause of the winner's curse, and the ability to perform Bayesian updating is dependent upon the agents' cognitive capacity. In this case, obviously, two learning algorithms are involved, and they are assumed to be associated with different types of cognitive loading.

Intuitively, intelligence can affect the way in which agents learn from the environment's feedback, because different learning algorithms, as decision making, have different degrees of complexity. In computational learning theory, there is even a formal treatment on the complexity of learning machine (Kearns, 1990; Hutter, 2000). Although these complexity measures are not necessarily computable, it is conceivable that some learning algorithms may be more complex than others. For example, Bayesian learning can generally be more complex than reinforcement learning.

Due to the general negligence of intelligence effects in ACE, there is also no effort being made to consider a mixture of various learning algorithms, which can reasonably reflect the empirical lessons drawn from market or game experiments, and to explore its consequence. To the best of our knowledge, Chan et al. (1999) is probably the only study of this kind. In a context of agent-based artificial stock markets, they consider three different types of agents, namely, momentum traders (chartists), empirical Bayesian traders and K-nearest-neighbour (KNN) traders.

The efficient markets hypothesis implies that there are no profitable strategies, and hence learning, regardless of its formalism, does not matter. As a result, the three types of traders, momentum traders, empirical Bayesian and KNN traders, should behave equally well, at least in the long run. However, when the market is not efficient, and learning may matter, it is expected that smarter agents can take advantage of dumber agents. In their experiments, Chan et al. (1999) found that momentum traders, who never learn, performed the worst during the transition period when the market is not efficient. Furthermore, the empirical Bayesian traders were also outperformed by the KNN traders. Although the two types of traders started learning at the same time and competed against each other to discover the true price, the KNN traders were evidently able to exploit predictability more quickly than the empirical Bayesian traders.

Like Feltovich (2005), Chan et al. (1999) did not make any explicit reference to agents' heterogeneity in intelligence; therefore, the way in which they introduced the three types of agents is not empirically driven. One of the next steps of ACE should be to attempt to empirically ground the mixture of different learning algorithms in either field data or experimental data so as to ensure the empirical relevance of the then-established agent-based models of heterogeneously intelligent agents.

6. Modularity in Agent-based Computational Economics

6.1 *Modularity: Legacy of Herbert Simon*

As we mentioned at the very beginning of this paper, the integrated framework presented here is inspired by Herbert Simon, who conducted a number of pioneering interdisciplinary studies in economics, psychology, computer science, artificial intelligence and complex systems. Among many of his great works, the one to which he devoted almost his entire academic life is *modularity* and its relationship with complex systems. He started this work and continued it to the end of his life (Callebaut and Rasskin-Gutman, 2005). Herbert Simon viewed *hierarchy* as a general principle of complex structures (Simon, 1965). Hierarchy, he argued, emerges almost inevitably through a wide variety of evolutionary processes, for the simple reason that hierarchical structures are *stable*. To demonstrate the importance of a *hierarchical structure* or *modular structure* in production, Simon offered his well-known story about a competition between Hora and Tempus, two imaginary watchmakers. In this story, Hora prospered because he used the modular structure in his design of watches, whereas Tempus failed to prosper because his design was not modular. Therefore, the story is mainly about a lesson: the advantage of using a *modular design* in production.

Modularity is becoming more important today because of the increased complexity of modern technology. Using the computer industry as an example, Baldwin and Clark (2000) show that the industry has experienced previously unimaginable levels of innovation and growth because it embraced the concept of modularity. Kamrani (2002) also asserts that embracing the principle of modular design can enable organizations to respond rapidly to market needs and allow the changes to take place in a cost-effective manner.

Nevertheless, the idea of modularity is not restricted to economics, and it has drawn no less attention from psychologists (Fodor, 1983, 2000) and neuroscientists (Churchland and Sejnowski, 1992; Brocas and Carrillo, 2008a). The recent progress in neuroscience has allowed us to identify a number of brain modules at various levels of granularity. In addition, various hypotheses regarding *the modularity of mind* also exist, such as the famous *massive modularity hypothesis* (Williams, 1966; Sawkins, 1976). The recent literature has indicated that a trend integrating economics, psychology and neural science has emerged as a new interdisciplinary research subject, and an easy way to see the drive of this collaboration is from the familiar *dual system conjecture*.

6.2 *Dual System Conjecture*

The dual system conjecture generally refers to the hypothesis that human thinking and decision making are governed by two different but interacting systems. This conjecture has been increasingly recognized as being influential in psychology (Kahneman, 2003), neural science (McClure *et al.*, 2004) and economics. The two systems are an *affective system* and a *deliberative system* (Loewenstein and O'Donoghue, 2005) or a *reflexive system* and a *reflective system* (Lieberman, 2003). The affective system is considered to be myopic, activated by environmental stimuli, and primarily driven by affective states. The deliberative system is generally described as being goal oriented and forward looking. The former is associated with the areas of the brain that we have labelled the ventral striatum (nucleus accumbens, ventral caudate and ventral putamen), the right striatum, neostriatum and amygdala, among others, whereas the latter is associated the areas of the brain that we have the labelled ventromedial and dorsolateral prefrontal and anterior cingulate, among others.

The dual system of the brain has become the neuroeconomic area which economic theorists take the most seriously. This has also helped with the formation of the new field known as *neuroeconomic theory*. A number of dual-process models have been proposed in economics with applications to *intertemporal choice* (Loewenstein and O'Donoghue, 2005; Fudenberg and Levine, 2006; Brocas and Carrillo, 2008a), *risk preferences* (Loewenstein and O'Donoghue, 2005) and *social preferences* (Loewenstein and O'Donoghue, 2005). All these models view economic behaviour as being determined by the interaction between two different systems.

The application of the dual system conjecture to learning is just the beginning. Earlier, we have mentioned the cognitive loading between different learning algorithms, such as reinforcement learning versus Bayesian learning (Section 5.2). This issue has been recently discussed in experimental economics (Charness and Levin, 2005), and now also in neuroeconomics (Bossaerts *et al.*, 2008).

6.3 *Software Agents with Neurocognitive Dual System*

Although agents with dual systems have been considered a new research direction in neuroeconomic theory (Brocas and Carrillo, 2008a, 2008b), software agents or autonomous agents in agent-based modelling mostly largely follow a single system. However, the dual system interpretation exists for many agent-based economic models. Consider the fundamentalist–chartist model as an example, where the fundamentalist's and chartist's behaviour can be differentiated by the associated neural systems, say, assuming the former is associated with a deliberative system whereas the latter is associated with the affective system.

Another example is the *individual learning* versus *social learning*. These two learning schemes have been frequently applied to model the learning behaviour in experiments and their fitness to the experimental data are different (Hanaki, 2005). Agent-based simulation has also showed that their emergent patterns were different. For example, in the context of an artificial stock market, Yeh and Chen (2001) show that agents using individual learning behave differently from agents using social learning in market efficiency, price dynamics and trading volume. If individual learning can be associated with, say, the deliberative system, and social learning can be connected to the affective system, then the dual system can also be applied to agent-based modelling. This issue opens the future to collaboration between agent-based economics and neuroeconomics.

6.4 *From Modular Mind/Brain to Modular Preference*

At present, modularity is still not a part of agent-based economic modelling. This absence is a little disappointing because ACE is regarded as a complement to mainstream economics in terms of articulating the mechanism of evolution and automatic discovery. One way to make progress is to enable autonomous agents to discover the modular structure of their surroundings, and hence they can adapt by using modules.

This is almost equivalent to causing their 'brain' or 'mind' to be designed in a modular way as well.

The only available work in agent-based economic modelling which incorporates the idea of modularity is the *agent-based models of innovation* initiated by Chen and Chie (2004). They proposed a *modular economy* whose demand side and supply side both have a *decomposable* structure.[8] Although the decomposability of the supply side, i.e. production, has already received intensive treatment in the literature, the demand side has not. Inspired by the study of *neurocognitive modularity*, Chen and Chie (2004) assume that *the preference of consumers can be decomposable*.[9] In this way, the demand side of the modular economy corresponds to a market composed of a set of consumers with *modular preference*.

In the modular economy, the assumption of modular preference is made in the form of a dual relationship with the assumption of modular production. Nevertheless, whether in reality the two can have a nice mapping, e.g. a one-to-one relation, is an issue related to the distinction between *structural modularity* and *functional modularity*. Although in the literature this distinction has been well noticed and discussed, 'recent progress in developmental genetics has led to remarkable insights into the molecular mechanisms of morphogenesis, but has at the same time blurred the clear distinction between structure and function' (Callebaut and Rasskin-Gutman 2005, p. 10).

The modular economy considered by Chen and Chie (2004) does not distinguish two kinds of modularity, and they are assumed to be identical. One may argue that the notion of modularity that is suitable for preference is structural, i.e. *what it is*, whereas the one that is suitable for production is process, i.e. *what is does*. However, this understanding may be partial. Using the LISP parse-tree representation, Chen and Chie (2004) have actually integrated the two kinds of modularity. Therefore, consider drinking coffee with sugar as an example. Coffee and sugar are modules for both production and consumption. Nevertheless, for the former, producers *add* sugar to coffee to deliver the final product, whereas for the latter, the consumers drink the mixture by knowing the existence of both components or by 'seeing' the development of the product.

Chen and Chie (2007) tested the idea of augmented GP (augmented with automatic automatically defined terminals) in a modular economy. Chen and Chie (2007) considered an economy with two oligopolistic firms. Although both of these firms are autonomous, they are designed differently. One firm is designed with simple GP, whereas the other firm is designed with augmented GP. These two different designs match the two watchmakers considered by Simon (1965). The modular preferences of consumers not only define the search space for firms, but a search space with different hierarchies. Although it is easier to meet consumers' needs with very low-end products, the resultant profits are negligible. To gain higher profits, firms have to satisfy consumers up to higher hierarchies. However, consumers become more and more heterogeneous when their preferences are compared at higher and higher hierarchies, which calls for a greater diversity of products.[10] It can then be shown that the firm using modular design performs better than the firm not using modular design, as Simon predicted.

7. Concluding Remarks

The literature on complexity in economics has been superbly surveyed and collected in Rosser (2004), which includes emergent complexity in agent-based economic models. Although this work has also included a few agent-based economic models with autonomous agents, emergent complexity is mostly discussed at the macro level. In this paper, we argue that the advantage of using autonomous agents is that it enables us to explore the possible emergent complexity at the micro level. In addition, the use of autonomous agents also bridges the gap between agent-based economic simulation and human-subject economic experiments. We particularly emphasize some recent augmentations of autonomous agents, inspired by experimental economics and neuroeconomics, by incorporating the *intelligence heterogeneity of human intelligence* and the *modularity of brain, mind and preference*. This work leads to the development of neurocognitive software agents, and starts with a 'molecular' foundation of aggregate dynamics. More work could be done along these lines in the future. For example, personality, social preference and culture can be included. Hence, the emergent complexity in economics and psychology can be firmly connected, and, hopefully, this is one of the aims further pursued by the economics profession.

Acknowledgements

The idea of the paper was generated when the first author was invited to be a speaker in a CIFREM Tutorial Workshop on *Agent-based Modelling in Economics and Finance* at CIFREM, University of Trento, Italy, May 19–20, 2008. It was then fully developed during the sojourn of the first author as a Visiting Professor at CIFREM in the fall semester of Year 2009. The authors are grateful to K. Vela Velupillai and Stefano Zambelli for their very generous hosting and the very insightful discussions. An early version of the paper was presented at *Workshop on Nonlinearity, Complexity and Randomness* organized by the *Algorithmic Social Sciences Research Unit*, CIFREM/Department of Economics, University of Trento, Italy, 27–28 October, 2009. The authors are also grateful to conference participants for their feedbacks. This final version is revised in light of the two referees' very painstaking reviews, for which the authors are most grateful. NSC research grant no. 98-2410-H-004-045-MY3 is gratefully acknowledged.

Notes

1. ACE is only part of the more broad field known as *computational economics*. For example, it appears only in two out of the eighteen chapters in Kendric, Mercado, and Amman (2006).
2. Having said that, we must notice that behavioural finance does study the market outcomes emerging from cognitive biases (Hirshleifer, 2001; Barberis and Thaler, 2003; Stracca, 2004). Nonetheless, most behavioural financial models are still confined to the representative agent assumptions.
3. It has been shown that various versions of cellular automata are capable of universal computation. For example, see Kari (2005). However, the computational-theoretic foundation of agent-based economic models has not been rigorously addressed in the literature. Few exceptions are Velupillai (2000, 2010a, 2010b).

4. To some extent, this way of rule selection is similar to that of finding the best performing random number generators (algorithms).

5. For a survey on this class of agent-based financial models and their emergent complexities, see Hommes (2006).

6. Probably one of the most controversial issues is whether individual differences in cognitive ability have a high heritability. See Rushton and Jensen (2005) for the recent development. Of course, our survey from human-subject experiments to computational-agent modelling would not involve this issue.

7. The idea of using population size as a proxy variable for working memory is first proposed in Casari (2004), who literally treated the population size used in the genetic algorithm equivalent to the number of chunks that human can process at a time. According to the famous '7 $\pm$ 2' rule proposed by Miller (Miller, 1956), the capacity lies between five to nine. Casari (2004) then set the population size of genetic algorithms to 6, 'which implies that decision makers have a hardwired limitation in processing information at six strategies at a time. (Casari, 2004, p. 261)' This is the probably the earliest article which connects the *population size* used in evolutionary computation to *working memory capacity* in cognitive psychology. However, in Casari (2004), agents are still treated as homogeneous.

8. Although this assumption is easier for the purpose of modelling, it is too much stronger than the assumption of only *near decomposability* as what Herbert Simon has developed (Simon, 1965, 2002).

9. Whether one can build preference modules upon the brain/mind modules is of course an issue deserving further attention.

10. If the consumers' preferences are randomly generated, then it is easy to see this property through the combinatoric mathematics. On the other hand, in the parlance of economics, moving along the hierarchical preferences means travelling through different regimes, from a primitive manufacturing economy to a quality service economy, from the mass production of homogeneous goods to the limited production of massive quantities of heterogeneous customized products.

References

Arifovic, J., McKelvey, R. and Pevnitskaya, S. (2006) An initial implementation of the Turing tournament to learning in repeated two-person games. *Games and Economic Behavior* 57(1): 93–122.

Arthur, B. (1992) On learning and adaptation in the economy. Santa Fe Institute Economics Research Program. Working Paper 92-07-038.

Arthur, B., Durlauf, S. and Lane, D. (eds) (1997) *The Economy as an Evolving Complex System II*. Reading, MA: Addison-Wesley.

Axelrod, R. (1984) *The Evolution of Cooperation*. New York, NY: Basic Books.

Baldwin, C. and Clark, K. (2000) *Design Rules: The Power of Modularity* (Vol. 1). Cambridge, MA: The MIT Press.

Barberis, N. and Thaler, R. (2003) A survey of behavioral finance. In G. Constantinides, M. Harris and R. Stulz (eds), *Handbook of the Economics of Finance* (pp. 1053–1124), Amsterdam, Netherlands: North-Holland.

Becker, G. (1981) *A Treatise on the Family*. Cambridge, MA: Harvard University Press.

Becker, G. (1996) *Accounting for Tastes*. Cambridge, MA: Harvard University Press.

Benjamin, D. and Shapiro, J. (2005) Does cognitive ability reduce psychological bias? Working Paper, Harvard University.

Bossaerts, P., Beierholm, U., Anen, C., Tzieropoulos, H., Quartz, S., de Peralta, R. and Gonzalez, S. (2008) Neurobiological foundations for "dual system" theory in decision making under uncertainty: fMRI and EEG evidence. 2008 Annual Meeting of Society for Neuroeconomics, Park City, Utah, 25–28 September, 2008.

Brocas, I. and Carrillo, J. (2008a) The brain as a hierarchical organization. *American Economic Review* 98(4): 1312–1346.

Brocas, I. and Carrillo, J. (2008b) Theories of the mind. *American Economic Review: Papers & Proceedings* 98(2): 175–180.

Brock, W. and Hommes, C. (1998) Heterogeneous beliefs and routes to chaos in a simple asset pricing model. *Journal of Economic Dynamics and Control* 22(8-9): 1235–1274.

Callebaut, W. and Rasskin-Gutman, D. (eds) (2005) *Modularity: Understanding the Development and Evolution of Natural Complex Systems*. Cambridge, MA: MIT Press.

Camerer, C. (2003) *Behavioral Game Theory: Experiments in Strategic Interaction*. Princeton, NJ: Princeton University Press.

Casari, M. (2004) Can genetic algorithms explain experimental anomalies? An application to common property resources. *Computational Economics* 24(3): 257–275.

Casari, M., Ham, J. and Kagel, J. (2007) Selection bias, demographic effects, and ability effects in common value auction experiments. *American Economic Review* 97(4): 1278–1304.

Chan, N., LeBaron, B., Lo, A. and Poggio, T. (1999) Information dissemination and aggregation in asset markets with simple intelligent traders. Working Paper, MIT.

Charness, G. and Levin, D. (2005) When optimal choices feel wrong: a laboratory study of Bayesian updating, complexity, and affect. *American Economic Review* 95(4): 1300–1309.

Charness, G. and Levin, D. (2009) The origin of the winner's curse: a laboratory study. *American Economic Journal: Microeconomics* 1(1): 207–236.

Chen, S. (2008) Financial applications: stock markets. In B. Wang (ed), *Wiley Encyclopedia of Computer Science and Engineering* (pp. 481–498). New York: John Wiley & Sons.

Chen, S.-H. and Chie, B.-T. (2004) Agent-based economic modeling of the evolution of technology: the relevance of functional modularity and genetic programming. *International Journal of Modern Physics B* 18(17-19): 2376–2386.

Chen, S.-H. and Chie, B.-T. (2007) Modularity, product innovation, and consumer satisfaction: an agent-based approach. In H. Yin, P. Tino, E. Corchado, M. Byrne and X. Yao (eds), *Intelligent Data Engineering and Automated Learning* (pp. 1053–1062). Heidelberg: Springer.

Chen, S.-H. and Yeh, C.-H. (2001) Evolving traders and the business school with genetic programming: a new architecture of the agent-based artificial stock market. *Journal of Economic Dynamics and Control* 25(3-4): 363–394.

Chen, S.-H., Zeng, R.-J. and Yu T. (2008) Co-evolving trading strategies to analyze bounded rationality in double auction markets. In R. Riolo (ed), *Genetic programming theory and practice VI* (pp. 195–213). New York: Springer.

Churchland, P. and Sejnowski, T. (1992) *The Computational Brain*. Cambridge, MA: MIT Press.

Clithero, J., Tankersley, D. and Huettel, S. (2008) Foundations of neuroeconomics: from philosophy to practice. *PLoS Biology* 6(11): 2348–2353.

Cornelissen, G., Dewitte, S. and Warlop, L. (2007) Social value orientation as a moral intuition: decision-making in the dictator game. Economics Working Papers series 1028, Department of Economics and Business, Universitat Pompeu Fabra, Spain.

Dawkins, R. (1976) *The selfish gene*. Oxford, UK: Oxford University Press.

Duffy, J. (2006) Agent-based models and human subject experiments. In L. Tesfatsion and K. Judd (eds), *Handbook of computational economics: Agent-based computational economics* (pp. 949–1011). Oxford, UK: Elsevier.

Feltovic, N. (2005) Slow learning in the market for lemons: a note on reinforcement learning and the winner's curse. In S.-H. Chen, L. Jain and C.-C. Tai (eds), *Computational Economics: A Perspective from Computational Intelligence* (pp. 149–160). Hershey, PA: Idea Group Publishing.

Fodor, J. (1983) *The Modularity of Mind: An Essay on Faculty Psychology*. Cambridge, MA: MIT Press.

Fodor, J. (2000) *The Mind Doesn't Work That Way: The Scope and Limits of Computational Psychology*. Cambridge, MA: MIT Press.

Francois, P. and Zabojnik, J. (2005) Trust, social capital, and economic development. *Journal of the European Economic Association* 3(1): 51–94.

Frederick, S. (2005) Cognitive reflection and decision making. *Journal of Economic Perspectives* 19(4): 25–42.

Fudenberg, D. and Levine, D. (2006) A dual-self model of impulse control. *American Economic Review* 96(5): 1449–1476.

Gardner, M. (1970) Mathematical games: the fantastic combinations of John Conway's new solitaire game "Life". *Scientific American* 223: 120–123.

Hanaki, N. (2005) Individual and Social Learning. *Computational Economics* 26(3-4): 213–232.

He, X. and Li, Y. (2008) Heterogeneity, convergence and autocorrelations. *Quantitative Finance* 8(1): 59–79.

Hirshleifer, D. (2001) Investor psychology and asset pricing. *Journal of Finance* 56(4): 1533–1597.

Hommes, C. (2006) Heterogeneous agent models in economics and finance. In L. Tesfatsion and J. Kenneth (eds), *Handbook of Computational Economics: Agent-Based Computational Economics* (pp. 1109–1186). Oxford, UK: Elsevier.

Hutter, M. (2000) A theory of universal artificial intelligence based on algorithmic complexity. *CoRR*, cs.AI/0004001, Available at http://arxiv.org/abs/cs.AI/0004001 (last accessed 17 October 2010).

Jones, G. (2008) Are smarter groups more cooperative? Evidence from prisoner's dilemma experiments, 1959–2003. *Journal of Economic Behavior and Organization* 68(3-4): 489–497.

Jones, G. and Schneider, W. (2006) Intelligence, human capital, and economic growth: a Bayesian averaging of classical estimates (BACE) approach. *Journal of Economic Growth* 11(1): 71–93.

Kagel, J. and Levin, D. (1986) The winner's curse and public information in common value auctions. *American Economic Review* 76(5): 894–920.

Kagel, J. and Levin, D. (2002) Bidding in common value auctions: a survey of experimental research. In J. Kagel and D. Levin (eds), *Common Value Auctions and the Winner's Curse* (pp. 501–586). Princeton, NJ: Princeton University Press.

Kahneman, D. (2003) Maps of bounded rationality: psychology for behavioral economics. *American Economic Review* 93(5): 1449–1475.

Kamrani, A. (2002) *Product Design for Modularity*. New York: Springer.

Kari, J. (2005) Theory of cellular automata: a survey. *Theoretical Computer Science* 334(1-3): 3–33.

Kearns, J. (1990) *Computational Complexity of Machine Learning*. Cambridge, MA: MIT Press.

Kendrick, D. Mercado, P. and Amman, H. (2006) *Computational Economics*. Princeton, NJ: Princeton University Press.

Kirman, A. (1993) Ants, rationality, and recruitment. *Quarterly Journal of Economics* 108(1): 137–156.

Landes, D. (2000) Culture makes almost all the difference. In L. Harrison and S. Huntington (eds), *Culture Matters*. New York: Basic Books.

Li, H. and Rosser, B. (2004) Market dynamics and stock price volatility. *European Physical Journal B* 39(3): 409–413.

Lieberman, M. (2003) Reflective and reflexive judgment processes: a social cognitive neuroscience approach. In J. Forgas, K. Williams and W. von Hippel (eds), *Social Judgments: Explicit and Implicit Processes* (pp. 44–67). New York: Cambridge University Press.

Littlewood, J. (1953) *A Mathematician's Miscellany*. London, UK: Methuen & Co. Ltd.

Loewenstein, G. and O'Donoghue, T. (2005) Animal spirits: affective and deliberative processes in economic behavior. Working Paper. Carnegie Mellon University.

Lynn, R. (2006) *Race Differences in Intelligence: an Evolutionary Analysis*. Washington, DC: Washington Summit Publishers.

Lynn, R. and Vanhanen, T. (2002) *IQ and the Wealth of Nations*. Santa Barbara, CA: Praeger.

McClure, S., Laibson, D., Loewenstein, G. and Cohen, J. (2004) Separate neural systems value immediate and delayed monetary rewards. *Science* 306(5695): 503–507.

Miller, G. (1956) The magical number seven, plus or minus two: some limits on our capacity for processing information. *Psychological Review* 101(2): 343–352.

Miller, J. and Page, S. (2007) *Complex Adaptive Systems: An Introduction to Computational Models of Social Life*. Princeton, NJ: Princeton University Press.

Nagel, R. (1998) A survey of experimental guessing games: a study of bounded rationality and learning. In D. Budescu, I. Erev and R. Zwick (eds), *Games and Human Behavior: Essays in Honor of Amnon Rapoport* (pp. 105–142). Hillsdale, NJ: Lawrence Erlbaum Associates.

Ohtsubo, Y. and Rapoport, A. (2006) Depth of reasoning in strategic form games. *Journal of Socio-Economics* 35: 31–47.

Pashler, H. (1998) *The Psychology of Attention*. Cambridge, MA: MIT Press.

Ram, R. (2007) IQ and economic growth: further augmentation of the Mankiw-Romer-Weil model. *Economics Letters* 94(1): 7–11.

Rosser, B. Jr. (2004) *Complexity in Economics*. Northampton, MA: Edward Elgar Publishing.

Rushton, P. and Jensen, A. (2005) Thirty years of research on race differences in cognitive ability. *Psychology, Public Policy, and Law* 11(2): 235–294.

Schelling, T. (1978) *Micromotives and Macrobehavior*. New York: W.W. Norton.

Segal, N. and Hershberger, S. (1999) Cooperation and competition between twins: findings from a prisoner's dilemma game. *Evolution and Human Behavior* 20: 29–51.

Simon, H. (1965) The architecture of complexity. *General Systems* 10: 63–76.

Simon, H. (1997) *Models of Bounded Rationality, Vol. 3*. Cambridge, MA: MIT Press.

Simon, H. (2002) Near decomposability and the speed of evolution. *Industrial and Corporate Change* 11(3): 587–599.

Smith, V. (2006) *Papers in Experimental Economics*. Cambridge: Cambridge University Press.

Stanovich, K. (1999) *Who is Rational? Studies of Individual Differences in Reasoning*. Hillsdale, NJ: Lawrence Erlbaum Associates.

Stracca, L. (2004) Behavioral finance and asset prices: where do we stand? *Journal of Economic Psychology* 25(3): 373–405.

Tesfatsion, L. and Judd, K. (eds) (2006) *Handbook of Computational Economics, Vol. 2: Agent-Based Computational Economics*. Oxford, UK: Elsevier.

Velupillai, K. (2000) *Computable Economics*. Oxford, UK: Oxford University Press.

Velupillai, K. (2010a) *Computable Foundations for Economics*. London, UK: Routledge.

Velupillai, K. (2010b) Foundations of boundedly rational choice and satisficing decisions. *Advances in Decision Sciences Volume* 2010 (July), Article ID 798030, March 30, 2010.

Von Neumann, J. completed by Burks, A. (1966) *Theory of Self Reproducing Automata*. Champaign, IL: University of Illinois Press.

Weede, E. and Kampf, S. (2002) The impact of intelligence and institutional improvements on economic growth. *Kyklos* 55(3): 361–380.

Williams, G. (1966) *Adaptation and Natural Selection*. Princeton, NJ: Princeton University Press.

Wolfram, S. (ed.) (1986) *Theory and Application of Cellular Automata*. Reading, MA: Addison-Wesley.

Yeh, C-H. and Chen, S-H. (2001) Market diversity and market efficiency: the approach based on genetic programming. *Journal of Artificial Simulation of Adaptive Behavior* 1(1): 147–165.

8

NON-LINEAR DYNAMICS, COMPLEXITY AND RANDOMNESS: ALGORITHMIC FOUNDATIONS

K. Vela Velupillai

1. Non-linear Dynamics, Complexity and Randomness – General Algorithmic Considerations

It should be mentioned that [the development of KAM (Kolmogorov–Arnold–Moser) theory and the 'hyperbolic revolution'] vary with particular vigour in the theory of dynamical systems. In their 'purest' form they occur in differential dynamics as quasi-periodicity, for which a certain regularity is characteristic, and as hyperbolicity, which is connected with those phenomena that are descriptively named *'quasi-randomness,' 'stochasticity,' or 'chaos'*.... Kolmogorov.... was the only one ... who made an equally large contribution to the study of both regular and chaotic motions (but in different parts of the theory of dynamical systems – the differential and the ergodic).... [T]he *differences between regularity and chaos* do not simply lie on the surface, but *are buried deep within*, so that it is difficult for even the best specialists to switch from one to the other.

The question arises: Is there some other 'sufficiently substantial' class of motions that could occupy an intermediate position between the quasi-periodic and the hyperbolic motions (or, perhaps, lie somewhere to the side of both)? Could horocyclic flows and (or) nilflows (or, *perhaps something of the sort that we do not yet know about*) play this role?
(Anosov, 2006, pp. 2–3; italics added)

Arguably, no one man contributed more to the theoretical foundations and frontiers of the triptych of non-linear dynamics, complexity – at least an important variant of it – and randomness, the latter two in algorithmic modes, than Kolmogorov. But

Nonlinearity, Complexity and Randomness in Economics, First Edition.
Stefano Zambelli and Donald A.R. George.
© 2012 John Wiley & Sons. Published 2012 by John Wiley & Sons, Ltd.

even he missed out on two related foundational developments that contributed to the algorithmic unification of dynamics and complexity: the varieties of surprising outcomes that were inspired by the famous Fermi–Pasta–Ulam (FPU) computational experiment,[1] on the one hand, and the developments in ordinary differential equations (ODEs) from the point of view of constructive and computable analysis, on the other. In the latter case, the constructive and computable approach to ODEs also had, at least as a by-product, considerations of the computational complexity of the solution procedures that were routinely invoked in their analysis.

There is also the recent development in research at the frontiers of the interface between dynamical systems theory, the theory of numerical analysis and computability (cf. e.g. Stuart and Humphries, 1996). There are those – like the authors of Blum *et al.* (1998) – who believe that the tradition of computation represented by the theory of numerical analysis is not captured by the notion of effective calculability in computability theory. On the other hand, the classical theory of numerical analysis is squarely algorithmic. There is now a systematic approach to the study of dynamical systems by exploiting a 'duality' between the intrinsic dynamics of algorithms and their underpinning in computability theory. If this 'duality' is then linked to the algorithmic basis of the classical theory of numerical analysis, much of the *ad hockery* of arbitrary discretization and computation of economic dynamic models can be avoided.

When Roger Penrose wondered *whether the Mandelbrot set is recursive* (Penrose, 1989, p.124, ff), the issue became one of the *algorithmic decidability* of the attractors of a certain class of complex dynamical systems, generated by *iterated function systems* (IFS). Although the theory of complex dynamical systems, in the sense of – say – rational maps on the Riemann sphere (see, e.g. McMullen, 1993) are almost as old as 'modern' dynamical systems theory as pioneeringly developed by Poincarè in the late 19th century, interpreting its dynamics algorithmically and linking that vision with computation is of much more recent origin (cf. Blum *et al.,* 1998). These issues of the decidability and computability of IFS continue a noble tradition in computability theory, the birth of which owes much to the valiant attempts made by a series of eminent logicians and mathematicians to encapsulate, formally, certain intuitive notions, such as effectivity, calculability and so on. They are also related to the classical mathematician's eternal quest for the correct formal definition of, for example, the intuitive notion of continuity. We know now that Bourbaki did not capture the entire intuitive content of continuity by 'his' definition of continuity (cf. Gandy, 1994). Penrose feels that the *Mandelbrot set* – therefore, also, related IFS that generate *Julia, Fatou* and other similar sets – is *naturally recursive* in an intuitive sense that is not captured by the formal notion of a recursive set as defined in computability theory.

Surely Anosov's thoughts on dynamical systems, a small part of which is quoted earlier, belongs to this tradition of wondering whether the richness of actually occurring dynamics have all been adequately encapsulated in the existing formalisms of dynamical systems theory.

Whether the economist's easy reliance on harnessing existing formalisms to force economic dynamics into a possibly illegitimate straitjacket of dynamical systems theory or a stochastic process, thereby distorting natural economic processes and dressing them in the clothes of theories that have emasculated the intrinsic dynamics belongs to this tradition or not is one of the main motivations for this paper. But we are aware that this is a question that requires the full force of methodological, epistemological and philosophical enquiry, coupled to experimental and mathematical investigations that need much more space than can be devoted to them in one article. We try to take a few small steps in what we hope is a direction that will ultimately help us face the main question more systematically.

A possibly pernicious line of thought in defining economic complexity by relying on formal (non-linear) dynamical systems theory is the concentration on defining the notion of dynamic complexity in terms of the attractors of such systems. This way of defining and studying the complexity of economic processes has led to unnecessary reliance on so-called chaotic dynamics and forcing economic assumptions so that a resulting economic dynamics would fulfil the necessary – and, often, also sufficient – conditions to generate such preconceived dynamics. Indeed, this has been the hallmark of non-linear dynamics in economics, from the earliest stages of non-linear macrodynamics to the more recent enthusiasms for varieties of complex economic dynamics underpinned by assumptions of fundamental non-linearities in microeconomics. In all of these attempts at generating seemingly complex economic dynamics, the attention has been squarely and systematically placed on the characterization of the attractors.

A counter-example to this tradition is to view economic processes as always being in transition regimes[2] and to model the dynamics with definably ultra-long transients towards trivial attractors. To disabuse the economists' practice and belief in concentrating the analysis of economic processes in terms of characterizing their attractors, we can cite the noble example of the Goodstein algorithm and the associated dynamical system whose attractor is the trivial set of a zero limit point (cf. Goodstein, 1944; Paris and Tavakol, 1993; Velupillai, 2010). If this approach to the study of economic processes is made systematic, then non-linearity, complexity and randomness become the basis of the study of economies eternally in transition. It may eventually become possible to do serious studies of economic processes devoid of the unnecessary excess baggage of steady state equilibria – whether of the deterministic or stochastic variety. Moreover, it will return the theory of economic quantities to its natural domain: the rational numbers.

In spite of these general observations and desiderata, the main contribution of the rest of this paper is confined to a study of a particular question which enables us to bring in non-linearity, complexity and randomness in algorithmic modes in a consistent and simple way. By starting from an intuitive criterion for complexity, suggested originally by Richard Day and imaginatively, if non-rigorously, advocated and applied by Barkley Rosser, we develop an algorithmic framework within which we are able to underpin the link between complexity, non-linear dynamics and a notion of randomness. In the next section, therefore, I summarize the intuitive content of the Day–Rosser suggestions for studying and defining dynamic economic complexity. In section three I attempt to model these suggestions in a way that unifies the non-linear complex dynamics of economic processes algorithmically – and provides a bridge towards the study of its algorithmically random content, too. The final section is – for the moment, at least – purely speculative, going beyond non-linearity, complexity and randomness, but remaining within the fold of the philosophy, epistemology and methodology of algorithmic mathematics to study the notion of *emergence* in such systems.

2. Non-linear Dynamics and Dynamic Complexity

What one is typically confronted with is some particular physical system whose constituents are governed by perfectly well-understood basic rules. These rules are usually *algorithmic*, in that they can be described in terms of functions simulatable on a computer, and their simplest consequences are mathematically predictable. But although the global behaviour of the system is *determined* by this algorithmic content, it may not itself be recognisably algorithmic. We certainly encounter this in the mathematics, which may be *non-linear* and not yield the exact solutions needed to retain predictive control of the system. We may be able to come up with a perfectly precise *description* of the system's development which does not have the predictive – or algorithmic – ramifications the atomic rules would lead us to expect. (Cooper, 2006, p. 194; italics in the original)

Barkley Rosser has opted for what he calls Richard Day's 'broad tent definition' of complexity in his work on *non-linear, complex* and *emergent* economics – both in microeconomics and macroeconomics – with an underlying focus also on the importance of discontinuities: (Rosser, 1999, pp. 170–171; italics added)

A 'broad tent' definition, following Richard H. Day (1994), is that a dynamical system is complex if it endogenously does *not* tend asymptotically to a fixed point, a limit cycle, or an explosion.

. . . .

Despite its 'broad tent' nature, this definition does not fit all of what some economists have called complexity. . . . .

However, Day's (1994) broad-tent definition remains attractive, because it is sufficiently broad that it includes not only most of what is now generally labelled complexity, but also its nonlinear dynamics predecessors. . . .

Although complexity is a multidisciplinary concept derived from mathematics and physics, the extra complications arising in economics because of the problem of interacting human calculations in decision-making add a layer of complexity that may not exist in other disciplines.

Richard Day's *magnum opus, Complex Economic Dynamics* (Vols I & II; 1994, 1999, in particular, section 25.2) has a consistent approach to dynamic complexity for modelling in economics, again both at the microeconomic and macroeconomic levels. In a recent reflection on *Complex Economic Dynamics* contrasting his vision with that of the dominant school of macroeconomics, Day observed: (Day, 2004, p. 204; italics added)

> A contrasting category of work [to the DSGE methodology] to which my own studies belong views the observed fluctuations and instabilities as being intrinsic to the development process, that economies do not converge to stable stationary situations or to ones of steady uninterrupted economic growth, and that they can be explained by the formal representation of *adaptive economizing and market mechanisms that function out-of-equilibrium.*

Day's characterization of dynamic complexity must, therefore, be understood against the backdrop of *adaptively economizing agents functioning in out-of-equilibrium situations.* This approach is summarized concisely as one where the 'definition of complexity' entails (italics added):[3]

> Types of change that are *not* periodic or balanced and that do *not* converge to a periodic or balanced pattern. Such *paths* are called *complex*. In particular they include processes that involve:
>
> - nonperiodic fluctuations
> - overlapping waves
> - switches in regime or *structural change*
>
> These types of changes.... are ubiquitous phenomena in the economics of experience.

In one of his more recent contributions to the subject (Rosser, 2010, p.185; italics added) whilst reiterating and finessing the above definition, and reaffirming his commitment to it, he goes beyond and further on the concept of complexity, by considering issues of 'emergent complexity', as well as being much more specific about the role of non-linearity:[4]

> In general, one advantage of the dynamic definition is that it provides a clearer distinction between systems that are complex and those that are not, although there are some fuzzy zones as well with it. Thus, while the definition given above categorizes systems with deterministically endogenous limit cycles as not complex, some observers would say that any system with a periodic cycle is complex as this shows endogenous business cycles in macroeconomics. Others argue that complexity only emerges with aperiodic cycles, the appearance of chaos, or discontinuities associated with bifurcations or multiple basins of attraction or catastrophic leaps or some form of non-chaotic aperiodicity. So, there is a gradation from very simple systems that merely converge to a point or a growth path, all the way to fully aperiodic or discontinuous ones. *In almost all cases, some form of non-linearity is present in dynamically complex systems* and is the source of the complexity, whatever form it takes. ....
>
> *The idea of either emergence or evolution, much less emergent evolution, is not a necessary part of the dynamic conceptualization of complexity, and certainly is not so for the various computational ones.*

However, in our opinion 'the idea of emergence', as it appeared in the works of the founding fathers – John Stuart Mill and George Henry Lewes – can be given an *algorithmic* interpretation and, hence, either a constructive mathematical or recursion theoretic conceptualization. Thus, any formal characterization of 'the idea of emergence' would have had to have been 'a necessary part of the dynamic conceptualization of complexity', since an algorithm is by definition a dynamic object, particularly in its classic formalization by Alan Turing. Many of the pioneers of computability theory posed the fundamental question to be asked as: 'What is a computable function?' and, then, go on to characterize them as a subset of the totality of mathematically definable functions. Turing, on the other hand, emphasized the *dynamic underpinnings* of any computational activity:

> The real question at issue is 'What are the possible processes which can be carried out in computing a number?' (Turing, 1936–1937, p. 245; italics added)

So far as I am concerned, every one of the more seriously formal definitions of complexity can, ultimately, be 'reduced' to a basis in computability theory or in Brouwerian constructive mathematics. Many of the frontiers of theoretical non-linear dynamics have become issues on the interface between dynamical systems theory, model theory, constructive analysis, computable analysis and numerical analysis. The dynamical system interpretation of numerical procedures, in turn, links it with issues of decidability and uncomputability, on the one hand, and computational complexity, on the other, in natural settings (cf. Stuart and Humphries, 1996; Blum *et al.*, 1998).

In the next section, I concentrate exclusively on formalizing the notion of dynamic complexity as suggested by Day and made the fulcrum of his many interpretations of complex economic dynamics by Barkley Rosser.

An important caveat, from the point of view of computability theory (or, perhaps, computable economics), must be stated here. The 'broad tent' definition is a kind of *negative criterion* for 'dynamic complexity'. In this 'negative criterion' sense, the search is for dynamical systems that are recursively enumerable but not recursive, at the least. Such systems bristle with algorithmic undecidabilities. To this if we append the slightly finer requirement of the distinction between recursive separability and recursive inseparability, we will also add some of the paradoxes of algorithmic dynamics, such as: computable dynamical systems giving rise to uncomputable outcomes.

3. A Complex (Non-linear) Dynamical System

> [A] fundamental problem in methodology [is that] the traditional theory of 'dynamical systems' is not equipped for dealing with constructive[5] processes.... We seek to solve this impasse by connecting dynamical systems with fundamental research in computer science ...... Many failures in domains of biological (e.g., development), cognitive (e.g., organization of experience), social (e.g., institutions), and economic science (e.g., markets) are nearly universally attributed to *some combination of high dimensionality and non-linearity. Either alone won't necessarily kill you, but just a little of both is more than enough. This, then, is vaguely referred to as complexity.*
> (Fontana and Buss, 1996, pp. 56–57; italics added)

Fortunately the Day–Rosser approach to the characterization of a complex dynamical system eschews any reliance on 'high dimensionality'! In fact, it is easy to show – even constructively – that non-linearity alone is sufficient to 'kill you' and that 'high dimensionality' is, at best, only an unnecessary adornment. Indeed, an appropriately constructed non-linear dynamical system, in fact, a piecewise-linear dynamical system, 'connected with fundamental research in computer science' can generate the kind of dynamical complexity characterized by the Day–Rosser definition *even in one-dimension*. The perceptive observation, 'connecting dynamical system with fundamental research in computer science', is crucial in this regard.

The essential features of the Day–Rosser characterization are simply the two workhorses of classic non-linear endogenous business cycle theories:

- Non-linearity
- Endogeneity

Even the 'new' twist suggested by Fontana and Buss of 'connecting dynamical systems with fundamental research in computer science', in the context of juxtaposing non-linear dynamics with complexity, has a respectable pedigree in economic dynamics. Now almost 60 years ago, Richard Goodwin pointed out:[6]

> [I]f our methods for determining the successive approximations [to a solution] are made analogous to the structure of economic decisions, then we may regard the sequence of steps as entirely parallel to an actual process of economic dynamics in time.... [And] we may regard economic dynamics as such a series of iterated trial solutions which actually succeed one another at realistically great, regular, intervals of time. (p.1)

and, hence:

> It is entirely permissible to regard the motion of an economy as a process of computing answers to the problems posed to it..... (p.2) (Goodwin, 1951, pp.1–2)

What I try to accomplish in this section are the following four tasks. First define, for an abstract (one-dimensional) dynamical system, the concept of *universality* via an equivalence with a dynamical system with a suitably initialized *Universal Turing Machine*. Next, show that the attractors of such dynamical systems satisfy the Day–Rosser criterion for dynamic complexity. Then, construct a *minimal dynamical system* capable of computation universality. Finally, going slightly beyond the Day–Rosser aims, I also show how the *algorithmic complexity* of such a minimal dynamical system, capable of computation universality, can be given formal content in terms of the *uncomputable Kolmogorov complexity* of the equivalent *Universal Turing Machine*.

I shall have to assume familiarity with the formal definition of a dynamical system (but, cf. e.g. the obvious and accessible classic (Hirsch *et al.*, 2004) or the more modern (Brin and Stuck, 2002), for the basic terms and concepts that are assumed here), the necessary associated concepts from dynamical systems theory and all the necessary notions from classical computability theory (for which the reader can, with profit and enjoyment, go to a classic like Rogers (1967) or, at the frontiers, to Cooper (2004)). Just for ease of reference the bare bones of relevant definitions for dynamical systems are given below in the usual telegraphic form.[7] An intuitive understanding of the definition of a '*basin of attraction*' is probably sufficient for a complete comprehension of the result that is of interest here – provided there is reasonable familiarity with the definition and properties of *Turing Machines* (or partial recursive functions or equivalent formalisms encapsulated by the *Church-Turing Thesis*).

Definition 1: *The Initial Value Problem (**IVP**) for an Ordinary Differential Equation (**ODE**) and **Flows**.*

Consider a differential equation:

$$\dot{x} = f(x) \tag{1}$$

where x is an unknown function of $t \in I$ (say, t: time and I an open interval of THE REAL LINE) and f is a given function of x. Then, a function x is a solution of (7) on the OPEN INTERVAL I if:

$$\dot{x}(t) = f(x(t)), \forall t \in I \tag{2}$$

The IVP for (1) is, then, stated as:

$$\dot{x} = f(x), \quad x(t_0) = x_0 \tag{3}$$

and a solution x(t) for (3) is referred to as a solution through x_0 at t_0. Denote x(t) and x_0, respectively, as:

$$\varphi(t, x_0) \equiv x(t), \text{ and } \varphi(0, x_0) = x_0 \tag{4}$$

*where $\varphi(t, x_0)$ is called the **flow** of $\dot{x} = f(x)$.*

Definition 2 (Dynamical System): *If f is a C^1 function (i.e. the set of all differentiable functions with continuous first derivatives), then the **flow** $\varphi(t, x_0), \forall t$, induces a **map** of $U \subset \mathbb{R}$ into itself, called a C^1 **dynamical system on** $\mathbb{R}$:*

$$x_0 \mapsto \varphi(t, x_0) \tag{5}$$

if it satisfies the following (one-parameter group) properties:

- $\varphi(0, x_0) = x_0$
- $\varphi(t + s, x_0) = \varphi(t, \varphi(s, x_0)), \quad \forall t$ & *s whenever both the left-hand and right-hand side maps are defined*
- $\forall t, \varphi(t, x_0)$ *is a C^1 map with a C^1 inverse given by: $\varphi(-t, x_0)$.*

Remark 3. *A geometric way to think of the connection between a **flow** and the induced **dynamical system** is to say that the flow of an **ODE** gives rise to a dynamical system on $\mathbb{R}$*

Remark 4. *It is important to remember that the **map** of $U \subset \mathbb{R}$ into itself may **not** be defined on all of $\mathbb{R}$. In this context, it might be useful to recall the distinction between partial recursive functions and total functions in classical recursion theory.*

Definition 5 (Invariant Set). *A set (usually compact) $S \subset U$ is **invariant** under the flow $\varphi(.,.)$ whenever $\forall t \in I, \varphi(.,.) \subset S$.*

Definition 6 (Attracting Set). *A closed invariant set* $A \subset U$ *is referred to as the* **attracting set** *of the* **flow** $\varphi(t, x)$ *if* $\exists$ *some neighbourhood* V *of* A, *s.t* $\forall x \in V$ & $\forall t \geq 0, \varphi(t, x) \in V$ *and:*

$$\varphi(t, x) \rightarrow A \text{ as } t \rightarrow \infty \tag{6}$$

Remark 7. *Recall that in dynamical systems theory contexts the attracting sets are considered the* **observable** *states of the dynamical system and its flow.*

Definition 8. *The basin of attraction of the attracting set* A *of a flow, denoted, say, by* Θ_A, *is defined to be the following set:*

$$\Theta_A = \bigcup_{t \leq 0} \varphi_t(V) \tag{7}$$

where: $\varphi_t(.)$ *denotes the flow* $\varphi(., .)$, $\forall t$.

Remark 9. *Intuitively, the basin of attraction of a flow is the* **set of initial conditions** *that eventually leads to its attracting set – that is, to its limit set (limit points, limit cycles, strange attractors etc). Anyone familiar with the definition of a Turing Machine and the famous Halting problem for such machines – or, alternatively, Rice's theorem – would immediately recognize the connection with the definition of basin of attraction and suspect that my main result will be obvious.*

Definition 10 (Dynamical Systems Capable of Computation Universality). *A dynamical system capable of computation universality is one whose defining initial conditions can be used to program and simulate the actions of any arbitrary Turing Machine, in particular that of a Universal Turing Machine.*

Proposition 11. *Dynamical systems characterizable in terms of limit points, limit cycles or 'chaotic' attractors, called 'elementary attractors', are* **not** *capable of universal computation.*

Proof. *Since the basin(s) of attraction of such dynamical systems are only recursive, they are incapable of universal computation.* ∎

Proposition 12. *Strictly linear dynamical systems are incapable of computation universality.*

Proof. *Strictly linear dynamical systems are formally equivalent to finite automata.* ∎

Proposition 13. *Only dynamical systems whose basins of attraction are poised on the boundaries of elementary attractors are capable of universal computation.*

Proof. *By construction, it is easy to show that such basins of attraction are recursively enumerable but not recursive.* ∎

Theorem 14. *There is no effective procedure to decide whether a given observable trajectory is in the basin of attraction of a dynamical system capable of computation universality.*

Proof. *The first step in the proof is to show that the basin of attraction of a dynamical system capable of universal computation is recursively enumerable but not recursive. The second step, then, is to apply Rice's theorem to the problem of membership decidability in such a set.*

First of all, note that the basin of attraction of a dynamical system capable of universal computation is recursively enumerable. This is so since trajectories belonging to such a dynamical system can be effectively listed simply by trying out, systematically, sets of appropriate initial conditions.

On the other hand, such a basin of attraction is not recursive. For, suppose a basin of attraction of a dynamical system capable of universal computation is recursive. Then, given arbitrary initial conditions, the Turing Machine corresponding to the dynamical system capable of universal computation would be able to answer whether (or not) it will halt at the particular configuration characterizing the relevant observed trajectory.

This contradicts the insolvability of the Halting problem for Turing Machines.

Therefore, by Rice's theorem, *there is no effective procedure to decide whether any given arbitrary observed trajectory is in the basin of attraction of such recursively enumerable but not recursive basin of attraction.* Only dynamical systems whose basins of attraction are poised on the boundaries of elementary attractors are capable of universal computation. ∎

Remark 15. *There is a classic mathematical 'fudge' in our proof of the recursive enumerability of the basin of attraction: how can one try out, 'systematically', the set of uncountable initial conditions lying in the appropriate subset of* $\mathbb{R}$*? Of course, this cannot be done and the theorem is given just to give an idea of the problem that we want to consider.* But 'it cannot be done' in the sense that time constraints would obviate any such 'trying out' of an uncountable many initial conditions. However, it is entirely feasible to construct an algorithm, to test 'systematically', the set of initial conditions lying on an 'appropriate' subset of $\mathbb{R}$. But the real finesse in theorizing along these lines is to find conditions under which 'an appropriate subset of initial conditions' can be located effectively. There is no theory – certainly no algorithmically based one – for this procedure and this is why, for example, the Fermi–Pasta–Ulam problem remains both a mathematical and an epistemological paradox (see Fermi *et al.*, 1955; Weissert, 1997).

Claim 16. *Only dynamical systems capable of computation universality are dynamically complex in the sense of Day–Rosser.*

The next natural question would be whether such systems exist. The reason – mentioned earlier, in Section 2, is that the Day–Rosser definition is a 'negative' one: a dynamically complex system is defined in terms of *what it does not do.* This is like checking for *non-membership* of a *recursively enumerable* but *non-recursive* set, which is impossible. Instead, the best way to answer such a question would be to *demonstrate by construction* the existence of such a system.

Keeping the framework and the question in mind, one way to proceed would be to constructivize the basic IVP problem for ODEs and then the theorem can be applied consistently. Alternatively, it is possible to work with ODEs within the framework of computable analysis and use *recursive (in)separability* judiciously to generate non-recursive solutions that are intrinsically complex to compute without *oracles*. Both of these methods will require the development of a wholly 'unfamiliar' set of concepts within an even more strange mathematical framework. It will require too much space and time to do so within the scope of this paper. Instead, we shall adopt a slightly devious method.

Consider the following Generalized Shift (GS) map (Moore, 1990; Moore, 1991):

$$\Phi : \wp \to \sigma^{F(\wp)}[\wp \oplus G(\wp)] \tag{8}$$

where $\wp$ is the (bi-infinite) symbol sequence, F is mapping from a finite subset of $\wp$ to the integers, G is mapping from a finite subset of $\wp$ into $\wp$ and σ is a shift operator.

The given 'finite subset of $\wp$', on which F and G operate is called the *domain of dependence* (DOD).

Let the given symbol sequence be, for example:

$$\wp \equiv \{.....p_{-1}pp_{=1}.....\} \tag{9}$$

Then:

$\wp \oplus G(\wp) \Rightarrow$ replace DOD by G($\wp$).

$\sigma^{F(\wp)} \Rightarrow$ *shift* the sequence left or right by the amount F($\wp$).

Remark 17. *In practice, a GS is implemented by denoting a distinct position on the initially given symbol sequence as, say, p_0 and placing a 'reading head' over it. It must also be noted $p_i = \wp, \forall i = 1, 2, \ldots$ could, for example, denote whole words from an alphabet etc., although in practice it will be 0,1 and $\circ$ ('dot'). The 'dot' will be signifying that the 'reading head' will be placed on the symbol to the right of it.*

The following results about GS maps are relevant for this discussion:

Proposition 18. *Any GS is a **non-linear** (in fact, **piecewise linear**) dynamical system capable of universal computation; hence they are universal dynamical systems and are equivalent to some constructible Universal Turing Machine.*

Thus the GS is capable of universal computation and it is **minimal** in a precisely definable sense (see Moore, 1990, 1991 for full details). It is also possible to construct, for each such GS dynamical system,[8] an equivalent universal Turing machine (UTM) that can simulate its dynamics, for sets of initial conditions.

Next, consider the definition of the Kolmogorov complexity of a finite object (Kolmogorov, 1968, p. 465):

$$K_\phi(y|x) = \begin{cases} \min \phi(p, x) = y l(p) \\ \infty \neg \exists p \text{ s.t } \phi(p, x) = y \end{cases} \tag{10}$$

where $\phi(p, x) = y$ is a partial recursive function or, equivalently (by the Church–Turing Thesis), a Turing Machine – the 'method of programming' – associating a (finite) object y with a *program p* and a (finite) object x; the minimum is taken over all programs capable of generating y, on input x, to the partial recursive function, p. Consider the above (minimal) universal dynamical system as canonical for any question about membership in attracting sets, A. What is the complexity of $K_U(p|x)$? By definition it should be:

$$K_U(y|x) = \begin{cases} \min_{U(p,x)=y} l(p) \\ \infty \neg \exists p \text{ s.t } \phi(p, x) = y \end{cases}$$

The meaning, of course, is: the minimum over all programs, p, implemented on U, with the given initial condition, x, which will stop at the halting configuration, y.

Unfortunately, however, $K_\phi(y|x)$ is *a non-recursive real number!*

How can we decide, algorithmically, whether any observed trajectory is generated by the dynamics of a system capable of computation universality? Consider the observable set of the dynamical system, $y \in A$; given the UTM, say U, corresponding to $\wp$; the question is: for what set of initial conditions, say x, is y the halting state of U. Naturally, by the theorem of the *unsolvability of the Halting problem*, this is an *undecidable* question.

Remark 19. *Why is it important to show the existence of the minimal program? Because, if the observed y corresponds to the minimal program of the dynamical system, that is, of U, then it is capable of computation universality; if there is no minimal program, the dynamical system is not interesting! A monotone decreasing set of programs that can be shown to converge to the minimal program is analogous to a series of increasingly complex finite automata converging to a TM. What we have to show is that there are programs converging to the minimal program from above and below, to the border between two basins of attractions.*

Shortly after Kolmogorov's above-mentioned paper was published, Zvonkin and Levin (1970, p. 92, theorem 1.5,b) provided the result and proof that rationalizes the basic principle of the *computable approximation* to the uncomputable $K_\phi(y|x)$. The significant relevant result is:

Theorem 20. *Zvonkin–Levin*
$\exists$ *a general recursive function* $H(t, x)$, *monotonically decreasing in t, s.t:*

$$\lim_{t \to \infty} H(t, x) = K_\phi(y|x) \tag{11}$$

Remark 21. *This result guarantees, the existence of 'arbitrarily good upper estimates' for $K_\phi(y|x)$, even although $K_\phi(y|x)$ is uncomputable. We are not sure this is a claim that is constructively substantiable.[11] How can a non-computable function be approximated? If any one non-computable function can be approximated uniformly, then by 'reduction' it should be possible, for example, to 'approximate', say, the Busy Beaver function. I suspect an intelligent and operational interpretation of the Zvonkin–Levin theorem requires a broadening of the notion of 'approximation'.* My view on this is further strengthened by some of the remarks by Cover and Thomas, where one reads:

> The shortest program is not computable, although as more and more programs are shown to produce the string, the estimates from above of the Kolmogorov complexity *converge to the true Kolmogorov complexity*, (the problem, of course, is that *one may have found the shortest program and never know that no shorter program exists*). (Cover and Thomas, 1991, p. 163, italics added)

These remarks border on the metaphysical! How can one *algorithmically* approximate to a true value that which cannot be known *algorithmically* – by definition?

But formally, at least, we can obviate the above result on the algorithmic impossibility of inferring, from observable trajectories, whether they have been generated by a dynamical system capable of computation universality. In fact, the formality is encapsulated elegantly and effectively in the way Jorma Rissanen developed the theory of stochastic complexity in Rissanen (1978, 1986). Thus, we can try to approximate to the undecidable by a monotone computable process; that is, we can approximate to the dynamical system capable of computation universality by a sequence of observation on simpler dynamical systems. Unfortunately, however, the melancholy fact noted in the last footnote may haunt the empiricist forever!

What I have demonstrated can be summarized as a *Generalised Day–Rosser Proposition* as follows:

Proposition 22. *Generalised Day–Rosser Proposition*

Dynamical systems that are dynamically complex in the sense of the Day–Rosser definition are computation universal. There exist *constructible* dynamical systems that are definably minimal and capable of computation universality. Their Kolmogorov complexity can be defined unambiguously, but cannot be computed exactly. *The inference problem for such systems possesses strong undecidability properties.* However, the Kolmogorov complexity can be approximated by a sequence of monotone decreasing general recursive functions.

4. Beyond Dynamic Complexities – Towards an Algorithmic Formalization of Emergence

> Professor Leontief ... maintains that we may utilize dynamical systems that are *unstable throughout* and cites *capitalism* as an example. (Goodwin, 1953, p. 68; italics added)

Day–Rosser dynamical systems are '*unstable throughout*' in the sense of being situated on the borderline between *decidable* dynamical systems. Their Kolmogorov complexities can be defined and, although uncomputable, can be approximated *effectively*.

Moreover, the Day–Rosser definition is independent of dimension. Much of the hype surrounding complex dynamics is against the backdrop of the necessity of systems with interacting fundamental units, coupled non-linearly. All of the formalism in the main section of this paper has been in terms of a scalar dynamical system. A one-dimensional, piece-wise linear, dynamical system was shown to satisfy the Day–Rosser characterization of dynamic complexity.

How, from the dynamic complexity of a one-dimensional dynamical system could we generate emergent behaviour, however conceived?

I have a simple – even simplistic – answer to this seemingly deep or difficult question, at least from the point of view of the formalism developed above. We can define emergent behaviour as that exhibited by the behaviour of a dynamical system in its **transition** from one that is incapable of computation universality to one that is capable of such universal behaviour. In other words emergent behaviour is that which is manifested in *the transition from the computable to the incomputable* – or, from the decidable to the undecidable. This is the kind of approach that has been suggested by Barry Cooper in his recent work (see Cooper, 2006). We endorse and accept this vision, and our formalism was inspired by having this vision as the backdrop for our interpretation of the classics of the emergence literature, in particular the pioneering works of Mill (1890), Lewes (1891) and Morgan (1927), referred to as the *British Emergentist* tradition (McLaughlin, 1992)

At this juncture it may well be apposite to remark[9] on the recent attempt by Boschetti and Gray (2007a) to discuss, define and claim that '(strongly) emergent systems may include processes which are not computable in a classical sense' (Boschetti and Gray (2007a), p.4). On the basis of this, they advocate a version of the 'Turing Test' to 'detect' emergence. I think this exercise is deeply flawed, particularly because these authors do not have a complete grasp of the meaning – mathematical, philosophical and epistemological – of computation and its rigorous, algorithmic definition.

Detecting, *algorithmically*, any notion of emergence, in the sense defined by the *British Emergentists' tradition*, and in any of its modern variants (e.g. Sperry, 1981) we conjecture can be shown to be *provably undecidable*. This is, for the moment a 'conjecture', but it is coupled to, as a kind of dual, to the result on Goodstein's Theorem (Goodstein, 1944). The strategy of proof I am in the process of developing proceeds, as in the definition of dynamic complexity earlier, along a negative criterion: given a suitably rich encapsulation of emergence in a formal definition, if a dynamical system is capable of transition from a non-emergent regime to an emergent one can be algorithmically detected,[10] then the definition is trivial (exactly paralleling the content of Rice's Theorem or a version of the Halting Problem for Turing Machines). This is why I have stated very explicitly, in the extended statement that is Proposition 22, that: *The inference problem for such systems possesses strong undecidability properties.*

It may be useful, also, to wonder whether there might be some 'mileage' to be gained by harnessing a vision in that interface between dynamical systems theory, computability, cellular automata dynamics and the theory of formal languages.[11] It is true that the pioneering work on cellular automata modelling for studying self-reconstruction and self-reproduction, at the hands of von Neumann and Ulam (e.g. von Neumann, 1966), in particular, was intimately tied to computability theory. Moreover, even in the later development by John Conway (Berlekamp *et al.*, 1982) and Wolfram (1985), the notion of *Universal Computation* was crucial, in studying the dynamical evolution of cellular automata-based dynamical systems. There are strong links to the work I report here; but my results on undecidability were not within the scope of these earlier, pioneering, works. If anything, they were focusing on decidability properties, to put it cryptically and, possibly, somewhat unfairly. The emergence of a cellular automata configuration that was capable of computation universality, based on the dynamically coupled evolution of elements that are by themselves not capable of computation universality, was the strong result in the early work by von Neumann and Ulam and the later work by John Conway.

My concern, that of detecting the transition between regimes, was not addressed by them.

The concept of *emergence*, crucial in the modern sciences of complexity, came to have its current connotations as a result of these (and a few other) clearly identifiable sequence of classic works by this trio (and one or two others, as indicated below). A representative sample of key observations, pertaining to this notion, is given below, partly because the economic literature on *Complexity*, of whatever hue, has paid no attention whatsoever to these origins. In particular, not even a meticulous and fastidious scholar as Hayek, in (1952), often referred to as a fountainhead for the role of emergence in the cognitive sciences, has made any reference to Lloyd Morgan and thereby, mysteriously, omitted Mill, of whom he was one of the great admirers and students. A representative sample of crucial definitions, in these classics, may go part of the way towards substantiating the vision we are advocating, *especially the one by Lewes*, the man who introduced the word *'emergent'*, from which Lloyd Morgan derived *'emergence'*:

> [T]here are laws which, like those of chemistry and physiology, owe their existence to.. *heteropathic laws*.... The Laws of Life will never be deducible from the mere laws of the ingredients, but the prodigiously *complex* Facts of Life may all be deducible from comparatively *simple* laws of life;...(Mill, 1890, Bk. III, Ch. VI, p. 269; italics added)

> Thus, although each effect is the resultant of its components, the product of its factors, we cannot always trace *the steps of the process*, so as to see in the product the mode of operation of each factor. In this latter case, I propose to call the effect *an emergent*. It arises out of the combined agencies, but in a form which does not display the agents in action. (Lewes, 1891, Problem V, Ch. III, p. 368, italics added)

> The concept of *emergence* was dealt with.. by J.S. Mill in his Logic.. under the discussion of *'heteropathic laws'* in causation. The word *'emergent'* as contrasted with *'resultant,'* was suggested by G.H. Lewes in his Problems of Life and Mind'. .... What makes emergents emerge?.. *What need [is there] for a directive Source of emergence. Why should it not proceed without one?* (Morgan, 1927, p. 2, 32, italics added)

The trio of Mill, Lewes and Lloyd Morgan, together with Broad (1929) and Alexander (1920) made up what has come to be called the *'British Emergentist'* school. Their rise and fall has been eloquently and almost persuasively argued by Brian McLaughlin (1992), standing on the shoulders of the philosophical critiques of the 1920s, launched primarily by Pepper (1926), Stace (1939) and Bayliss (1929). However none of these critiques of the pioneers were blessed with the visions or, in the case of McLaughlin, knowledge of, algorithmic mathematics. My vision is informed and underpinned by an algorithmic epistemology, for dynamics, inference and formalization. From such a standpoint, the *British Emergentists* were prescient in their approach to the formalization of emergence, coupled to the dialectic between the simple and the complex, in a natural dynamic context. They *rise and rise*; there was never any fall of the *British Emergentisits*!

Emergence, order, self-organization, turbulence, induction, evolution, (self-organized) criticality, adaptive, non-linear, networks, irreversible and non-equilibrium are some of the 'buzz' words, in various permutations and combinations, that characterize the conceptual underpinnings of the 'new' sciences of complexity that seem to pervade some of the frontiers in the natural, social and even the human sciences. Not since the heyday of Cybernetics and the more recent ebullience of chaos applied to a theory of everything, has a concept become so prevalent and pervasive in almost all fields, from Physics to Economics, from Biology to Sociology, from Computer Science to Philosophy as Complexity seems to have become. Even though lip service is paid to the poverty of axiomatics and the deductive method, almost without exception the mathematics employed by the practitioners of the new sciences of complexity is the classical variety: real analysis, founded on axiomatic set theory, supplemented by one or another variety of the axiom of choice. These theoretical technologies are, *ab initio*, non-algorithmic. This dichotomy – or is it, perhaps, a schizophrenia – pervades the work of, for example, those advocates of agent-based modelling who claim that the generation of patterns mimicking data at one level, based on foundations at a simpler level, is the best approach to the study of emergence, complexity and dynamics.

I disagree.

Einstein, perceptively, summarized a particular epistemology that he followed in his scientific endeavours:

If then it is the case that the axiomatic basis of theoretical physics cannot be an inference from experience, but must be free invention, have we any right to hope that we shall find the correct way?.... To this I answer with complete assurance, that in my opinion there is *the* correct path and, moreover, that it is in our power to find it. Our experience up to date justifies us in feeling sure that in Nature is actualized the ideal of mathematical simplicity. It is my conviction that pure mathematical construction enables us to discover the concepts and the laws connecting them which give us the key to the understanding of the phenomena of Nature.

Einstein in his *Herbert Spencer Lecture*, '*On the Methods of Theoretical Physics*', given at Oxford University on June 10, 1933. (Einstein, 1934, p.167; italics in original)

Economists, too, advocating a complexity vision would have the economic theorist discard the axiomatic, deductive method altogether. These economists also claim and assert that the epistemological and methodological poverty of so-called 'deductive mathematics' in an epoch where the ubiquity of the digital computer makes what they claim to be 'inductive and abductive methods' far superior in tackling formally intractable economic problems. For a supreme theorist like Einstein, grappling with no less empirically unruly phenomena than those faced by the economist, an epistemological underpinning, like the one explicitly acknowledged earlier, provides a justification for the methods of axiomatic, mathematical theorizing. Any advocacy of a new vision and its methods, without an epistemological basis to underpin them, runs the risk of having to be hoisted by its own petard and, therefore, of living dangerously. In a certain clearly substantiable sense, Richard Day and Barkley Rosser stand on the giant shoulders of Charles Sanders Peirce, one in that line of great American mathematical epistemologists, descending towards Warren McCulloch and Norbert Wiener, in the immediate epoch before our own times.

Acknowledgements

Many fruitful conversations on the interaction between dynamical systems theory, computability theory and the notion of complexity with Joe McCauley and Stefano Zambelli were decisive in disciplining my own thoughts. Incisive, detailed, comments and suggestions by two anonymous referees were most useful for the revision. Naturally, none of these worthies are even remotely responsible for the remaining infelicities.

Notes

1. It is rarely acknowledged that economists were prescient in this line of research via the remarkable analysis of '*coupled markets*' – integrating considerations of interdependence and (non-linear) dynamics – that was pioneered by Richard Goodwin almost fully a decade before even Fermi, Pasta and Ulam (cf. Goodwin, 1947). In the concluding section of his pioneering analysis, Goodwin observed:

   > To go from two identical markets to *n* non-identical ones will require the prolonged services of *yet unborn calculating machines*. (Goodwin, 1947, p. 204; italics added)

   This classic paper by Goodwin was made famous by Herbert Simon in his own sustained research on causality and *near-decomposability*, eventually also to form the 'backbone' of his analysis of evolution (cf. e.g. Simon (1953) and (1997; especially I.3 & I.4))

2. I may as well 'confess' my adherence to the importance of viewing economic dynamics as 'transition dynamics' in twin paradoxical modes: the Austrian 'traverse dynamics' and the Keynesian 'transition dynamics'. The Austrian notion of 'traverse dynamics' is a well-mined analytical tradition. It was in a famous footnote in Chapter 17 of the GT that Keynes stressed the importance of transition regimes (and made the reference to Hume as the progenitor of the equilibrium concept in economics):

   > [H]ume began the practice amongst economists of stressing the importance of the equilibrium position as compared with the ever-shifting transition towards it, though he was still enough of a mercantilist not to overlook the fact that *it is in the transition that we actually have our being*: ...

   (Keynes, 1936, p. 343, footnote 3; italics added)

3. This characterization was stated in an e-mail response by Dick Day to a query from the author for a succinct statement summarizing his general vision of dynamic complexity, on 11 February 2009. In trying to understand Richard Day's visions of dynamic complexity, it must be remembered that he is, together with Herbert Simon, James March, Richard Cyert, Sidney Winter and Richard Nelson, one of the original founders of what was once called 'behavioural economics'. What is now called 'behavioural economics' is a bastardization of the original, computationally constrained approach to behaviour by individuals and organizations. It is not without significance that Day is the founding father of the *Journal of Economic Behavior and Organization* – and Rosser is his anointed successor.

4. One of the many starting points for the themes he develops in Rosser (2010) is the concluding conjecture in Velupillai (2009, p. 1415; italics in original):

> The 'fallacy of composition' that drives a felicitous wedge between micro and macro, between the individual and the aggregate, and gives rise to *emergent* phenomena in economics, in non-algorithmic ways – as conjectured, originally more than a century and a half ago – by John Stuart Mill (1890) and George Herbert Lewes (1891), and codified by Lloyd Morgan in his *Gifford Lectures* (1927) – may yet be tamed by *unconventional models of computation*.

This paper is a step in the direction of showing the feasibility of a formal answer to that conjecture.

5. Fontana and Buss are not referring to 'constructive' in its mathematical senses of Brouwerian constructive mathematics – or any other variant, such as Bishop-style or Russian constructivism. Their reference to 'constructive' is, at best, interpretable in terms of computability theory, but even this is possible only by a serious stretching of the imagination.

6. However, it must be remembered that Goodwin was thinking of an *analog computer* when he made this statement.

7. In the definition of a dynamical system given below I am not striving to present the most general version. The basic aim is to lead to an intuitive understanding of the definition of a basin of attraction so that the main theorem is made reasonably transparent. Moreover, the definition given below is for scalar ODEs, easily generalizable to the vector case.

8. They can also encapsulate smooth dynamical systems in a precise sense. I have described the procedure, summarizing a variant of Chris Moore's approach, in Velupillai (2000, Chapter 4).

9. A perceptive referee commented: 'Boschetti and Gray (2007a) also proposed a Turing test for emergence. Maybe the authors would like to see whether it is relevant or not for what they proposed'. I am most grateful to the referee for bringing this work to my attention and for posing an interesting question, which I try to answer in the main body of the paper, albeit somewhat briefly. The reasons for the brevity is not that I was constrained by space, but that the contents of the Boschetti and Gray (2007a) work cannot be interpreted without placing it in the context of its companion piece, Boschetti and Gray (2007b), which is replete with elementary errors in the mathematics and philosophy of computability theory and the foundations of mathematics. Almost all of what these two authors state and claim about Turing and Gödel, in the latter reference, can be shown to be false or misleading. Moreover, every claim they make about computing beyond the Turing limit is easily shown to be false. It is obvious that these two authors are totally ignorant of the deep and powerful objections raised against Penrose's 'Lucasian' misconceptions by Putnam (1995) and Davis (undated). Moreover, they are also blissfully innocent of all the powerful results of Rubel (1988, 1989) and Pour-El (1974) on the connection between General Purpose Analog Computers and Digital Computers (GPAC) and how the limitations of the latter in the language of computability theory are not transcended by the former. Much of these details are discussed in detail in Velupillai (2004). The authors also make thoroughly invalid claims on the possibilities of so-called 'hyper-computation', in another form of going beyond the Turing limits of computation, Here, too, an elementary perusal of, say Davis (2004), could have prevented their extravagant claims. In view of the gross errors and misconceptions in the companion

piece, which should be considered the foundations upon which the 'Turing Test' exercise is advocated, we do not think it worthwhile to devote too much space for them.

10. This is one of the many reasons why I think the whole Boschetti and Gray approach is severely misguided and *algorithmically meaningless*.

11. On this point, too, I have been inspired by the perceptive comments of one of the referees to face the possibilities, but here, too, somewhat cryptically. I shall not deal with the issues that are related to the 'Chomsky Hierarchy' simply because I do not think there is anything to be gained from that perspective for the problems I try to tackle here. In a crude sense, the reason is that there is no intrinsic transition dynamics in approaching the problem I address here from the point of view of the theory of formal languages.

References

Alexander, S. (1920) *Space, Time and Deity: The Gifford Lectures at Glasgow,* Vol. I & Vol. II. London: Macmillan & Co.

Anosov, D.V. (2006) Dynamical systems in the 1960s: the hyperbolic revolution (translated by R. Cooke). In A.A. Bolibruch, Yu. S. Osipov, and Ya. G. Sinai (eds.), *Mathematical Events of the Twentieth Century*, Chapter 1, (pp. 1–17). Berlin, Heidelberg and Phasis Moscow: Springer-Verlag.

Bayliss, C.A. (1929) The philosophic functions of emergence. *The Philosophical Review*, 38(4): 372–384.

Berlekamp, E.R., Conway, J.H. and Guy, R.K. (1982) *Winning Ways for Your Mathematical Plays – Volume 2: Games in Particular*. London: Academic Press.

Blum, L., Cucker, F., Shub, M. and Smale, S. (1998) *Complexity and Real Computation*. New York & Berlin: Springer-Verlag.

Boschetti, F. and Gray, R. (2007a) A Turing test for emergence. In M. Prokopenko (ed.), *Advances in Applied Self-organizing Systems* (pp. 349–364). London: Springer-Verlag.

Boschetti, F. and Gray, R. (2007b) Emergence and computability. *Emergence: Complexity and Organization* 9(1–2): 120–130.

Brin, M. and Stuck, G. (2002) *Introduction to Dynamical Systems*. Cambridge: Cambridge University Press.

Broad, C.D. (1929) *The Mind and its Place in Nature – The Tarner Lectures delivered at Trinity College, Cambridge, 1923*. Kegan Paul, Trench. London: Trubner & Co., Ltd.

Cooper, S.B. (2004) *Computability Theory*. Boca Raton & London: Chapman & Hall/CRC.

Cooper, S.B. (2006) Computability and emergence. In: Dov M. Gabbay, Sergei S. Goncharov and Michael Zakharyaschev (eds.), *Mathematical Problems from Applied Logic I – Logics for the XXIst Century* (pp. 193–231). New York: Springer-Verlag.

Cover, T. and Thomas, J. (1991) *Elements of Information Theory*. New York & Chichester: John Wiley & Sons, Inc.

Davis, M. (2004) The myth of hypercomputation. In Christof Teuscher (ed.), *Alan Turing: Life and Legacy of a Great Thinker* (pp. 195–211). Berlin & Heidelberg: Springer-Verlag.

Davis, M. (undated) How subtle is Gödel's theorem: more on Roger Penrose. Available at: *cs.nyu.edu/cs/faculty/davism/penrose2.ps*

Day, R.H. (1994) *Complex Economic Dynamics, Vol I: An Introduction to Dynamical Systems and Market Mechanisms*. Cambridge, MA: The MIT Press.

Day, R.H. (1999) *Complex Economic Dynamics, Vol. II: An Introduction to Macroeconomic Dynamics* (with contributions by Tzong-Yau Lin, Zhang Min and Oleg Pavlov). Cambridge, MA: The MIT Press.

Day, R.H. (2004) *The Divergent Dynamics of Economic Growth: Studies in Adaptive Economizing, Technological Change and Economic Development*. Cambridge: Cambridge University Press.

Einstein, A. (1934) On the method of theoretical physics. *Philosophy of Science* 1(2): 163–169.

Fermi, E., Pasta, J. and Ulam, S. (1955) *Studies of Non Linear Problems*. Los Alamos Preprint, LA-1940, May.

Fontana, W. and Buss, L. (1996) The barrier of objects: from dynamical systems to bounded organizations. In J. Casti and A. Karlqvist (eds.), *Barriers and Boundaries* (pp. 56–116). Reading, MA: Addison-Wesley.

Gandy, R. (1994) The confluence of ideas in 1936. In *The Universal Turing Machine – A Half-Century Survey* (Second Edition) (pp. 51–102). Wien & New York: Springer-Verlag.

Goodstein, R.L. (1944) On the restricted ordinal theorem. *Journal of Symbolic Logic*. 9(2): 33–41.

Goodwin, R.M. (1947) Dynamical coupling with especial reference to markets having production lags. *Econometrica* 15(3): 181–204.

Goodwin, R.M. (1951) Iteration, automatic computers and economic dynamics. *Metroeconomica* 3(1): 1–7.

Goodwin, R.M. (1953) Static and dynamic linear general equilibrium models. In The Netherlands Economic Institute, H. E. Stenfert and N.V. Kroese (eds.), *Input-Output Relations: Proceedings of a Conference on Inter-Industrial Relations held at Driebergen, Holland*, (pp. 54–87). Leiden: H.E. Stenfert Kroese N.V.

Hayek, F.A. (1952) *The Sensory Order: An Inquiry into the Foundations of Theoretical Psychology*. Chicago, Illinois: University of Chicago Press.

Hirsch, M.W., Smale, S. and Devaney, R.L. (2004) *Differential Equations, Dynamical Systems & An Introduction to Chaos*. New York & London: Elsevier-Academic Press.

Keynes, J.M. (1936) *The General Theory of Employment, Interest and Money*. London: Macmillan & Co. Limited.

Kolmogorov, A.N. (1968) Three approaches to the definition of the concept of the "Amount of Information". In *Selected Translations in Mathematical Statistics and Probability*, Vol. 7 (pp. 293–302). Rhode Island: American Mathematical Society Providence.

Lewes, G.H. (1891) *Problems of Life and Mind*. New York: Houghton, Miffin & Co.

Lloyd, M.C. (1927) *Emergent Evolution: The Gifford Lectures* (2nd Edition). London: Williams & Norgate.

McLaughlin, B.P. (1992) The rise and fall of British emergentism. In Ansgar Beckermann, Hans Flohr and Jaegwon Kim (eds.), *Emergence or Reduction: Essays on the Prospects of Nonreductive Physicalism* (pp. 49–93). Berlin: Walter de Gruyter.

McMullen, C.T. (1993) Frontiers in complex dynamics. *Lecture Presented to the AMS-CMS-MAA Joint Meeting*, Vancouver, Canada. August 16, 1993.

Mill, J.S. (1890) *A System of Logic* (8th Edition). New York: Harper & Brothers Publishers.

Moore, C. (1990) Unpredictability and undecidability in dynamical systems. *Physical Review Letters* 64(4): 2354–2357.

Moore, C. (1991) Generalized shifts: unpredictability and undecidability in dynamical systems. *Nonlinearity* 4: 199–230.

von Neumann, J. (1966) *Theory of Self-Reproducing Automata*. Edited and completed by Arthur W. Burks. Urbana: University of Illinois Press.

Paris, J. and Tavakol, R. (1993) Goodstein algorithm as a super-transient dynamical system. *Physics Letters A* 180(1–2): 83–86.

Penrose, R. (1989) *The Emperor's New Mind: Concerning Computers, Mind, and the Laws of Physics*. Oxford: Oxford University Press.

Pepper, S.C. (1926) Emergence. *The Journal of Philosophy* 23(9): 241–245.

Pour-El, M.B. (1974) Abstract computability and its relation to the general purpose analog computer (Some connections between logic, differential equations and analog computers). *Transactions of the American Mathematical Society* 199: 1–28.

Putnam, H. (1995) Review of shadows of the mind by roger penrose. *Bulletin (New Series) of the American Mathematical Society* 32(3): 370–373.

Rissanen, J. (1978) Modelling by shortest data description. *Automatica* 14(5): 465–471.

Rissanen, J. (1986) Stochastic complexity and modeling. *The Annals of Statistics* 14(3): 1080–1100.

Rogers, H. Jr. (1967) *Theory of Recursive Functions and Effective Computability*. Cambridge, MA: The MIT Press.

Rosser, J.B. Jr. (1999) On the complexities of complex economic dynamics. *Journal of Economic Perspectives* 13(4): 169–192.

Rosser, J.B. Jr. (2010) Constructivist logic and emergent evolution in economic complexity. In Stefano Zambelli (ed.), *Computable, Constructive and Behavioural Economic Dynamics*. London: Routledge.

Rubel, L.A. (1988) Some mathematical limitations of the general-purpose analog computer. *Advances in Applied Mathematics* 9: 22–34.

Rubel, L.A. (1989) Digital simulation of analog computation and Church's thesis. *Journal of Symbolic Logic* 54(3): 1011–1017.

Simon, H.A. (1953) Causal ordering and identifiability. In Wm. C. Hood and Tjalling C. Koopmans (eds.), *Studies in Econometric Method*, Chapter III (pp. 40–74). Cowles Foundation Monograph, #14, New Haven: Yale University Press.

Simon, H.A. (1997) *Models of Bounded Rationality: Empirically Grounded Economic Reason* (Vol 3). Cambridge, Massachusetts: The MIT Press.

Sperry, R.W. (1981) Some effects of disconnecting the cerebral hemispheres. *Nobel Prize Lecture*, Stockholm, 8 December, 1981.

Stace, W.T. (1939) Novelty, indeterminism and emergence. *The Philosophical Review* 48(3): 296–310.

Stuart, A.M. and Humphries, A.R. (1996) *Dynamical Systems and Numerical Analysis*. Cambridge: Cambridge University Press.

Turing, A. (1936–1937) On computable numbers, with an application to the Entscheidungs problem. *Proceedings of the London Mathematical Society* Series 2, 42: 236–265.

Velupillai, K. (2000) *Computable Economics*. Oxford: Oxford University Press.

Velupillai, K.V. (2004) Computation and economic dynamics: resurrecting the *Icarus* tradition. *Metroeconomica* 55(2–3): 239–264.

Velupillai, K.V. (2009) Uncomputability and undecidability in economic theory. *Applied Mathematics and Computation* 215(4): 1404–1416.

Velupillai, K.V. (2010) The Minsky moment: a critique and a reconstruction. Forthcoming In: Geoff Harcourt and Neville Norman (eds.), *The OUP Handbook on Post-Keynesian Economics* (p. 2011). Oxford: Oxford University Press.

Weissert, T.P. (1997) *The Genesis of Simulation in Dynamics: Pursuing the Fermi-Pasta-Ulam Problem*. New York: Springer-Verlag.

Wolfram, S. (1985) Undecidability and intractability in theoretical physics. *Physical Review Letters* 54(8): 735–738.

Zvonkin, A.K. and Levin, L.A. (1970) The complexity of finite objects and the development of the concepts of information and randomness by means of the theory of algorithms. *Russian Mathematical Surveys* 25(6): 83–124.

9

STOCK-FLOW INTERACTIONS, DISEQUILIBRIUM MACROECONOMICS AND THE ROLE OF ECONOMIC POLICY

Toichiro Asada, Carl Chiarella, Peter Flaschel, Tarik Mouakil,
Christian Proaño and Willi Semmler

1. Introduction

The aim of this paper is to give an overview of the "KMG" (Keynes-Metzler-Goodwin) approach to macrodynamic modelling. It focuses in particular on the KMGT ('Keynes-Metzler-Goodwin-Tobin) portfolio model that incorporates financial markets in a Tobinian way. The original KMG model of Chiarella and Flaschel (2000) focuses particularly on the real side of the economy. It starts from Keynesian AD-AS analysis, introduces the interaction of Metzlerian sales expectations–inventory cycles, and then finally adds a detailed formulation of the working of the wage–price spiral in a growing economy (the Goodwin component). This approach is nonlinear in the same sense that the Goodwin growth cycle is nonlinear. In addition it exhibits further nonlinearities in the form of products of state variables as they appear, for example, in the wage share when output per unit of capital becomes an endogenous variable through the KM components of the model.

In the original KMG model three asset markets are considered (equities, bonds and money) but they are depicted in a rudimentary way and have little influence on the real side of the model. The equities market is presented only in nominal terms and the perfect-substitute mechanism through which the price of equities is determined does not yet feed back into the real side of the economy. Stock prices do not play an active role in the KMG model, due to the absence of wealth and capital gains effects on aggregate demand and due to the absence of Tobin's q in consumption and investment behaviour. In the same way, though asset holding households are supposed to hold government bonds, the feedback of their rate of change in households portfolios – determined by the government budget constraint – is suppressed via a suitably chosen

Nonlinearity, Complexity and Randomness in Economics, First Edition.
Stefano Zambelli and Donald A.R. George.
© 2012 John Wiley & Sons. Published 2012 by John Wiley & Sons, Ltd.

taxation rule such that there is no interest income effect on asset holders' consumption. The only financial market that influences the real side of the economy in the KMG model is the money market (via an LM curve theory of interest) through the negative effect of the interest rate on the rate of investment. However this financial market does not explicitly interact with the other two since the demand for money simply provides an LM curve that gives rise to a stable relationship between the nominal rate of interest, the output–capital ratio and supplied real balances per unit of capital.

In Tobin's portfolio choice theory by contrast, the demand for each asset is defined in such a way that the total amount of assets that households want to hold is equal to their wealth. This balance sheet constraint underlying portfolio choice is one of the two pillars of Tobin's approach to macroeconomic modelling. The second pillar, or flow constraint, states that the net amount of assets accumulated (liabilities issued) by one sector must equal its net savings (expenditures). In the KMGT model the stock constraint concerns only capital holders, while the flow constraint has to be fulfilled for all the sectors of the economy (namely asset holders, workers, firms and the government).

The KMGT model just outlined, see Asada *et al.* (2010a) chapter 10, for full details, thus attempts to remedy such shortcomings by using the insights of Tobin's 'Old Keynesian Analysis'. First, although wealth and interest income effects are still ignored, bond and equity stock dynamics now feed back into the real part of the economy through the introduction of Tobin's q into the function defining the investment behaviour of firms. Second, the three financial markets now interact with each other thanks to the introduction of Tobinian gross-substitute type of portfolio choice. The demand for each asset varies positively with its own real rate of return and negatively with the rates of other assets by way of this gross-substitute assumption. In particular the demand for bonds, and hence the interest rate on bonds, are now influenced by variations in the price of equities.

We use this Tobinian macroeconomic portfolio approach, coupled with the interaction of heterogeneous agents on the financial markets, to characterize the potential for financial market instability. Though the study of the latter has been undertaken in many partial models, we focus here on the interconnectedness of all three markets. Furthermore, we study the potential for labour market and fiscal policies to have a role in stabilizing an unstable macroeconomy. Amongst various stabilization policies we in particular propose a certain type of fiscal policy and a 'scala mobile' wage policy.

Standard, though quite high-dimensional,[1] stability analysis is brought to bear to demonstrate the narrow limits of private sector stability and the stabilizing effects of the suggested fiscal policy measures. The paper builds on work by Asada *et al.* (2010a, 2010b) by using models of this research agenda as a starting point for the proper design of a macrodynamic framework and labour market, fiscal and monetary policies in a framework which allows in general for large swings in financial and real economic activity. It builds on baseline models of the dynamic interaction of labour market, product market and financial markets with risky assets. We revive a framework of a macroeconomic portfolio approach that Tobin (1969) had suggested, but also build on recent work on the interaction of heterogeneous agents in the financial market. We allow for heterogeneity in share and goods price expectations and study the financial, nominal and real cumulative feedback chains that may give rise to the potential for an unstable economy. The work connects to traditional Keynesian business cycle analysis as suggested by Tobin in particular, including however also the Goodwin (1967) distributive cycle. Moreover, Metzlerian aspects concern the quantity adjustment process on the market for goods which is of a delayed disequilibrium type. In a previous model, developed by Asada *et al.* (2010a), there were no long-term bonds on the asset market. This extension towards the presence of a further risky asset is now built into the current model variant.

The paper will develop as follows. Section 2 presents the baseline KMGT model. In Section 3, we introduce long-term bonds as the primary financing instrument of the government. Section 4 discusses the intensive form of the model. In Section 5, we investigate the stability properties of varies fiscal policy measures. Section 6 draws some conclusions. The proofs of the various theorems are given in Asada *et al.* (2010b) and Asada *et al.* (2010c). Taken together, the paper therefore provides a survey of the baseline structure of the KMGT portfolio model, its extension towards the inclusion of a further risky asset besides equities, its modification towards an inclusion of fiscal policy measures and finally also monetary policy measures.

2. Macroeconomic Portfolio Choice and Keynesian Business Cycle Theory; the KMGT Model

In the tradition of Tobin (1969) and his later work we will depart from standard theory and provide the structural form of a growth model using a portfolio approach that incorporates heterogeneous agent behaviour on asset markets. In order to discuss the details we split the model into appropriate modules that refer to the sectors of the economy, namely households, firms and the government (the fiscal and monetary authority). Beside presenting a detailed structure of the asset market, we also represent the wage–price interactions, and connect the dynamics of the financial market to those of the labour and product markets.

2.1 *Households*

As discussed in the introduction we disaggregate the sector of households into worker households and asset holder households. We begin with the description of the behaviour of workers:

Worker households

$$\omega = w/p \tag{1}$$

$$C_w = (1 - \tau_w)\omega L^d \tag{2}$$

$$S_w = 0, \tag{3}$$

$$\hat{L} = n = \text{const.} \tag{4}$$

Equation (1) gives the definition of the real wage ω before taxation, where w denotes the nominal wage and p the actual price level. We operate in a Keynesian framework with sluggish wage and price adjustment processes, and the assumption that the labour demand of firms can always be satisfied out of the given labour supply. Then, according to equation (2), real income of workers equals the product of real wages times labour demand, which net of taxes $\tau_w \omega L^d$, equals workers' consumption, since we do not allow for savings of the workers as postulated in equation (3). No savings by workers implies that their wealth is zero at every point in time. This in particular means that the workers do not hold any assets and that they consume instantaneously their disposable income. We finally assume in equation (4) a constant growth rate n of the labour force L, coupled with the assumption that labour is supplied inelastically at each moment in time. We stress here that such an assumption is still rooted in the neoclassical tradition and has only be dispensed with in other variants of the KMG approach, see Chiarella and Flaschel (1998) in particular. Our reformulations of the old neoclassical synthesis from the KMG perspective thus do not always question all the assumptions made in this synthesis as, for example, in Sargent (1987).

The income, consumption and wealth of the asset holders are described by:[2]

Asset holder households

$$r_k^e = (Y^e - \delta K - \omega L^d)/K \tag{5}$$

$$C_c = (1 - s_c)\left[r_k^e K + iB/p - T_c\right], \quad 0 < s_c < 1 \tag{6}$$

$$S_p = s_c[r_k^e K + iB/p - T_c] \tag{7}$$

$$= (\dot{M} + \dot{B} + p_e \dot{E})/p \tag{8}$$

$$W_c = (M + B + p_e E)/p, \quad W_c^n = pW_c. \tag{9}$$

The first equation (5) of this module defines the expected rate of return on real capital, r_k^e, as the ratio of the currently expected real cash flow and the real stock of business fixed capital K. The expected cash flow is given by expected real revenues from sales Y^e diminished by real depreciation of capital δK and the real wage ωL^d. We assume that firms pay out all expected cash flow in the form of dividends to the asset holders. These dividend payments are one source of income for asset holders. The second source is given by real interest payments on short term bonds (iB/p) where i is the nominal interest rate. Summing up these interest incomes and taking account of lump sum taxes T_c in the case of asset holders (for reasons of simplicity) we obtain the disposable income of asset holders given by the terms in the square brackets of equation (6), which together with a postulated fixed propensity to consume $(1 - s_c)$ out of this income gives us the real consumption of asset holders.

Real savings of asset owners is their real disposable income minus their consumption as expressed in equation (7). The asset owners can allocate the real savings in the form of money change $\dot{M}$, or buy other financial assets, namely short-term bonds $\dot{B}$ or equities $\dot{E}$ at the price p_e, the only financial instruments that we allow for in the present reformulation of the KMG growth model. Hence, the savings of asset holders must be distributed to these assets as stated in equation (8). Real wealth of asset holders is thus defined in equation (9) as the sum of real cash balances, real short term bond holdings and real equity holdings of asset holders. Note that the short term bonds are assumed to be fixed price bonds with a price of one: $p_b = 1$, and a flexible interest rate i. Equation (9) states that actual nominal wealth equals the stocks of financial assets held by the asset holders. We assume, as is usual in portfolio approaches, that the asset holders demand assets of an amount that equals in sum their nominal wealth as stated in equation (9). In other words, they reallocate their wealth in view of new information on the rates of returns on their assets and take account of their wealth constraint.

Next we introduce portfolio holdings. Following the general equilibrium approach of Tobin (1969) we can express the demands of asset owning households for financial assets as

$$M^d = f_m(i, r_e^e)W_c^n \tag{10}$$

$$B^d = f_b(i, r_e^e)W_c^n \tag{11}$$

$$p_e E^d = f_e(i, r_e^e)W_c^n \tag{12}$$

$$W_c^n = M^d + B^d + p_e E^d. \tag{13}$$

The demand for money balances of asset holders M^d is determined by a function $f_m(i, r_e^e)$ which depends on the interest rate on short run bonds i and the expected rate of return on equities r_e^e. The value of this function times the nominal wealth W_c^n gives the nominal demand for money M^d, so that f_m describes the portion of nominal wealth that is allocated to pure money holdings.

We do not assume that the financial assets of the economy are perfect substitutes, but rather that they are imperfect substitutes. This is implicit in the approach that underlies the above block of equations. But what is the motive for asset holders to hold a fraction of their wealth in the form of money, when there is a riskless interest bearing asset? In our view it is reasonable to employ a speculative motive: Asset holders want to hold money in order to *be able* to buy other assets or goods with zero or very low transaction costs. This of course assumes that there are (implicitly given) transaction costs when fixed price bonds are turned into money.

The nominal demand for bonds is given by $f_b(i, r_e^e)$ and the nominal demand for equities by $f_e(i, r_e^e)$, which again are functions that describe the fractions of nominal wealth that are allocated to these forms of financial wealth.

What remains to be modelled in the household sector is the expected rate of return on equities r_e^e which, as usual, consists of real dividends per unit of equity ($r_k^e pK / p_e E$) plus expected capital gains, π_e, the latter being nothing other than the expected growth rate of equity prices. Thus we can write

$$r_e^e = \frac{r_k^e pK}{p_e E} + \pi_e. \tag{14}$$

In order to complete the modelling of asset holders' behaviour, we need to describe the evolution of π_e. In the tradition of recent work on heterogeneous agents in asset markets, we here assume that there are two types of asset holders, who differ with respect to their expectation formation of equity prices.[3] There are behavioural traders, called *chartists*, who in principle employ some form of adaptive expectations mechanism, which here we simply take as

$$\dot{\pi}_{ec} = \beta_{\pi_{ec}}(\hat{p}_e - \pi_{ec}) \tag{15}$$

where $\beta_{\pi_{ec}}$ is the adjustment speed toward the actual growth rate of equity prices. The other asset holders, the *fundamentalists*, employ a forward looking expectation formation mechanism

$$\dot{\pi}_{ef} = \beta_{\pi_{ef}}(\eta - \pi_{ef}) \tag{16}$$

where η is the fundamentalists' expected long run growth rate of share prices, obtained from some (costly) analysis of fundamental factors. Assuming that the aggregate expected rate of share price increase is a weighted average of the two expected rates, where the weights are determined according to the sizes of the groups, we postulate

$$\pi_e = \alpha_{\pi_{ec}}\pi_{ec} + (1 - \alpha_{\pi_{ec}})\pi_{ef}. \tag{17}$$

Here for simplicity $\alpha_{\pi_{ec}} \in (0, 1)$ is the ratio of chartists to all asset holders is assumed to be constant. Brock and Hommes (1997) allow these functions to evolve according to some 'success' criterion.

2.2 *Firms*

We consider the behaviour of firms by means of two submodules. The first describes the production framework and investment by firms in business fixed capital, the second introduces the Metzlerian approach of inventory dynamics concerning expected sales, actual sales and the output of firms.

Firms: production and investment

$$r_k^e = (pY^e - wL^d - p\delta K)/(pK) \tag{18}$$

$$Y^p = y^p K \tag{19}$$

$$u = Y/Y^p \tag{20}$$

$$L^d = Y/x \tag{21}$$

$$e = L^d/L = Y/(xL) \tag{22}$$

$$q = p_e E/(pK) \tag{23}$$

$$I = i_q(q-1)K + i_u(u - \bar{u})K + nK \tag{24}$$

$$\hat{K} = I/K \tag{25}$$

$$p_e \dot{E} = pI + p(\dot{N} - \mathcal{I}). \tag{26}$$

Firms are assumed to pay out dividends according to expected profits (expected sales net of depreciation and minus the wage sum, see equations 5 to 7, for the module of the asset owning households). The rate of expected profits r_k^e is expected real profits per unit of capital as stated in equation (18). Firms produce output utilizing a production technology that transforms labour demanded L^d combined with business fixed capital K into output. For convenience we assume that the production takes place with a fixed proportion technology.[4] According to equation (19) potential output Y^p is given at each moment of time by a fixed coefficient y^p times the existing stock of physical capital. Accordingly, the utilization of productive capacity is given by the ratio u of actual production Y and the potential output Y^p. The fixed proportions in production give rise to a constant output-labour coefficient x, by means of which we can deduce labour demand from goods market determined output as in equation (21). The ratio L^d/L thus defines the rate of employment in the model.

The economic behaviour of firms must include their investment decision with regard to business fixed capital, which is determined independently of the savings decision of households. We here model investment decisions per unit of capital as a function of the deviation of Tobin's q (see Tobin (1969)) from its long run value of 1, and the deviation of actual capacity utilization from a normal rate of capital utilization. We add an exogenously given trend term, here given by the natural growth rate n in order to allow this rate to determine the growth path of the economy in the usual way. Tobin's average q is defined in equation (23) as the ratio of the nominal value of equities and the reproduction costs for the existing stock of capital. Investment in business fixed capital is reinforced when q exceeds one, and is reduced when q is smaller than one. This influence is represented by the term $i_q(q-1)$ in equation

(24). The term $i_u(u - \bar{u})$ models the component of investment which is due to the deviation of the utilization rate of physical capital from its non accelerating inflation value $\bar{u}$. The last component, nK, takes account of the natural growth rate n which is necessary for steady state analysis if natural growth is considered as exogenously given. Capital stock growth is given in (25) by net investment per unit of capital I/K in this demand determined model of the short-run equilibrium position of the economy. Equation (26) is the budget constraint of the firms. Investment in business fixed capital and unintended changes in the inventory stock $p(\dot{N} - \mathcal{I})$ must be financed by issuing equities, since equities are the only financial instrument of firms in this section.

Next we model the inventory dynamics following Metzler (1941) and Franke (1996). This approach is a very useful concept for describing the goods market disequilibrium dynamics with all of its implications. In the following we take $\alpha_{n^d}, \beta_n, \beta_{y^e} \geq 0$:

Firms output adjustment

$$N^d = \alpha_{n^d} Y^e \tag{27}$$

$$\mathcal{I} = nN^d + \beta_n(N^d - N) \tag{28}$$

$$Y = Y^e + \mathcal{I} \tag{29}$$

$$Y^d = C + I + \delta K + G \tag{30}$$

$$\dot{Y}^e = nY^e + \beta_{y^e}(Y^d - Y^e) \tag{31}$$

$$\dot{N} = Y - Y^d \tag{32}$$

$$S_f = Y - Y^e = \mathcal{I}. \tag{33}$$

Equation (27) states that the desired stock of physical inventories, denoted by N^d, is assumed to be a fixed proportion of the expected sales. The planned investment $\mathcal{I}$ in inventories follows a sluggish adjustment process toward the desired stock N^d according to equation (28). Taking account of this additional demand for goods, equation (29) writes the production Y as equal to the expected sales of firms plus planned inventories $\mathcal{I}$. To explain the expectation formation for goods demand, we need the actual total demand for goods which in equation (30) is given by consumption (of private households and the government) and gross investment by firms.

Equation (31) models the dynamics of expected sales as the outcome of an error correction process, that also incorporates the natural growth rate n in order take account of the fact that this process operates in a growing economy. The adjustment of sales expectations is driven by the prediction error $(Y^d - Y^e)$, with an adjustment speed β_{y^e}. Actual changes in the stock of inventories are given in equation (32) by the deviation of production from goods demanded.

The savings of the firms S_f is as usual defined by their income minus consumption. Because firms are assumed to not consume anything, their income equals their savings

Table 1. The Four Activity Accounts of the Firms.

Uses	Resources
Production Account of Firms	
Depreciation $p \delta K$	Private consumption pC
Wages wL^d	Gross investment $pI + p \delta K$
Gross accounting profits $\Pi = r_k^e pK + p\mathcal{I}$	Inventory investment $p\dot{N}$
	Public consumption pG
Income Account of Firms	
Dividends $r_k^e p_y K$	Gross accounting profits Π
Savings $p\mathcal{I}$	
Accumulation Account of Firms	
Gross investment $pI + p \delta K$	Depreciation $p \delta K$
Inventory investment $p\dot{N}$	Savings $p\mathcal{I}$
	Financial deficit FD
Financial Account of Firms	
Financial deficit FD	Equity financing $p_e \dot{E}$

and is given by the excess of production over expected sales, $Y - Y^e$. According to the production account in Table 1 the output of firms is given by $\omega L^d + p\delta K + r_k^e pK + p\mathcal{I} = pY^e + p\mathcal{I} = pY^d + p\dot{N}$ and their income (= savings) is given by $p\mathcal{I}$.

2.3 Fiscal and Monetary Authorities

The role of the government in this paper is to provide the economy with public (non-productive) services within the limits of its budget constraint. Public purchases (and interest payments) are financed through taxes, through newly printed money, or newly issued fixed-price bonds ($p_b = 1$). The budget constraint gives rise to some repercussion effects between the public and the private sector. Thus we have

$$T = \tau_w \omega L^d + T_c \qquad (34)$$

$$T_c - iB/p = t_c K, \qquad t_c = \text{const.} \qquad (35)$$

$$G = gK, \qquad g = \text{const.} \qquad (36)$$

$$S_g = T - iB/p - G \qquad (37)$$

$$\hat{M} = \mu \qquad (38)$$

$$\dot{B} = pG + iB - pT - \dot{M}. \qquad (39)$$

In equation (34) we model the tax income consisting of taxes on wage income and lump sum taxes on capital income T_c. The latter quantity is determined net of government interest payments as a constant fraction of the capital stock in equation (35).[5] With regard to the real purchases of the government for the provision of government services we assume, again as in Sargent (1987), that these are a fixed proportion g of real capital. This fiscal policy is in a sense neutral and is to be contrasted with that of the independent fiscal authority that we posit and discuss in Section 5. We can thus represent fiscal policy by means of simple parameters in the intensive form representation of the model and in the steady state considerations to be discussed later. The real savings of the government (which is a deficit if it has a negative sign) is defined in equation (37) by real taxes minus real interest payments minus real public services. For reasons of simplicity the growth rate of money is given by a constant μ. So equation (38) is the monetary policy rule of the central bank and shows that money is assumed to enter the economy via open market operations of the central bank, which buys short-term bonds from the asset holders when issuing new money. Then the changes in the short-term bonds supplied by the government are given residually in equation (39), which is the budget constraint of the government sector.[6]

2.4 Wage–Price Interactions

We now turn to a module of our model that can be the source of significant destabilizing forces within the complete model. These are the three laws of motion of the wage–price spiral. Using the approach of Rose (1967)[7] of two short-run Phillips curves, one a wage Phillips curve and the other a price Phillips curve, the relevant dynamic equations can be written as

$$\hat{w} = \beta_w(e - \bar{e}) + \kappa_w \hat{p} + (1 - \kappa_w)\pi^c \tag{40}$$

$$\hat{p} = \beta_p(u - \bar{u}) + \kappa_p \hat{w} + (1 - \kappa_p)\pi^c \tag{41}$$

$$\dot{\pi}^c = \beta_{\pi^c}(\alpha \hat{p} + (1 - \alpha)(\mu - n) - \pi^c) \tag{42}$$

where $\beta_w, \beta_p, \beta_{\pi^c} \geq 0, 0 \leq \alpha \leq 1$ and $0 \leq \kappa_w, \kappa_p \leq 1$. This approach assumes that relative changes in money wages are influenced by demand pressure in the market for labour and price inflation (cost–pressure) terms. Price inflation in turn depends on demand pressure in the market for goods and on money wage (cost–pressure) terms. Wage inflation therefore is described in equation (40) on the one hand by means of a demand pull term $\beta_w(e - \bar{e})$, which states that relative changes in wages depends positively on the gap between actual employment e and its NAIRU (Non Accelerating Inflation Rate of Unemployment) value $\bar{e}$. On the other hand, the cost-push element in wage inflation is the weighted average of short-run (perfectly anticipated) price inflation $\hat{p}$ and medium run expected overall inflation π^c, where the weights are given by κ_w and $1 - \kappa_w$, respectively. The price Phillips curve equation (41) is similar, also displaying demand pressure and cost–pressure components. The demand pull term is given by the gap between capital utilization and its NAIRU value, $(u - \bar{u})$, and the cost-push element is the κ_p and $1 - \kappa_p$, respectively, weighted average of short run wage inflation $\hat{w}$ and expected medium run overall inflation π^c.

Equation (42) postulates a simple kind of forward looking expectations into the economy namely that changes in expected medium run inflation are due to an adjustment process towards a weighted average of the current inflation rate and steady state inflation with weights α and $(1 - \alpha)$, respectively. This adjustment is driven by an adjustment velocity β_{π^c}.

2.5 Capital Markets

We have not yet discussed how capital markets are organized and thus have not yet formulated the determination of the nominal rate of interest i and the price of equities p_e. Following Tobin's (1969) portfolio approach, and also Franke and Semmler (1999), we simply postulate that the equilibrium conditions

$$M = M^d = f_m(i, r_e^e)W_c^n, \quad W_c^n = M + B + p_e E \tag{43}$$

$$B = B^d = f_b(i, r_e^e)W_c^n \tag{44}$$

$$p_e E = p_e E^d = f_e(i, r_e^e)W_c^n, \quad r_e^e = \frac{pY^e - wL^d - p\delta K}{p_e E} + \pi_e^e \tag{45}$$

always hold and thus determine the two prices, i for bonds and p_e for equities, as statically endogenous variables of the model. Note here that all asset supplies are given magnitudes at each moment in time and recall from equation (14) that r_e^e is given by $\frac{r_k^e pK}{p_e E} + \pi_e$. Since all variables in the last expression apart from p_e are statically endogenously determined at each point in time, instantaneous variations in r_e^e are solely due to variations in the share price p_e. Our model thus supports the view that the secondary market is the market where the prices or interest rates for financial assets are determined such that these markets clear at all moments in time. Hence newly issued assets do not impact significantly on these prices.

Trade between the asset holders induces a process that makes asset prices fall or rise in order to equilibrate demand and supply. In the short run (in continuous time) the structure of wealth of asset holders (W_c^n) is, disregarding changes in the share price p_e, given to them and for the model. This implies that the functions $f_m()$, $f_b()$ and $f_e()$, introduced in equations (10) to (12) must satisfy the obvious conditions

$$f_m(i, r_e^e) + f_b(i, r_e^e) + f_e(i, r_e^e) = 1 \tag{46}$$

$$\frac{\partial f_m(i, r_e^e)}{\partial z} + \frac{\partial f_b(i, r_e^e)}{\partial z} + \frac{\partial f_e(i, r_e^e)}{\partial z} = 0, \quad \forall z \in \{i, r_e^e\}. \tag{47}$$

These conditions guarantee that the number of independent equations is equal to the number of statically endogenous variables (i, p_e) that the asset markets are assumed to determine at each moment in time.

We postulate that the financial assets display the gross substitution property, namely

$$\frac{\partial f_b(i, r_e^e)}{\partial i} > 0, \quad \frac{\partial f_m(i, r_e^e)}{\partial i} < 0, \quad \frac{\partial f_e(i, r_e^e)}{\partial i} < 0 \tag{48}$$

$$\frac{\partial f_e(i, r_e^e)}{\partial r_e^e} > 0, \quad \frac{\partial f_m(i, r_e^e)}{\partial r_e^e} < 0, \quad \frac{\partial f_b(i, r_e^e)}{\partial r_e^e} < 0 \tag{49}$$

which means that the demand for all other assets increases whenever the price of one asset rises. The above discussion concentrates on stocks and their impact on asset prices, including the balance sheet constraint of asset holders.

2.6 *The Comparative Statics of the Asset Markets*

We now focus on the short-run comparative statics of the financial markets module of the system. We derive in particular Tobin's q as the function $q = q(m, b, r_k^e, \pi_e)$ which will be needed to investigate the stability properties of the model around its steady state position in Sections 5 and 6.

We assume that the asset demand functions display the properties which guarantee a unique interior steady state solution; see Asada *et al.* (2010c) for more details. We now approximate these demand functions by linear functions in a neighbourhood of the steady state in order to derive the local stability properties in Sections 5 and 6. The *linearized versions of the asset demand functions* can be written as (recall that $r_e^e = r_k^e/q + \pi_e)^8$

$$f_m^l(i, r_e^e) = \alpha_{m0} - \alpha_{m1}i - \alpha_{m2}(r_k^e/q + \pi_e)$$

$$f_b^l(i, r_e^e) = \alpha_{b0} + \alpha_{b1}i - \alpha_{b2}(r_k^e/q + \pi_e)$$

$$f_e^l(i, r_e^e) = \alpha_{e0} - \alpha_{e1}i + \alpha_{e2}(r_k^e/q + \pi_e)$$

where the superscript l denotes the linearized form and where $\alpha_{ij} \geq 0 \quad \forall \quad i \in \{b, m, e\}, \ j \in \{0, 1, 2\}$. Because of the balance sheet constraint of asset holders it is sufficient to focus on the first two asset market equilibrium conditions in all subsequent equilibrium considerations. For money and bonds these two equilibrium conditions (from equations 43 and 44) read

$$m = (\alpha_{m0} - \alpha_{m1}i - \alpha_{m2}(r_k^e/q + \pi_e))(m + b + q) \tag{50}$$

$$b = (\alpha_{b0} + \alpha_{b1}i - \alpha_{b2}(r_k^e/q + \pi_e))(m + b + q). \tag{51}$$

Solving equations (50) and (51) for the interest rate i we obtain, respectively,

$$i_{LM} = \frac{\alpha_{m0} - \alpha_{m2}(r_k^e/q + \pi_e) - m/(m + b + q)}{\alpha_{m1}} \tag{52}$$

$$i_{BB} = \frac{-\alpha_{b0} + \alpha_{b2}(r_k^e/q + \pi_e) + b/(m + b + q)}{\alpha_{b1}}. \tag{53}$$

The LM-subscript denotes the interest rate that equates demand for real balances and real money supply (equation 50) and the BB-subscript denotes the interest rate that equates real bond demand and supply (equation 51). Figure 1 displays examples of these two functions as a function of Tobin's q.[9]

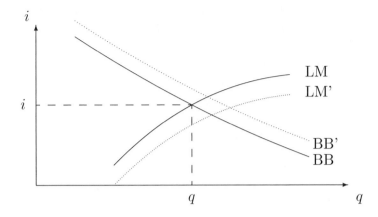

Figure 1. The LM and BB Curve Characterization of Tobin's Portfolio Approach.

The intersection of the LM-curve and the BB-curve then provides the equilibrium values for the short-term interest rate i and Tobin's q. The figure only shows one example of such functions and as we know that the functions are not linear in q we do not know yet whether the equilibrium exists and is unique. Note however that we are only considering a neighbourhood of the steady state solution for the variables i, q, m, b, r_k^e, π_e. In order to show that i and q exist and are uniquely determined for all m, b, r_k^e, π_e sufficiently close to the steady state solution we therefore have to show that the assumptions of the implicit function theorem are valid at the steady state.

Lemma 1. *Assume that there exists a unique steady state solution of the model described in Sections 2.1 to 2.5. Then there is also a unique solution (i, q) to the model's equations which clears the asset markets, for all values of m, b, r_k^e, π_e in an appropriately chosen neighbourhood of the interior steady state solution.*

We thus have the result that the financial markets can always be cleared through adjustments of the short-term interest rate and Tobin's q. But how do these two variables react in the short-run as the above statically given exogenous variables change over time? We consider this question first on the level of the partial equilibrium curves shown in Figure 1. We can derive for the dependence of the two interest functions i_{LM} and i_{BB} on the variables r_k^e, π_e, q and m the relationships

$$\underset{-\ \ -\ \ -\ \ +\ +}{i_{LM}(r_k^e,\ \pi_e,\ m,\ b,\ q)} \quad \text{and} \quad \underset{+\ \ +\ \ -\ \ +\ -}{i_{BB}(r_k^e,\ \pi_e,\ m,\ b,\ q)} \tag{54}$$

These results follow directly by taking the respective partial derivatives of the functions in equations (52) and (53), which together through the equilibrium condition $i_{\text{LM}} = i_{\text{BB}}$ yield

$$
\frac{\alpha_{m0} - \alpha_{m2}(r_k^e/q + \pi_e) - m/(m + b + q)}{\alpha_{m1}}
$$
$$
- \frac{-\alpha_{b0} + \alpha_{b2}(r_k^e/q + \pi_e) + b/(m + b + q)}{\alpha_{b1}} = 0. \tag{55}
$$

Application of the implicit function theorem then gives the following qualitative dependencies of Tobin's average q:

$$
\begin{array}{c}
q(r_k^e, \pi_e, m, b) \\
+ \ \ + \ \ + \ \ +
\end{array}
\quad \forall \, q > \left(\frac{\alpha_{b1}}{\alpha_{m1}} - 1\right) m
$$
$$
\begin{array}{c}
q(r_k^e, \pi_e, m, b) \\
+ \ \ + \ \ + \ \ -
\end{array}
\quad \forall \, q < \left(\frac{\alpha_{b1}}{\alpha_{m1}} - 1\right) m. \tag{56}
$$

The first situation in equation (56) must apply locally around the steady state if $(\frac{\alpha_{b1}}{\alpha_{m1}} - 1)m^o < 1$ holds true while the other one holds in the opposite case. We thus get the result that an increase in r_k^e, the basis for the dividend rate of return, unambiguously increases Tobin's q, as does an increase in the expected capital gains π_e. Furthermore, an increase in m also pushes q upwards and thus increases investment, just as an increase in m would do in the presence of a negative dependence of the rate of investment on the rate of interest, the Keynes effect in traditional models of the AS-AD variety. The positive influence of m on q thus mirrors the Keynes effect of traditional Keynesian short-run equilibrium analysis. The nominal rate of interest is however no longer involved in the real part of the model as it is here formulated which allows us to ignore its comparative statics in the current analysis. Comparative statics of the influence of an increase of bonds b on Tobin's q are ambiguous. There is however the following result which is of use when stability questions are approached.

Lemma 2. *In a neighbourhood around the steady state of the models in Sections 2.1 to 2.5, the partial derivative of Tobin's q with respect to cash balances exceeds the partial derivative of q with respect to bond holdings; that is*

$$
\frac{\partial q}{\partial m} > \frac{\partial q}{\partial b}.
$$

We should stress that in the proof of this Lemma the gross substitution property, equations (48)–(49), plays an important role. Lemma 2 tells us that an open market policy of the government, which means that the central bank buys bonds by issuing money $(dm = -db)$, indeed has an expansionary effect on Tobin's q since

$$
\frac{\partial q}{\partial m} dm + \frac{\partial q}{\partial b}(-dm) > 0. \tag{57}
$$

Before we come to a reformulation and extension of the model, its steady state and its stability properties, as well as among other things the potentially destabilizing role

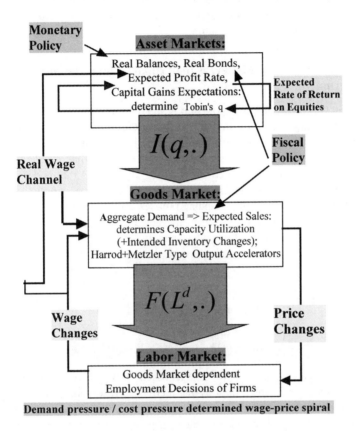

A Keynesian Portfolio Approach to Ec. Growth (no Keynes- or Mundell-Effect Channels yet)

Figure 2. Keynes' Causal Downward Nexus (from Self-Contained Financial Market Dynamics to Economic Activity), Feedback Chains (from Economic Activity to Expected Returns on Equities), Supply Side Dynamics (the Wage–Price Spiral) and Policy Rules in a Keynesian Model with Portfolio Dynamics.

of chartist-type capital gains expectations, we discuss the full structure of our model by means of Figure 2. This figure highlights the destabilizing role of the wage–price spiral, where now – due to the assumed investment behaviour – there is always a positive impact of real wages on aggregate demand and as a result wage flexibility will be destabilizing (if not counteracted by its effects on expected profits and their effect on financial markets and Tobin's q). Monetary policy, whether money supply oriented and thus determining the interest rate in the form $i(M, p)$ or of a Taylor type determining money supply of the form $M(i, \hat{p})$, should (via the gross substitution effects) contribute to the stability of financial markets. Fiscal policy impacts on the goods and the financial markets and may be of an orthodox type or of a Keynesian countercyclical kind.

There remains the discussion of the self-reference within the asset markets (that is the closed loop structure between capital gains expectations and actual capital gains) which is clearly of a destabilizing nature.

3. Long-Term Bonds, Not Money, as the Primary Financing Instrument of the Government

In this section we extend the basic portfolio KMG model of Asada *et al.* (2010c), which couples a KMG model of monetary growth with the dynamics of the stock market, towards the treatment of not only detailed real, but also detailed financial market structures (exhibiting now two risky assets) and the role that fiscal and monetary policy can play in such an extended framework. This moves the model much closer to what actually happens on financial markets from the macroeconomic point of view.

By contrast, Turnovsky (1995, chapter 2) makes use as representation of traditional Keynesian macroeconomics, of a – from the perspective of Keynes' (1936) General Theory – trivial dynamic portfolio model, namely

$$M^d = f_m(Y, i, r)(M + B + pK) \tag{58}$$

$$B^d = f_b(Y, i, r)(M + B + pK) \tag{59}$$

$$pK = f_k(Y, i, r)(M + B + pK). \tag{60}$$

In these asset demand functions we have as assets only two types of money and the value of the capital stock which implies that there is no risk involved in trading on such asset markets. Such a view on the working of financial markets is depriving Keynesian macroeconomics nearly all of its relevance, in particular from the perspective of the currently observed crisis in the financial and the real sectors of the world economy. Our subsequent step towards the inclusion of risk not only in equity holdings, but also in the holdings of government bonds therefore represent a compelling step forward from the Keynesian perspective.

There are thus good reasons to vary the restricted set of financial assets in order to account for long term bonds, also because it is often claimed that the market for long term bonds competes more directly with the equity market. Thus it seems natural to consider long term bonds in the portfolio setup of the model, replacing the short term bonds (government money) and using the broader monetary aggregate $M_2 = M + B$ in the following representation of financial markets. We thus now deal with the set of financial assets: money M_2, long term bonds B^l and equities E. We assume long term bonds to be perpetuities valued at any point in time with price p_b. A long term bond pays out one unit of money in every period of time and displays an expected rate of return, r_b^e with π_b being capital gain expectations so that

$$r_b^e = 1/p_b + \pi_b \tag{61}$$

This expected rate of return on long term bonds is the sum of the inverted bond price, which denotes their interest rate, and the expected capital gain, where the latter is the expected growth rate in long term bond prices π_b. The composition of M_2 will only matter when monetary policy is considered explicitly.

We start our consideration of the new situation by exploiting the modelling structure of the preceding section and only give detailed explanation where changes impact the structural equations.

3.1 Private Households

The worker households are not affected at all by asset market conditions, because they are assumed to consume all their income and save nothing. But the asset holder households will experience some changes. We start with the equations concerned with income, consumption and saving, which now read

$$C_c = (1 - s_c)[r_k^e K + B^l + iB - T_c] \tag{62}$$

$$S_c = s_c[r_k^e K + B^l + iB - T_c] \tag{63}$$

$$= (\dot{M}_2 + p_b \dot{B}^l + p_e \dot{E})/p \tag{64}$$

$$W_c = (M_2 + p_b B^l + p_e E)/p, \quad W_c^n = pW_c. \tag{65}$$

The sources of income consist of the dividend payments of firms to asset holders, $r_k^e K$, and the interest payments on the bonds holdings, $B^l + iB$. The income is diminished by a tax T_c. The consumption and savings of asset holders are determined by their saving propensity s_c according to equations (62) and (63). The savings are distributed to money, long term bonds and equity as shown in equation (64), while equation (65) gives the definition of asset holders' wealth.

As we have seen savings of assets holders enter their financial wealth. The desired nominal amounts of the financial assets are determined by means of demand functions which depend on the rates of return of the assets and wealth according to the demand functions[10]

$$M_2^d = f_m(r_b^e, r_e^e)W_c^n \tag{66}$$

$$p_b B^{ld} = f_{b^l}(r_b^e, r_e^e)W_c^n \tag{67}$$

$$p_e E^d = f_e(r_b^e, r_e^e)W_c^n \tag{68}$$

$$W_c^n = M_2^d + p_b B^{ld} + p_e E^d. \tag{69}$$

3.2 *Government*

With respect to the government, the taxation of asset holders is changed and hence the saving and the government budget equations must be adjusted accordingly. The equations for the government sector are

$$T = \tau_w \omega L^d + T_c \tag{70}$$

$$T_c = t_c K + (iB + B^l)/p, \quad \text{with } t_c = \text{const.} \tag{71}$$

$$G = gK, \quad g = \text{const.} \tag{72}$$

$$S_g = T - B^l/p - iB/p - G \tag{73}$$

$$\hat{M}_2 = \mu \tag{74}$$

$$\dot{M}_2 + p_b \dot{B}^l = pG + B^l + iB - pT. \tag{75}$$

The real tax levied on asset holders now consists of a fixed proportion on total capital $t_c K$ and of the stock of bonds. Again this is a useful trick to avoid interest payments in the consumption function of asset holders and, as we will see, plays a role in the government budget constraint. The saving of the government is then given by the income $T = \tau_w \omega L^d + T_c$ minus the government purchases for interest payments and provision of governmental services. From all this we can derive the government budget equation as stated in equation (75). All purchases minus income must be financed by issuing money or long term bonds.

3.3 *Asset Markets*

As we have seen in the modelling of the asset holders, the demands for financial assets depend crucially on the rates of return on long term bonds and equities. Thus, in order to reach an equilibrium at every point in time on money, bond and equity markets, the rates of return have to adjust to their equilibrium values instantaneously.

As in Section 2.5, the demand functions of the asset holders in the capital markets fulfil the adding up constraints

$$f_m + f_{b^l} + f_e = 1 \tag{76}$$

and

$$\frac{\partial f_m}{\partial z} + \frac{\partial f_{b^l}}{\partial z} + \frac{\partial f_e}{\partial z} = 0, \quad \forall \quad z \in \{r_b^e, r_e^e\}. \tag{77}$$

Again we assume that the gross substitution property of the demand functions, the analogue of equations (48)–(49), holds.

It should be pointed out that now there will be fundamentalist and chartist activity in both the market for equities and the market for long term bonds. We use the symbols π_{ef}, π_{bf}, π_{ec}, π_{bc} to denote the expectations of these two groups.

4. Intensive Form of the Model

For notational simplicity we shall use the symbol m in place of $m_2 = m + b$ in the following sections. We shift the new model into capital intensive form and again exploit the findings of Asada $et\ al.$ (2010c). But we have to derive explicitly the law of motion for the intensive form of long term bonds $\frac{B^l}{pK}$ by solving equation (75) in terms of $\dot{B}^l$ and making use of equations (70) and (71) to obtain

$$\dot{B}^l = \frac{1}{p_b}(p(g - t_c)K - \tau_w wL^d - \dot{M}_2). \tag{78}$$

Substituting this last relation into the definition

$$\dot{b}^l = \frac{\partial\left(\frac{B^l}{pK}\right)}{\partial t} = \frac{\dot{B}^l}{pK} - b^l(\hat{p} + I/K)$$

we obtain

$$\dot{b}^l = \frac{\frac{1}{p_b}(p(g - t_c)K - \tau_w wL^d - \dot{M}_2)}{pK} - b^l(\hat{p} + I/K) \tag{79}$$
$$= \frac{1}{p_b}(g - t_c - \tau_w \omega l^d - \mu m) - b^l(\hat{p} + I/K).$$

Note that b^l here is not the nominal value of long term bonds per unit of capital, but rather its real value per unit of capital. As we have to account explicitly for the price of the long term bonds, we do not aggregate the price and the number of long term bonds. Using the law of motion of goods prices (obtained by solving equations (40) and (41)) we see that the law of motion of long term bonds is

$$\dot{b}^l = \frac{1}{p_b}(g - t_c - \tau_w \omega l^d - \mu m) - b^l(\kappa[\beta_p(u - \bar{u}) + \kappa_p \beta_w(e - \bar{e})] + \pi^c + i(\cdot))$$

where κ equals $(1 - \kappa_w \kappa_p)^{-1}$ and we recall that $i(\cdot)$ equal I/K denotes the investment function.

With these preliminary considerations the entire model can now be set up. First we start with the statically endogenous variables needed later in the differential equations:

$$y = (1 + \alpha_{nd}(n + \beta_n))y^e - \beta_n v \tag{80}$$

$$l^d = y/x \tag{81}$$

$$c = (1 - \tau_w)\omega l^d + (1 - s_c)(y^e - \delta - \omega l^d - t_c) \tag{82}$$

$$i(\cdot) = i_q(q - 1) + i_u(u - \bar{u}) + n \tag{83}$$

$$y^d = c + i(\cdot) + \delta + g \tag{84}$$

$$r_e^e = \frac{r_k^e}{q} + \pi_e \tag{85}$$

$$r_b^e = \frac{1}{p_b} + \pi_b \tag{86}$$

$$\pi_e = \alpha_{\pi_e}\pi_{ec} + (1 - \alpha_{\pi_e})\pi_{ef} \tag{87}$$

$$\pi_b = \alpha_{\pi_b}\pi_{bc} + (1 - \alpha_{\pi_b})\pi_{bf} \tag{88}$$

$$e = l^d/l \tag{89}$$

$$u = y/y^p \tag{90}$$

$$r_k^e = y^e - \delta - \omega l^d. \tag{91}$$

Tobin's q and the price for long term bonds p_b are responsible for the equilibrium on the financial markets for money, long term bonds and equities at every point in time. The intensive form of the demand functions (66)–(68) reads

$$m^d = f_m(r_b^e, r_e^e)(m + p_b b^l + q) \tag{92}$$

$$p_b b^{ld} = f_{b^l}(r_b^e, r_e^e)(m + p_b b^l + q) \tag{93}$$

$$q = f_e(r_b^e, r_e^e)(m + p_b b^l + q). \tag{94}$$

Thus the solution of the following two equilibrium conditions gives a combination of q and p_b that equilibrates the money market and the bond market (note that we make use of equations 85 and 86):

$$f_m\left(\frac{1}{p_b} + \pi_b, \frac{r_k^e}{q} + \pi_e\right)(m + p_b b^l + q) - m = 0 \tag{95}$$

$$f_{b^l}\left(\frac{1}{p_b} + \pi_b, \frac{r_k^e}{q} + \pi_e\right)(m + p_b b^l + q) - b = 0. \tag{96}$$

The growth rates of wages and prices obtained by solving (40) and (41) are given again by

$$\hat{w} = \kappa\left(\beta_w(e - \bar{e}) + \kappa_w\beta_p(u - \bar{u})\right) + \pi^c \tag{97}$$

$$\hat{p} = \kappa\left(\beta_p(u - \bar{u}) + \kappa_p\beta_w(e - \bar{e})\right) + \pi^c. \tag{98}$$

From these one can derive the growth rate of real wages.

Finally the differential equations, for the core of the model can be given, ordered from an economic perspective, as:[11]

$$\hat{\omega} = \kappa[(1 - \kappa_p)\beta_w(e - \bar{e}) + (\kappa_w - 1)\beta_p(u - \bar{u})] \tag{99}$$

$$\hat{l} = n - i(\cdot) = -i_q(q - 1) - i_u(u - \bar{u}) \tag{100}$$

$$\dot{y}^e = \beta_{y^e}(y^d - y^e) + (n - i(\cdot))y^e \tag{101}$$

$$\dot{v} = y - y^d - i(\cdot)v \tag{102}$$

$$\dot{m} = m\mu - m(\kappa[\beta_p(u - \bar{u}) + \kappa_p\beta_w(e - \bar{e})] + \pi^c + i(\cdot)) \tag{103}$$

$$\dot{b}^l = \frac{1}{p_b}(g - t_c - \tau_w\omega l^d - \mu m)$$
$$- b\left(\kappa[\beta_p(u - \bar{u}) + \kappa_p\beta_w(e - \bar{e})] + \pi^c + i(\cdot)\right) \tag{104}$$

$$\dot{\pi}^c = \alpha\beta_{\pi^c}\kappa[\beta_p(u - \bar{u}) + \kappa_p\beta_w(e - \bar{e})] + (1 - \alpha)\beta_{\pi^c}(\mu - n - \pi^c) \tag{105}$$

$$\dot{\pi}_{bf} = \beta_{\pi_{bf}}(\bar{\eta}_b - \pi_{bf}) \tag{106}$$

$$\dot{\pi}_{ef} = \beta_{\pi_{ef}}(\bar{\eta}_e - \pi_{ef}) \tag{107}$$

$$\dot{\pi}_{bc} = \beta_{\pi_{bc}}(\hat{p}_b - \pi_{bc}) \tag{108}$$

$$\dot{\pi}_{ec} = \beta_{\pi_{ec}}(\hat{p}_e - \pi_{ec}). \tag{109}$$

It is possible to state the following theorem concerning the uniqueness of the steady state:

Theorem 1. *Assume that: the saving propensity of the asset holders s_c is sufficiently large; the government runs a primary deficit; the long term expectations for equity price inflation of the fundamentalists equal the steady state inflation rate of the prices of goods; the demand functions for financial assets are such that there holds*

$$\lim_{r_b^e \to 0}(f_m(r_b^e, r_k^e + \pi_e) + f_b(r_b^e, r_k^e + \pi_e)) < \bar{\phi},$$

$$\lim_{r_b^e \to \infty}(f_m(r_b^e, r_k^e + \pi_e) + f_b(r_b^e, r_k^e + \pi_e)) > \bar{\phi},$$

with $\bar{\phi} = \frac{g - t_c - \tau_w\omega l^d}{g - t_c - \tau_w\omega l^d + \mu}$, then the dynamical system (99) to (6eq:lb.piec) displays a unique interior steady state with ω^o, l^o, y^{eo}, v^o, b^o, $m^o > 0$.

The remainder of the paper is essentially devoted to finding fiscal, wage and monetary policies that can stabilize the dynamical systems (99)–(109) in situations where it turns unstable.

5. Keynesian Fiscal Policy Rules and Stability of Balanced Growth

In this section we focus on the local stability properties of the dynamical system (99) to (109), in particular seeking fiscal policies which may be stabilizing. Our strategy will be to build up to stability results for the full 11 dimensional dynamical system (99)–(109) by analysing a number of lower dimensional subsystems. Our approach is essentially the cascade of stable matrices technique outlined in Chiarella *et al.* (2006).

As we shall see in Theorem 3 one of our fiscal policy measures relies on the existence of an independent fiscal authority. Whilst such a concept may yet seen a farfetched policy in many advanced economies, it should be pointed out that it was not so long ago that the concept of an independent monetary authority, now in place in most advanced economies, seemed equally farfetched. Furthermore this idea is starting to be debated in a way similar to the debates that eventually led to independent monetary authorities; see for instance Debrun *et al.* (2009). Our analysis can be regarded as adding further weight to arguments in favour of the establishment of an independent fiscal authority.

The 3D subsystem **Theorem 2.** *We assume that the values of* ω, ν, π^c, π_{ec}, π_{ef}, π_{bc} *and* π_{bf} *are at their steady state values and set the parameters* $\beta_p, \beta_w, \beta_n, \beta_{\pi^c}, \beta_{\pi ec}, \beta_{\pi ef}, \beta_{\pi bc}, \beta_{\pi bf} = 0$, *so that* ω, ν, π^c, π_{ec}, π_{ef}, π_{bc} *and* π_{bf} *will remain at their steady state values and the dynamics for l do not feedback into the rest of the dynamical system. We moreover assume that the conditions for the existence of a steady state in Theorem 1 are fulfilled. Then the dynamical system*

$$
\begin{cases}
\dot{m} = m\mu - m(\pi_o^c + i(\cdot)) \\
\dot{b}^l = \dfrac{1}{p_b(\cdot)}(g - t_c - \tau_w \omega l^d - \mu m) - b^l\left(\pi_o^c + i(\cdot)\right) \\
\dot{y}^e = \beta_{y^e}(y^d(\cdot) - y^e) + (n - i(\cdot))y^e
\end{cases}
\tag{110}
$$

possesses a locally asymptotically steady state, if the following conditions hold: β_{y^e} *is sufficiently large,* i_u *sufficiently small, the parameter* α_{e1} *is sufficiently small, and the parameters* $\alpha_{m2}, \alpha_{b'2}$ *are sufficiently small (the last condition implying that the parameter* α_{e2} *is also sufficiently small, so that changes in* r_e^e *are relatively moderate).*

Theorem 3. *Assume an independent fiscal authority solely responsible for the control of business fluctuations (acting independently of the neutral business cycle fiscal policy of the government) which implements the following two rules for its activity oriented expenditures and their funding as a function of the utilization gap:*

$$
g^u = -g_u(u - \bar{u}), \quad t^u = g_u(u - \bar{u}).
$$

The budget of this authority is always balanced and we assume – due to the present form of the model – that the taxes t^u *are paid by (or in the boom received by) asset holding households. The stability condition on* i_u *(see equation 83) now involves the parameter* $i_u - g_u$. *Then an anti-cyclical policy* g^u *that is chosen in a sufficiently active way will* *enforce damped oscillations in the considered 3D subdynamics if the savings rate s_c of asset holders is sufficiently close to one and if stock markets are sufficiently tranquil, the latter being so if the parameters α_{e1}, α_{e2} are sufficiently small and the parameter α_{m1} is not too large.*

Theorems 2 and 3 tell us that an anti-cyclical fiscal policy that is chosen in a sufficiently active way will enforce damped oscillations in the considered three dimensional subdynamics if the savings rate of asset holders is sufficiently close to one and if stock market readjustments are sufficiently inelastic (and α_{m1} is not too large). Note that neither the steady state nor the laws of motions are changed through the introduction of such an independent business cycle authority, if $s_c = 1$ holds true, which we shall assume for simplicity in the following analysis.[12] We assume that the assumptions on the financial market parameters α hold if the Tobin taxes (to be considered below in Theorem 13) are chosen to be sufficiently large.

The 4D subsystem   Now we let real wages vary with a positive adjustment speed β_p and so obtain the system

$$
\begin{cases}
\dot{m} = m\mu - m\left(\kappa\beta_p\left(\dfrac{y}{y^p} - \bar{u}\right) + \pi_o^c + i(\cdot)\right) \\[3mm]
\dot{b}^l = \dfrac{1}{p_b}(g - t_c - \tau_w\omega l^d - \mu m) - b^l\left(\kappa\beta_p\left(\dfrac{y}{y^p} - \bar{u}\right) + \pi_o^c + i(\cdot)\right) \\[3mm]
\dot{y}^e = \beta_{y^e}(y^d - y^e) + y^e(n - i(\cdot)) \\[3mm]
\dot{\omega} = \omega\kappa(\kappa_w - 1)\beta_p\left(\dfrac{y}{y_p} - \bar{u}\right).
\end{cases}
\tag{111}
$$

Theorem 4. *Given the assumptions of Theorems 1 and 2 it follows that the 4D subsystem (111) possesses an asymptotically stable steady state if the adjustment speed of wages associated with capacity gaps, β_p, is sufficiently small.*

Note that an implication of this new condition for the considered four dimensional subdynamics is also obtained under the assumption $\kappa_w = 1$; that is workers always demand a full indexation of their nominal wages to the rate of price inflation. So we can assert in addition:

Theorem 5. *Assume that the cost-push term in the money wage adjustment rule (40) is given by the current rate of price inflation (which is perfectly foreseen) so that $\kappa_w = 1$. Then the 4D subdynamics exhibit damped oscillations around the steady state position of the economy.*

This type of income policy, known as a 'scala mobile',[13] thus implies stability instead of instability (as might be expected), since it considerably simplifies the real wage channel of the model. However we also need the following theorem in order to really tame the wage–price spiral of the model.

The 5D subsystem   We enlarge the dimensions of the dynamical system further by allowing β_w to have positive values. This assumption will cause the dynamics for l to feedback so that we obtain the 5D subsystem

$$
\begin{cases}
\dot{m} = m\mu - m\left(\kappa\left[\beta_p\left(\dfrac{y}{y^p} - u\right) + \kappa_p\beta_w\left(\dfrac{y}{xl} - \bar{e}\right)\right] + \pi_o^c + i(\cdot)\right) \\[2mm]
\dot{b}^l = \dfrac{1}{p_b}\left(g - t_c - \tau_w\omega\dfrac{y}{x} - \mu m\right) - b^l\left(\kappa\left[\beta_p\left(\dfrac{y}{y^p} - \bar{u}\right) + \kappa_p\beta_w\left(\dfrac{y}{xl} - \bar{e}\right)\right] + \pi_o^c + i(\cdot)\right) \\[2mm]
\dot{y}^e = \beta_{y^e}[c + i(\cdot) + \delta + g - y^e] + y^e(n - i(\cdot)) \\[2mm]
\dot{\omega} = \omega\kappa\left[(1 - \kappa_p)\beta_w\left(\dfrac{y}{xl} - \bar{e}\right) + (\kappa_w - 1)\beta_p\left(\dfrac{y}{y^p} - \bar{u}\right)\right] \\[2mm]
\dot{l} = l\left[-i_q(q - 1) - i_u\left(\dfrac{y}{y^p} - \bar{u}\right)\right]
\end{cases}
\tag{112}
$$

about which we may state:

Theorem 6. *Assume that the assumptions made in Theorem 4 hold, and in addition the parameter β_w takes positive values. Then the 5D subsystem (112) possesses an asymptotically stable steady state if β_w is sufficiently small.*

Theorem 7. *We assume that the economy is a consensus based one, meaning that labour and capital reach agreement with respect to the scala mobile principle in the dynamics of money wages. Assume that they also agree against this background that additional money wage increases should be small in a boom (when $u - \bar{u} > 0$) and vice versa in a recession. This policy makes the steady state of the 5D subdynamics (112) asymptotically stable.*

Such a consensus between capital and labour, that could be called a corporatist income policy, benefits both parties and in addition it would simplify negotiations over the general level of money wages.

The 6D subsystem   Next we allow the parameter β_n (see equation 80) to become positive, so activating the inventory dynamics and obtaining the six dimensional subdynamics

$$
\begin{cases}
\dot{m} = m\mu - m\left(\kappa\left[\beta_p\left(\dfrac{y}{y^p} - u\right) + \kappa_p\beta_w\left(\dfrac{y}{xl} - \bar{e}\right)\right] + \pi_o^c + i(\cdot)\right) \\[2mm]
\dot{b}^l = \dfrac{1}{p_b}\left(g - t_c - \tau_w\omega\dfrac{y}{x} - \mu m\right) - b^l\left(\kappa\left[\beta_p\left(\dfrac{y}{y^p} - u\right) + \kappa_p\beta_w\left(\dfrac{y}{xl} - \bar{e}\right)\right] + \pi_o^c + i(\cdot)\right) \\[2mm]
\dot{y}^e = \beta_{y^e}[c + i(\cdot) + \delta + g - y^e] + y^e(n - i(\cdot)) \\[2mm]
\dot{\omega} = \omega\kappa\left[(1 - \kappa_p)\beta_w\left(\dfrac{y}{xl} - \bar{e}\right) + (\kappa_w - 1)\beta_p\left(\dfrac{y}{y^p} - \bar{u}\right)\right] \\[2mm]
\dot{l} = l\left[-i_q(q - 1) - i_u\left(\dfrac{y}{y^p} - \bar{u}\right)\right] \\[2mm]
\dot{v} = y - y^d - i(\cdot)v
\end{cases}
\tag{113}
$$

about which we can assert:

Theorem 8. *Assume that the assumptions of Theorem 6 hold and in addition allow the parameter β_n take positive values. Then, the 6D subsystem (113) possesses an asymptotically stable steady state if β_n is sufficiently small.*

Theorem 9. *The static Metzlerian feedback between expected sales and output, given by equation (80), namely*

$$y = (1 + \alpha_{n^d}(n + \beta_n))y^e - \beta_n v$$

implies that a moderate production coefficient α_{n^d} or cautious inventory adjustment β_n (or both) can tame the Metzlerian output accelerator.

We here do not introduce any regulation of the Metzlerian sales-inventory adjustment process, but simply assume that parameter values (in particular β_n) are such that this inventory accelerator process is of a secondary nature in the business fluctuations generated by the dynamics, in particular if the control of the goods market accelerator (i_u) of Theorem 3 is working to stabilize the dynamics.

The 7D system Now letting the parameter β_{π^c} become positive, so that medium run inflationary expectations are taken into account, we obtain the seven dimensional subdynamics

$$
\begin{cases}
\dot{m} = m\mu - m\left(\kappa\left[\beta_p\left(\frac{y}{y^p} - u\right) + \kappa_p\beta_w\left(\frac{y}{xl} - \bar{e}\right)\right] + \pi^c + i(\cdot)\right) \\[2mm]
\dot{b}^l = \frac{1}{p_b}\left(g - t_c - \tau_w\omega\frac{y}{x} - \mu m\right) - b^l\left(\kappa\left[\beta_p\left(\frac{y}{y^p} - \bar{u}\right) + \kappa_p\beta_w\left(\frac{y}{xl} - \bar{e}\right)\right] + \pi^c + i(\cdot)\right) \\[2mm]
\dot{y}^e = \beta_{y^e}[c + i(\cdot) + \delta + g - y^e] + y^e(n - i(\cdot)) \\[2mm]
\dot{\omega} = \omega\kappa\left[(1 - \kappa_p)\beta_w\left(\frac{y}{xl} - \bar{e}\right) + (\kappa_w - 1)\beta_p\left(\frac{y}{y^p} - \bar{u}\right)\right] \\[2mm]
\dot{l} = l\left[-i_q(q - 1) - i_u\left(\frac{y}{y^p} - \bar{u}\right)\right] \\[2mm]
\dot{v} = y - y^d - i(\cdot)v \\[2mm]
\dot{\pi}^c = \alpha\beta_{\pi^c}\kappa[\beta_p(u - \bar{u}) + \kappa_p\beta_w(e - \bar{e})] + (1 - \alpha)\beta_{\pi^c}(\mu - n - \pi^c)
\end{cases}
\tag{114}
$$

about which we can prove:

Theorem 10. *Assume that all assumptions of Theorem 8 are fulfilled, and in addition allow β_{π^c} take positive values. Then the 7D subsystem (114) possesses a local asymptotically stable steady state if β_{π^c} is sufficiently small.*

If it turns out that β_{π^c} is not sufficiently small then it is possible to obtain stability by decreasing sufficiently the weight α on current inflation in the rule (42) for the formation of medium-run expectations. Thus we have:

Theorem 11. *Assume that the business cycle is controlled in the way we have described it so far in Theorems 1 to 10 except that β_{π^c} is not sufficiently small. The steady state will be locally asymptotically stable if α in the rule (42) for the inflationary climate is chosen sufficiently small.*

Thus the economy will exhibit damped fluctuations if in addition to the conditions of Theorems 1 to 10 the parameter α in the law of motion for the inflationary climate expression π^c is chosen sufficiently small. There is a reasonable possibility of this if the business cycle is damped and actual inflation, here only depends on the market for goods so that[14]

$$\hat{p} \approx \beta_p(u - \bar{u})/(1 - \kappa_p) + \pi^c$$

is moderate. A stronger orientation of the change in the inflationary climate on a return to the steady state rate of inflation (achieved by a smaller value of α) thus helps to stabilize the economy. Alternatively, the adjustment speed of the inflationary climate β_{π^c} may be assumed to be sufficiently small, corresponding to what we have already assumed for the wage price spiral in the preceding theorems.

Note here that expectations formation on financial markets are still ignored, since π_{bf}, π_{bc}, π_{ef}, π_{ec} are still all assumed to be static. It is however obvious that an enlargement of the dynamics by these expectations does not destroy the stability properties that have been demonstrated in Theorem 11 if only fundamentalists are active, since this enlarges the Jacobian solely by a negative entry in its diagonal. Continuity then implies that introducing a proportion of chartists that is relatively small as compared to the fundamentalists will still preserve the damped fluctuations we have shown to exist in the above sequence of theorems. Thus for the full system of dynamic laws for the expectations in equity price inflation and bond price inflation given by equations (87)–(88) we can state:

Theorem 12. *Allowing the adjustment speeds of the fundamentalists expectations towards the actual growth rate of bond prices $\beta_{\pi_{bf}}$ and equity prices $\beta_{\pi_{ef}}$ to be positive, and assuming the proportion of chartists $(\alpha_{\pi_b}, \alpha_{\pi_e})$ is sufficiently small the dynamical system (99)–(100) will display an asymptotically stable steady state.*

In order to get this result enforced by policy action, independently of the size of the chartist population, we introduce Tobin taxes on the capitals gains of equities (at a rate τ_e) and long-term bonds (at a rate τ_b) so that the dynamics of chartists' expectations in both markets read

$$\begin{cases} \dot{\pi}_{ec} = \beta_{\pi_{ec}}((1 - \tau_e)\hat{p}_e - \pi_{ec}) \\ \dot{\pi}_{bc} = \beta_{\pi_{bc}}((1 - \tau_b)\hat{p}_b - \pi_{bc}). \end{cases} \tag{115}$$

Such a tax may be monitored through a corresponding tax declaration scheme which not only taxes capital gains, but also as written here subsidizes capital losses (and thus is not entirely to the disadvantage of the asset holders of the model). The financial market accelerator can be tamed through the introduction of appropriate levels of Tobinian taxes on capital gains:

Theorem 13. *The Tobin tax implies that damped business fluctuations remain damped for all tax rate parameters τ_e, τ_b chosen sufficiently large (below 100%).*

Note here however that this rule introduces a new sector to the economy, which accumulates or deccumulates reserve funds R according to the rule

$$\dot{R} = \tau_e \dot{p}_e E + \tau_b \dot{p}_b B^l.$$

In order to keep the laws of motion of the economy unchanged (and so allow the application of the above stability propositions) we shall assume that the sector involving the reserve funds is independent of the other public institutions. For the steady state value ρ^o of the funds of this new sector, when expressed per value unit of capital pK, we obtain

$$\rho^o = (R/pK)^o = \tau_e(\mu - n)/\mu < 1.$$

This easily follows from the law of motion

$$\hat{\rho} = \hat{R} - \hat{p} - \hat{K} = \frac{\dot{R}}{pK}\frac{pK}{R} - \hat{p} - \hat{K}$$

since there holds $\hat{p} + \hat{K} = \mu$ and $\hat{E} = n, q = 1, \hat{p}_e = \hat{p}$ in the steady state. It is assumed that the reserves of this institution are sufficiently large so that they will not become exhausted during the damped business fluctuations generated by the model.

The stability results demonstrated in the above theorems are intuitively very appealing in view of what we know about Keynesian feedback structures and from what has been discussed in the preceding sections, since it basically states that the wage spiral must be damped, the Keynesian dynamic multiplier must be stable and not too much distorted by the emergence of Metzlerian inventory cycles, that the Harrodian knife-edge growth accelerator must be weak, and that inflationary and capital gains expectations are fundamentalist in orientation and money demand must be subject to small transaction costs and fairly unresponsive to rate of return changes on financial assets (that is money demand is not close to a liquidity trap). Such assumptions represent indeed fairly natural conditions from a Keynesian perspective.[15]

On this basis we have shown in the above theorems the result that independently conducted countercyclical fiscal policy can limit the fluctuations on the goods market, that an appropriate consensus between capital and labour can tame the wage–price spiral and that a Tobin tax can tame the financial market accelerator. Metzlerian inventory dynamics and fluctuations in the inflationary climate that surrounds the economy must also be weak and thus not endanger asymptotic stability.

6. Conclusions

Summing up, we have seen that it is not the individual behaviour of economic agents (firms, households, institutions) but rather the interconnectedness of agents and sectors that produces the stabilizing or destabilizing feedback effects of modern macro economies. Left to itself, the macroeconomy has experienced large boom–bust cycles, with extensive externalities when the bubble has burst, as we have seen in recent times. In the context of our proposed KMGT model we argue that boom–bust cycles can be dampened. In terms of policy of institutions, we have shown that countercyclical labour market and fiscal policies, with a tranquilized wage–price spiral, a Tobin tax on capital gains and the implementation of a Tobin rule in place of a Taylor rule, taken together, could be powerful means to make the business cycle not only less volatile, but damped and convergent to the balanced growth path of the economy.

More specifically, in Section 5, we have considered the stability of the steady state of the KMGT model and shown that it is asymptotically stable under the following conditions: (1) Harrod/Metzler accelerators sufficiently small, (2) money demand sufficiently inelastic, (3) equity markets sufficiently tranquil, (4) inflationary climate update sufficiently sluggish and (5) fundamentalists dominate chartists. Furthermore, we have also been able to identify the following policy conditions for the existence of an attracting balanced growth path: (a) strong tax financed countercyclical fiscal policy, (b) implementation of a corporatist Scala Mobile wage policy and (c) Tobin tax on capital gains is sufficiently strong.

The reader interested in delving more deeply into the issues raised in this paper from the partial, the integrated and the financial perspectives is referred to the forthcoming collection of papers in Chiarella Flaschel and Semmler (2011a); Chiarella Flaschel and Semmler (2011b); Chiarella Flaschel and Semmler (2011c). In future work we will continue the analysis of appropriate policy measures and then also investigate the role of monetary policy and show how it must be designed in order to further improve the stability properties of the economy we have considered in this paper. We already claim here in this respect that the monetary authority must be prepared to trade – in place of fix-price bonds – in risky assets if it really wants to influence the economy, both from the perspective of the real and the financial markets.

Notes

1. To our knowledge local stability analysis in dimensions higher than 4 is only possible so far in our KMGT approach, due to the fact that we avoid the then intractable Routh–Hurwitz conditions by identifying parameter regions of the models where our cascade of stable matrices approach, to be described below, becomes applicable.
2. In the following discussion we use lower case letters to represent an upper case quantity in per capita terms; thus $y = Y/K$, $m = M/pK$, $b = B/pK$ etc.
3. See Brock and Hommes (1997) and Chiarella Dieci and He (2009) for more discussion of this categorization. Abreu and Brunnermeier (2003) also use behavioural and fundamentalist traders.
4. This assumption saves one differential equation and avoids a certain amount of 'roundaboutness' in the basic analysis without altering in any essential way the basic results; on this point see Chiarella and Flaschel (2000), Chapter 5.
5. See, for example, (p.18 Sargent 1987) for the introduction of such net of interest taxation rules.
6. See Köper (2003) for an explicit treatment of government interest payments.

7. See also Rose (1990).
8. We note that the parameters of such functions must be chosen (particularly in numerical investigations) such that a meaningful relationship between the interest rate i^o and the rate of return on equities r_e^{eo} is established in the steady state.
9. The dashed lines show how these curves simultaneously shift when one of the statically exogenous variables r_k^e, π_e, q, m rises or b falls.
10. Note that here we only treat short-term bonds implicitly as a component of the enlarged money supply $M2$ and hence we suppress explicit treatment of the rate of interest i that appears in Section 2.
11. In equations (106) and (107) $\bar{\eta}_b$ and $\bar{\eta}_e$ represent the fundamentalists expected long term growth rate of the prices of long bonds and equities. These are a natural generalization of the quantity η appearing in equation (16)
12. If $s_c = 1$ does not hold then certain feedback loops in the dynamics of the system become active; similar stability results can still be obtained but a different proof technique will be required.
13. In Italian this term literally means 'escalator', but by extension it also means 'cost-of-living index', which is its intended meaning here.
14. Keep in mind that β_w is assumed to be small so we ignore the term $\beta_w \kappa_p (e - \bar{e})/(1 - \kappa_p)$ appearing in the expression for $\hat{p}$.
15. For the chartists we only conjecture, that positive but small adjustment speeds of their expectations on asset price growth rates will preserve asymptotic stability. But here the dynamics is much more complex than that for the fundamentalists, since there are complicated feedback channels involved. These feedback channels generally give rise to Hopf-bifurcations and thus in particular to a cyclical loss of stability when those parameters that we have assumed to be sufficiently small in the stability propositions of this section, are made sufficiently large.

References

Abreu, D. and Brunnermeier, M. (2003) Bubbles and crashes. *Econometrica* 71: 173–204.
Asada, T., Chiarella, C., Flaschel, P. and Franke, R. (2010a) *Monetary Macrodynamics*. London, UK: Routledge.
Asada, T., Chiarella, C., Flaschel, P., Köper, C., Proaño, C. and Semmler, W. (2010b) Stabilizing an unstable economy: policy rules to safeguard real and financial market stability. Working Paper, School of Finance and Economics, University of Technology, Sydney, Australia.
Asada, T., Chiarella, C., Flaschel, P., Mouakil, T., Proaño, C. and Semmler, W. (2010c) Stabilizing an unstable economy: on the choice of proper policy measures. *Economics, The Open-Access, Open-Assessment E-journal* 3: 1–43.
Brock, W. and Hommes, C. (1997) A rational route to randomness. *Econometrica* 65: 1059–1095.
Charpe, M., Chiarella, C., Flaschel, P. and Semmler, W. (2010) *Financial Assets, Debt and Liquidity Crises. A Keynesian Approach*, forthcoming. Cambridge, UK: Cambridge University Press.
Chiarella, C. and Flaschel, P. (1998) Dynamics of 'natural' rates of growth and employment. *Macroeconomic Dynamics* 2: 345–368.
Chiarella, C. and Flaschel, P. (2000) *The Dynamics of Keynesian Monetary Growth. Macro Foundations*. Cambridge, UK: Cambridge University Press.
Chiarella, C., Flaschel, P., Groh, G. and Semmler, W. (2000) *Disequilibrium, Growth and Labor Market Dynamics. Macro Perspectives*. Heidelberg, Germany: Springer.

Chiarella, C., Flaschel, P. and Franke, R. (2005) *Foundations for a Disequilibrium Theory of the Business Cycle. Qualitative Analysis and Quantitative Assessment*. Cambridge, UK: Cambridge University Press.

Chiarella, C., Flaschel, P., Franke, R. and Semmler, W. (2006) A high-dimensioal model of real-financial market interaction: the cascades of stable matrices approach, In C. Chiarella, P. Flaschel, R. Franke and W. Semmler (eds), *Quantitative and Empirical Analysis of Nonlinear Dynamic Macromodels* (pp. 359–383). Amsterdam, Netherlands: Elsevier.

Chiarella, C., Dieci, R. and He, X. (2009) Heterogeneity, market mechanisms, and asset price dynamics. In T. Hens and K. R. Schenk-Hoppé (eds), *Handbook of Financial Markets: Dynamics and Evolution*. Holland: North-Holland.

Chiarella, C., Flaschel, P. and Semmler, W. (2011a) *Reconstructing Keynesian Macroeconomics. Volume I: Partial Perspectives*. London, UK: Routledge.

Chiarella, C., Flaschel, P. and Semmler, W. (2011b) *Reconstructing Keynesian Macroeconomics. Volume II: Integrated Approaches*. London, UK: Routledge.

Chiarella, C., Flaschel, P. and Semmler, W. (2011c) *Reconstructing Keynesian Macroeconomics. Volume III: Financial Markets and Banking*. London, UK: Routledge.

Debrun, X., Hauner, D. and Kumar, M.S. (2009) Independent fiscal agencies. *Journal of Economic Surveys* 23(1): 44–81.

Franke, R. (1996) A Metzlerian model of inventory growth cycles. *Structural Change and Economic Dynamics* 7: 243–262.

Franke, R. and Semmler, W. (1999) Bond rate, loan rate and Tobin's q in a temporary equilibrium model of the financial sector. *Metroeconomica* 50(3): 351–385.

Metzler, L.A. (1941) The nature and stability of inventory cycles. *Review of Economic Statistics* 23: 113–129.

Rose, H. (1967) On the non-linear theory of the employment cycle. *Review of Economic Studies* 34: 153–173.

Rose, H. (1990) *Macroeconomic Dynamics: A Marshallian Synthesis*. Cambridge, UK: Blackwell.

Sargent, T.J. (1987) *Macroeconomic Theory*, 2nd edn. New York: Academic Press.

Tobin, J. (1969) A general equilibrium approach to monetary theory. *Journal of Money, Credit, and Banking* 1: 15–29.

10

EQUILIBRIUM VERSUS MARKET EFFICIENCY
Randomness versus Complexity in Finance Markets

Joseph L. McCauley

1. Introduction

Rational expectations (Sargent, 1987) generally confuses stationary markets with efficient markets. Efficient markets and equilibrium markets are mutually contradictory; if you have efficiency then you cannot have equilibrium (McCauley, 2009). An efficient market admits no equilibria at all, therefore admits no stationary price, whereas a stationary market must fluctuate about an equilibrium price. Rational expectations teaches contradictory ideas because equilibrium is seriously self-contradictorily defined therein (McCauley, 2009). One of the favourite notions of rational expectations is that nearly everything, including finance markets, should be deregulated. The world has experienced the flaw in that assumption since September 2007.

Historically seen, rational expectations was an attempt to put randomness into the straightjacket of the neoclassical economic model (McCann, 1994). Avoiding historic misconceptions, we will state the only correct formal mathematical definition of market equilibrium. We will exhibit below the predictions of both stationary/ equilibrium markets and efficient markets, and explain how the latter describe real markets empirically. Real markets are stochastic and non-stationary, are non-stationary 'random processes' with non-stationary differences (Bassler *et al.*, 2007, 2008).

2. 'Value' in a Stochastic Market

Let $(x_1, \ldots, x_n)$ represent observed points in a time series at times $(t_1, \ldots, t_n)$ where $t_k < t_{k+1}$. Finance markets generate time series that reflect a certain class of stochastic

Nonlinearity, Complexity and Randomness in Economics, First Edition.
Stefano Zambelli and Donald A.R. George.

process, as we will explain below. First, following Kolmogorov, a stochastic process $x(t)$ is precisely specified/defined by the infinite hierarchy of n-point densities (Stratonovich, 1963; Gnedenko, 1967)

$$f_{n-1}(x_1, t_1; \ldots; x_{k-1}, t_{k-1}; x_{k+1}, t_{k+1}; \ldots; x_n, t_n) = \int dx_k f_n(x_1, t_1; \ldots; x_n, t_n) \qquad (1)$$

so that, for example,

$$f_1(x, t) = \int dy f_2(y, s; x, t) \qquad (2)$$

and

$$f_n(x_n, t_n; \ldots; x_1, t_1) = p_n(x_n, t_n \mid x_{n-1}, t_{n-1}; \ldots; x_1, t_1) f_{n-1}(x_{n-1}, t_{n-1}; \ldots; x_1, t_1)$$

$$= p_n(x_n, t_n \mid x_{n-1}, t_{n-1}; \ldots x_1, t_1) \ldots p_2(x_2, t_2 \mid x_1, t_1) f_1(x_1, t_1) \qquad (3)$$

where p_n is the transition density depending on n points. In finance, $x(t) = \ln p(t)/p_c(t)$ is the log return, where $p(t)$ is the price of the underlying asset (stock, bond or foreign exchange) at time t. The price $p_c(t)$ locates the peak of the 1-point returns density $f_1(x, t)$ at time t and so is consensus value, or just 'value'. 'Value' is simply the price that the largest fraction of agents agrees on at any given point of time, the most probable price. There is no assumption of market clearing or equilibrium, and this definition of value is not restricted to equilibrium. In particular, it applies to both non-stationary and hypothetical stationary markets (McCauley, 2009).

Could value be known then we could distinguish undervalued from overvalued. But as radio engineers knew in the 1930s, even 1-point densities cannot be measured, there is too much scatter in data points. Instead, only certain averages can be reliably measured (Bassler et al., 2007; McCauley, 2008a). We know in principle what we mean by the notion of 'value' but we cannot expect to be able to measure it. What do we need in order to pin down an underlying class of stochastic dynamics generating the market?

The 1-point density defines value, but a 1-point density cannot pin down an underlying stochastic process. Completely different classes of process can exhibit the same 1-point density (Hänggi and Thomas, 1977; McCauley, 2010). Pair correlations provide the lowest level of specification of a specific process or a class of processes, so we need at least the 2-point density f_2 or the 2-point conditional density p_2 in order to have any hope of understanding the underlying dynamics. In practice, the 2-point density cannot be extracted from data due to scatter, so we need to measure the pair correlations $\langle x(t + T)x(t) \rangle$ from time series analysis.

3. Stationarity and Statistical Equilibrium

The generalization to random processes of a deterministic equilibrium is a stationary random process. In such a process prices fluctuate about an equilibrium price that we can identify as 'value'. In this case value is time invariant because the 1-point density is time independent. That is, 'value' would be fixed once and for all in a stationary market.

The definition of equilibrium is both simple and clear: all averages are time invariant. So in a stationary process, all densities f_n and all transition densities p_n of all orders n must be time-translationally invariant (Stratonovich, 1963; Gnedenko, 1967; McCauley, 2009):

$$f_n(x_1, t_1 + T; \ldots; x_n, t_n + T) = f_n(x_1, t_1; \ldots; x_n, t_n) \tag{4}$$

and $p_2(x_n, t_n | x_{n-1}, t_{n-1}) = p_2(x_n, t + T | x_{n-1}, 0)$ as well.

It follows that the *normalizable* 1-point density $f_1(x)$ is t-independent, so that the mean $\langle x(t) \rangle$, variance $\sigma^2 = \langle (x^2(t)) \rangle - \langle (x(t)) \rangle^2$, and all 1-point averages are constants.

The 1-point density describes fluctuations about statistical equilibrium. A warning: stationary processes may be Markovian, but *time-translationally invariant Markov processes are generally not stationary*. In a time-translationally invariant Markov process a *normalizable t-independent* 1-point density generally does not exist (McCauley, 2009). The Wiener process (known in economics as 'white noise') is the simplest example of a non-equilibrium Markov process.

With stationarity, time-translational invariance of the transition density $p_2(x_n, t + T | x_{n-1}, 0)$. implies pair correlations

$$\langle x(t + T)x(t) \rangle = \langle x(T)x(0) \rangle \tag{5}$$

depending on lag time T alone, independent of starting time t. In practice, constant mean and variance and a pair correlation depending on time lag alone are the empirical signatures of statistical equilibrium. However, an equilibrium market could not clear pointwise.

4. Trading Strategy in an Equilibrium Market

The notion of recurrence is important in equilibrium markets. The analogue to this in dynamical systems theory that comes closest is Poincare recurrence.

A trading strategy that allows you to beat an equilibrium market is the following: one knows that the prices will repeatedly fluctuate about equilibrium. When the price drops a standard deviation from value, then buy. Hold until the price hits value plus one standard deviation and then sell. Such fluctuations are systematically guaranteed, you can even calculate the *recurrence time* (McCauley, 2012) by using Ito's lemma along with the construction of a martingale.

As an example we can calculate the first passage time for the Wiener process $B(t)$ by constructing a martingale $M(t)$. A martingale is the generalization of the idea of a fair game, $\langle M(t) \rangle = M(t_0)$, drift-free motion. We as k for the first passage time for hitting either the point $B(t) = -A$ or $B(t) = B$: with $B(0) = 0$, $-B < 0 < A$, we calculate the average time t required for $x = A$ or $x = -B$. This is also called the hitting time. Let $P(A, t) = 1 - P(-B, t)$ denote the probability that $x = -A$. Construct any martingale from x, $M(t) = h(B, t)$ by using Ito's lemma,

$$dM = \frac{\partial h}{\partial B} dB \qquad (6)$$

$$\frac{\partial h}{\partial t} + \frac{1}{2} \frac{\partial^2 h}{\partial B^2} = 0 \qquad (7)$$

Then

$$\langle M(\tau) \rangle = h(-B, \tau)P(-B, \tau) + h(A, \tau)P(A, \tau) = h(0, 0) \qquad (8)$$

Solving the boundary value problem

$$\begin{aligned} h(-B, t) &= 0 \\ h(A, t) &= 1 \end{aligned} \qquad (9)$$

yields the hitting probabilities as

$$P(A, \tau) = h(0, 0)/h(A, \tau) \qquad (10)$$

With $h(B, t) = c_1 B + c_2$, the boundary value problem yields

$$P(A, \tau) = \frac{B}{A + B}$$

$$P(-B, \tau) = \frac{A}{A + B} \qquad (11)$$

Averaging $M = B^2(t) - t$ then yields the hitting time

$$\langle \tau \rangle = AB \qquad (12)$$

With recurrence guaranteed, you could suck money out of an equilibrium market as with a vacuum cleaner, with little or no risk. You need only have enough cash to survive without having to sell before the expected price increase appears (bet/cash should always be small). Because you are only trading on equilibrium fluctuations, the buy/sell strategy can be repeated *ad infinitum*. It is clear that an equilibrium market cannot be efficient, if by efficient we mean a market that is hard or impossible to beat (Mandelbrot, 1966).

Maybe the Dollar was stationary on the gold standard (McCauley, 2008b, 2009). We do not know and cannot find out. We do know that no finance market has been stationary since at least the late 1950s. Mauri Osborne noticed in 1958 that the stock prices are roughly log-normally distributed (Osborne, 1964) with a standard deviation varying with the square root of time (non-stationary process). This is the model used by Black and Scholes to price options in 1973 (Black and Scholes, 1973) when options trading began on a large scale. Some traders claimed that this model worked well until the market crash of 1987. Finance markets are non-stationary. Equilibrium is found neither in the most well-known model nor in real data. What class of model characterizes a finance market?

5. Efficient Markets

Here and in all that follows we assume a normal liquid market, a market where the noise traders (Black, 1986) trade frequently enough that bid/ask spreads are very small relative to price (McCauley, 2009). A crash is not a normal liquid market. In a crash liquidity dries up. To zeroth order, there are many limit orders to sell with few or no buyers in a market crash. A market crash is not a fluctuation due to fat tails in a 1-point returns distribution, a market crash is instead a liquidity drought. This should be fairly clear even to laymen since 9/2011.

Due to the sparseness of data it is impossible to model a crash falsifiably. This may be practical example of complexity: events can occur that cannot be derived mathematically (von Neumann, 1966). There are, however, non-mathematical signs that a bubble is about to burst. These signs take the form of unusually risky behaviour. Before the stock market crash of 2000 ordinary people quit their jobs, mortgaged their houses a second time, and used the cash to 'day trade'. Leading up to the derivatives crash of 2007–2008, agents bought houses for the short term to resell for a profit. That is, houses were bought and resold as if they were hot stocks. This sort of behaviour has been described non-mathematically in the literature (McKay, 1980; Kindleberger, 1996). The market crash of 1929 led to a liquidity crisis (Eichengreen, 1996; McCauley, 2008b, 2009). The reason that crashes between 1960 and 2000 did not lead to a liquidity crisis, but the 2007–2008 crash did, is described in references (McCauley, 2008b, 2009).

By the efficient market hypothesis, we mean a detrended *normal liquid market* that is either very hard or impossible to beat systematically. This means that there are no *readily available* correlations or patterns that can be exploited systematically for profit. A Markovian market would be unbeatable in this sense because a detrended Markov market has no memory to exploit in a trading strategy. A detrended Markov process is generally non-stationary without time-translational invariance, and recurrence of prices cannot be predicted or expected. More generally, a detrended Markov process is a martingale, but the reverse is not necessarily true. Martingales behave Markovian at the level of pair correlations even if the entire process has non-Markov features, like memory of an initial condition in the distant past (McCauley, 2010, 2012).

To formulate the dynamics of hard to beat markets, we assume that the increment autocorrelations vanish, where by increments we mean differences in levels $x(t, T) = x(t + T) - x(t)$, $x(t, -T) = x(t) - x(t - T)$. The statement that trading during an earlier time interval provides no signals for traders in a later non-overlapping time interval *at the level of pair correlations* is simply that

$$\langle (x(t_1) - x(t_1 - T_1))(x(t_2 + T_2) - x(t_2)) \rangle = 0 \tag{13}$$

if there is no time interval overlap, $[t_1 - T_1, t_1] \cap [t_2, t_2 + T_2] = \emptyset$, where $\emptyset$ denotes the empty set on the line. This is very different condition than assuming that the increments statistically independent, and is much weaker than assuming that the market is Markovian. With (13), past returns cannot be used to predict future returns.

Consider any stochastic process $x(t)$ where the differences are uncorrelated, meaning that equation (13) holds. From this condition we obtain the autocorrelation function for levels (returns). Let $t > s$, then

$$\langle x(t)x(s)\rangle = \langle(x(t) - x(s))x(s)\rangle + \langle x^2(s)\rangle = \langle x^2(s)\rangle > 0 \qquad (14)$$

since $x(s) - x(t_0) = x(s)$, so that $\langle x(t + T)x(t)\rangle$ is simply the variance in levels $x(t)$ at the earlier time t. *This condition is equivalent to a Martingale process:*

$$\int dy y p_2(y, t + T \,|\, x, t) = x \qquad (15)$$

$$\langle x(t + T)x(t)\rangle = \int\int dx dy x y p_2(y, t + T); x, t) f_1(x, t)$$

$$\int x f_1(x, t)\, dx \left(\int y dy\, p_2(y, t + T); x, t\right) = \int x^2 f_1(x, t)\, dx \qquad (16)$$

At the level of pair correlations, a martingale cannot be distinguished from a drift free Markov process. Note also that equation (13) can be interpreted as asserting that earlier returns have no correlation with future gains. This condition cannot be assumed, it must be deduced via data analysis.

Next, we emphasize the key point for data analysis and modelling. Combining

$$\langle(x(t + T) - x(t))^2\rangle = +\langle(x^2(t + T)) + \langle x^2(t)\rangle - 2\langle x(t + T)x(t)\rangle \qquad (17)$$

with (17) we get

$$\langle(x(t + T) - x(t))^2\rangle = \langle x^2(t + T)\rangle - \langle x^2(t)\rangle \qquad (18)$$

which depends on both t and T, excepting the rare case where $\langle x^2\rangle$ is linear in t. *Uncorrelated differences are generally non-stationary* (this is bad news for cointegration).

It is easy to show that, with one rare exception, time-translationally invariant martingales are non-stationary processes. The daily and weekly behaviour of this mean square fluctuation has been described in (Bassler *et al.*, 2007, 2008) for foreign exchange (FX) markets.

The difference correlations of a stationary process do not vanish,

$$\langle x(t, T)x(t, -T)\rangle = \langle x(2T)x(0)\rangle - \sigma^2 \qquad (19)$$

reflecting pair correlations that can be traded on for profit. Price recurrence is the basis for a successful trading strategy in a hypothetical stationary market. Real liquid markets are martingales, non-stationary with non-stationary differences.

A successful mathematics-based trading strategy should carry with it the prediction of the first passage time, which is related to the idea of recurrence. For a martingale without time-translational invariance the standard procedure for calculating the first passage time fails. The question how even to formulate the first passage time for a general non-stationary process is fraught with difficulties.

6. Recurrence in Finance Markets

A first passage time is a relaxation of the condition of recurrence, albeit is related in spirit. Given the present price of a stock, what is the average waiting time for the stock to hit an entirely different price? Clearly, formulating this problem requires as a first step that we know the dynamical model that generates the stock prices. All that we know is that we have the martingale class, with the first difference $x(t, T) = x(t + T) - x(t)$ given as (Bassler *et al.*, 2007)

$$\langle x^2(t, T) \rangle \approx T \int D(x, t) f_1(x, t) \, dx \qquad (20)$$

for $T \ll t$ we cannot say *which* martingale. Precisely the t-dependence of (20) has been measured for FX markets (Bassler *et al.*, 2007, 2008; McCauley, 2009).

If forced to extrapolate, then we would choose the exponential martingale with Hurst exponent $H = 1/2$ (McCauley, 2009). In this case the diffusion coefficient is given by

$$D(x, t) = 1 + |x| / t^{1/2} \qquad (21)$$

This martingale describes a non-stationary process where the variance grows linearly with the time, so is not at all approximable by stationarity. The first and all other differences for this martingale are also non-stationary.

Clearly, we have a non-time-translationally invariant martingale. Could we formulate and solve the problem of first passage time for a martingale without time-translational invariance then we could either develop a profitable trading strategy, or at least decide that it is too risky to place a bet. We might also be able to address the following problem: if two stocks appear to be significantly relatively mispriced, then how long should we expect to wait to see the discrepancy disappear? Here is the fundamental difficulty with trying to formulate and solve all such questions.

The standard method (Stratonovich, 1963; Durrett, 1984; McCauley, 2012) for formulating a first passage time assumes a time-translationally invariant stochastic process, a process where $D(x, t) = D(x)$. In that case the first passage time problem can be reduced to the solution of an ordinary differential equation. If the diffusion coefficient depends inseparably on both x and t, then that method cannot be used. In a word, we do not even understand how to formulate the problem. There is therefore no reliable mathematical prediction to tell us that we should bet on a return to parity of two stocks that are (subjectively) judged to be relatively mispriced. This degree of ignorance does not prevent trading houses from promoting short and long trades based on the idea of mispricing. Long Term Capital Management's experience of the Gamblers' Ruin in October 1997 was based on a misplaced belief in recurrence that was shown to be wrong when liquidity dried up for Russian bonds (Dunbar, 2000). First passage times for non-time-translationally invariant martingales might be another example of complexity, we do not know.

Acknowledgments

This contribution is based on lectures given to economics students at Trento in May, 2010. I am grateful to Vela Velupillai for inviting me to speak to his class and for encouraging me to think further about 'recurrence' in stochastic processes, and especially to Ventkatachlam Ragupathy for sending me a copy of his notes of my lecture.

References

Bassler, Kevin E., McCauley, Joseph L. and Gunaratne, Gemunu H. (2007) Nonstationary increments, scaling distributions, and variable diffusion processes in financial markets. *PNAS* 104: 17287–17290.

Bassler, Kevin E., Gunaratne, Gemunu H. and McCauley, Joseph L. (2008) Empirically based modeling in finance and beyond and spurious stylized facts. *International Review of Finnalcial Analysis* 17: 767–783.

Black, F. (1986) Noise. *Journal of Finance* 3: 529–543.

Black, F. and Scholes, M. (1973) The pricing of options and corporate liabilities. *Journal of Political Economy* 81: 637–654.

Dunbar, N. (2000) *Inventing Money, Long-Term Capital Management and the Search for Risk-Free Profits*. New York: Wiley.

Durrett, R. (1984) *Brownian Motion and Martingales in Analysis*. Belmont, CA: Wadsworth.

Eichengreen, B. (1996) *Globalizing Capital: A History of the International Monetary System*. Princeton, NJ: Princeton University Press.

Gnedenko, B.V. (1967) *The Theory of Probability*. Translated by B.D. Seckler. New York: Chelsea.

Hänggi, P. and Thomas, H. (1977) Time evolution, correlations, and linear response of non-Markov processes. *Zeitschrift für Physik* B26: 85–92.

Kindleberger, C.P. (1996) *Manias, Panics, and Crashes, A History of Financial Crises*. New York: Wiley.

Mandelbrot, B. (1966) The variation of certain speculative prices. *Journal of Business* 39: 242–255.

McCann, C.R. Jr. (1994) *Probability Foundations of Economic Theory*. London, UK: Routledge.

McCauley, Joseph L. (2008a) Time vs. ensemble averages for nonstationary time series. *Physica A* 387: 5518–5522.

McCauley, Joseph L. (2008b) Nonstationarity of efficient financial markets: FX market evolution from stability to instability. *International Review of Financial Analysis* 17: 820–837.

McCauley, Joseph L. (2009) *Dynamics of Markets: The New Financial Economics*. Cambridge, UK: Cambridge University Press.

McCauley, Joseph L. (2010) NonMarkov Ito processes with 1-states memory. *Physics Procedia* 3: 1659–1676.

McCauley, Joseph L. (2012) *Stochastic Differential Equations and Applications for Physics and Finance*. Cambridge, UK: Cambridge University Press (forthcoming).

McKay, C. (1980) *Extraordinary Popular Delusions and the Madness of Crowds*. New York: Harmony Books.

Osborne, M.F.M. (1964) In P. Cootner (ed.), *The Random Character of Stock Market Prices*. Cambridge, MA: MIT.

Sargent, T.J. (1987) *Macroeconomic Theory*. New York: Academic.

Stratonovich, R.L. (1963) *Topics in the Theory of Random Noise*. Translated by R.A. Silverman. New York: Gordon & Breach.

von Neumann, J. (1966) *Theory of Self-Reproducing Automata*, edited and completed by Arthur W. Burks. Urbana and London: University of Illinois Press.

11

FLEXIBLE ACCELERATOR ECONOMIC SYSTEMS AS COUPLED OSCILLATORS

Stefano Zambelli

1. Introduction

The very term 'macrodynamics' has – in the Anglo-Saxon world – an origin that comes even before the term 'macroeconomics'.[1] The term macroeconomics itself is from the definition of macrodynamics given by Frisch (1933, p. 156), where he distinguishes between micro-dynamics and macrodynamics. *'The macrodynamic analysis, . . . , tries to give an account of the fluctuations of the whole economic system taken in its entirety'*.

Since that seminal work, it has become clear that the basic ingredients forming a 'macrodynamic' could emanate from permuting and combining a variety of analytical concepts. The sometimes mutually exclusive ingredients could be listed as: continuous versus discrete (or mixed); linear versus nonlinear; low versus high dimension; simple versus complex; stochastic versus deterministic (or mixed); endogenous versus exogenous: analytically tractable versus intractable; closed versus open; decidable, computable versus undecidable; with or without equilibrium (or equilibria); stable versus unstable and so on.

In Frisch's seminal paper, we find some guiding lines with respect to the method to be followed. There we find a methodological suggestion about how to proceed in order to construct a proper *propagation* mechanism.

'The complete macrodynamic problem, . . . , consists in describing as realistically as possible the kind of relations that exist between the various magnitudes in the Tableau Èconomique exhibited in Figure 1, and from the nature of these relations to explain the movements, cyclical or otherwise, of the system. . . . In the present paper . . . I shall confine myself to systems that are still more simplified than the one exhibited in Figure 1. I shall commence by a system that represents, so to speak, the extreme limit of simplification, but which is, however, completely determinate . . . I shall then introduce little by little more complications into the system . . . This procedure has one interesting feature:

Nonlinearity, Complexity and Randomness in Economics, First Edition.
Stefano Zambelli and Donald A.R. George.

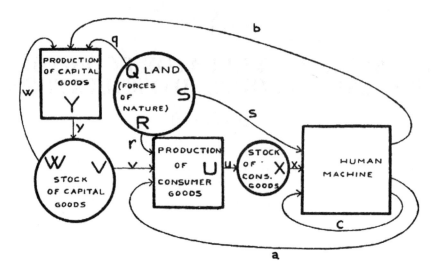

Figure 1. Tableau Economique.

Source: Frisch (1933, p.174)

it enables us to draw some conclusion about those properties of the system that may account for the cyclical character of the variations. Indeed, the most simplified cases are characterized by monotonic evolution without oscillations, and it is only by adding certain complications *to the picture that we get systems where the theoretical movement will contain oscillations. It is interesting to note at what stage in this hierarchie order of theoretical set-ups the oscillatory movement come in*' (Frisch, 1933, p. 158).

It is well known (see, e.g. Velupillai, 2003, p. 32) that dynamical systems may be characterized by their basins of attraction, which may be grouped into four (Wolfram) classes (class 1 limit points – class 2 limit cycles – class 3 strange attractors – class 4 configurations posed at the borderline of strange attractors). And inside each class further classifications are possible. In this paper, the genesis of different economic models belonging to the above classification – obtained by adding *certain complications* – will be analysed.

2. Frisch's Rocking Horse: A Linear Accelerator Time-to-Build Model

2.1 *The Horse*

Frisch used '*Propagation Problems and Impulse Problems*' (PPIP) not only to show how things ought to be done in general, but also as a methodological example to be used with those with whom he had some public and/or private debates. In the pages of the *Journal of Political Economy*, Frisch (1931, 1932a, 1932b) had intellectual exchanges with Clark (1931, 1932), in which he wanted to show, using the mathematical method, that Wesley Mitchell, Alvin Hansen and Clark himself had reached wrong conclusions with respect to the causality in the accelerator model, which was a well-accepted model explaining booms and depressions at that time.

The logical problem in the Hansen–Mitchell–Clark theory was its claim that '*in order to bring about an absolute shrinkage in the demand of intermediate product, all that may be needed is that the final demand should slacken its rate of growth*' (Clark 1917, pp. 222–223). This had to be so because according to them, '*every producer of things to be sold to producers has two demands to meet . . . Both these demands come ultimately from the consumer, but they follow different laws. The demand for maintenance and replacement of existing capital varies with the amount of the demand for finished products, while the demand for new construction or enlargement of stocks depends upon whether or not the sales of the finished product[s] are growing*' (p. 220).

This debate was summarized and expanded in PPIP, where Frisch first presented a '*Simplified System without Oscillations*' and, subsequently, '*A Macrodynamic System Giving Rise to Oscillations*'.

The two systems of equations are reproduced here – the notations are same as that of the original paper, Frisch (1933).

'*Simplified System without Oscillations*'

$$y(t) = mx(t) + \mu \dot{x}(t) \tag{1}$$

$$\dot{x}(t) = c - \lambda(rx(t) + sy(t)) \tag{2}$$

$$z(y) = \int_0^\varepsilon D(\tau) y(t - \tau) \, d\tau \tag{3}$$

'*A Macrodynamic System Giving Rise to Oscillations*'

$$y(t) = mx(t) + \mu \dot{x}(t) \tag{1}$$

$$\dot{x}(t) = c - \lambda(rx(t) + sz(t)) \tag{2'}$$

$$z(y) = \int_0^\varepsilon D(\tau) y(t - \tau) \, d\tau \tag{3}$$

The '*Simplified System without Oscillations*' is, as Frisch pointed out, a first order differential equation that cannot produce cyclical behaviour.[2] Clearly this is a system belonging to the sub-class 1, which has a basin of attraction towards which the system converges monotonically, i.e. without any type of oscillations.

Frisch does discuss the types of economic mechanisms or theories that would be necessary so as to expand the model and hence construct a system that will be able to generate cyclical behaviour. Among the different possibilities, Frisch chose the 'time to build' factor and he did so by introducing the 'advancement function' $D(\tau)$ and by allowing the 'carry-on-activity' to feed back into the system. $D(\tau)$ is fundamental because it expresses the economic activity that is necessary in order to transform an investment decision made at time $t - \varepsilon$ into an actual delivery at time t. Frisch simplified the problem by introducing a linear description which was expressed by $D(\tau) = 1/\varepsilon$. Hence (3) can be substituted with

$$\dot{z}(t) = \frac{y(t) - y(t - \varepsilon)}{\varepsilon} \tag{4}$$

The system is now a linear system that does not allow persistence of oscillations and actually – as demonstrated in Zambelli (1992, 2007) – does not generate oscillations at all, neither damped nor undamped, for economically meaningful range of parameters. In short, Frisch failed in his objectives: His *'Simplified System without Oscillations'* never became *'A Macrodynamic System Giving Rise to Oscillations'*. The system simply generates a dynamical system of class 1, coverging monotonically to a limit point basin of attraction.

2.2 *The Forcing Term*

In order to account for the persistence of oscillations, the above system has to be constantly removed away from equilibrium: a forcing term has to be introduced. This forcing term can be itself cyclical or exhibit irregular ups and downs. This is what Frisch suggested in one of the sections of his paper. But, clearly, a model of the cycle that relies on an external, exogenously given forcing factor, does not provide a satisfactory explanation of the cyclical behaviour. In other words, it is not sufficient to constantly change the initial conditions of the dynamical system, so as to provide a theoretical explanation of the existence of cycles. This clearly becomes a tautological explanation: cycles exist because cycles exist. Unfortunately, this is now the bread and butter of standard macroeconomics (Real Business Cycles, Stochastic Dynamic General Equilibrium and so on). What one does here is to introduce exogenous 'randomness', which does not help at all in the understanding of the economic mechanisms.

3. Hicks–Goodwin 'Perpetual Motion': A Nonlinear Model

A simple examination of equation (1) shows that the linear case is a very special and unlikely one. In fact, the relationship is likely to be nonlinear because it simply states how the two variables have to be linked together, but clearly, no restriction on the functional form of either $y(t)$ or $x(t)$ is imposed. Given that the cardinality of the set of nonlinear functions is higher than the cardinality of linear functions, the likelihood that either $x(t)$ or $y(t)$ is linear is of measure 0. What equation (2) or (2′) does is to impose linearity to an otherwise potentially nonlinear relation. This is not in itself methodologically inappropriate, provided there is an economic reason to do so. Goodwin and Hicks have provided an economic justification, that was actually already present in Clark,[3] according to which there is no economic reason for the accelerator principle to be linear.

3.1 *Goodwin's (1951) Flexible Multiplier Accelerator Model*

Equation (1) above would be recognized by a modern economist as, following Hicks (1950) and Goodwin (1951),

$$I(t) = \dot{K}(t) = F(Y(t), \dot{Y}(t)) \tag{5}$$

with the standard meaning for the symbols, $I(t)$ is aggregate investment, $K(t)$ is aggregate capital and $Y(t)$ is aggregate output.[4]

A reasonable functional form which is consistent with Goodwin's flexible accelerator idea may be given by:[5]

$$I(t) = \dot{K}(t) = \varphi(vY(t) - K(t))$$

$$\frac{\delta\varphi(vY(t) - K(t))}{\delta(vY(t) - K(t))} > 0 \quad \text{and} \quad \frac{\delta\varphi(0)}{\delta(vY(t) - K(t))} = v$$

$$\lim_{vY(t)-K(t)\to+\infty} \varphi(v(Y(t) - K(t)) = k^{**}; \quad \lim_{vY(t)-K(t)\to-\infty} \varphi(v(Y(t) - K(t)) = k^{*} \tag{6}$$

The idea behind the above functional form is similar to that of the flexible accelerator of the original article by Goodwin (1951), where $vY(t)$ is the desired capital level and $K(t)$ the existing level. Under normal conditions, i.e. near normal production capacity exploitation, the net investment adjusts fast to the production needs, so that around the equilibrium condition, i.e. $vY(t) - K(t) = 0$, a linear accelerator holds. In fact, $\delta\varphi(0)/\delta Y(t)$ is equal to the constant capital-output ratio v. When current demand is inadequate with respect to production capacity, either because it is too high or too low, the investments levels tend to either k^{**} or k^{*} : the production or destruction of capital goods per time unit cannot go above or below these physical limits.

An explicit functional form consistent with the above description may be derived from the composition of two logistic functions.

The total demand at time $t + \vartheta + \varepsilon$ is given by

$$Y((t + \vartheta) + \varepsilon) = C((t + \vartheta) + \varepsilon) + I((t + \vartheta) + \varepsilon) \tag{7}$$

where ε is the Robertson lag and $\vartheta + \varepsilon$ the Lundberg lag.

The lag between the moment in which income is earned and spent may be described as follows:

$$C((t + \vartheta) + \varepsilon) = C_0 + cY(t + \vartheta) \tag{8}$$

The fact that it takes *time to build* and consequently, there is a lag between the moment at which an investment decision is made and the capital goods are actually delivered may be described as follows:

$$I((t + \vartheta) + \varepsilon) = \dot{K}(t) = \varphi(vY(t) - K(t)) \tag{9}$$

Substituting equations (8) and (9) into (7), we have the law of motion of our economy that is described by a mixed nonlinear difference-differential equation. In order to maintain the structure of the model as simple as possible, the mixed difference differential equation is approximated by a second order differential equation. After some simple truncations of Taylor series expansions, we obtain:

$$\varepsilon\vartheta\ddot{Y}(t) = -(\varepsilon + (1 - c)\vartheta)\dot{Y}(t) - (1 - c)Y(t) + C_0 + \varphi(vY(t) - K(t)) \quad (10)$$

The above equation has the same functional form as in the Goodwin model, but here an explicit and different definition for $cp(.)$ is given. The state space representation of equation (10) is given by:

$$\dot{Y}(t) = Z(t) \quad (11a)$$

$$\dot{Z}(t) = b[Co - (l - c)Y(t) - aZ(t) + \varphi(vY(t) - K(t))] \quad (11b)$$

$$\dot{K}(t) = \varphi(vY(t) - K(t)) \quad (11c)$$

$$b = \frac{1}{\varepsilon\theta}; \quad a = \varepsilon + \vartheta(1 - c)$$

One can check that the above model can account for cyclical behaviour. For a wide range of the parameter values, the dynamical system evolves towards a limit cycle. In fact, the analysis of the Jacobian shows that the equilibrium point is a repellor and that the variables evolve inside a closed compact set.

4. Coupled Oscillators in Goodwin's Model: The Two National Systems Case

Given the richness of the model, it seems to be appropriate to study the dynamic evolutions of two (three or more) coupled economies, which are characterized by different values of the structural parameters.

A natural way in which to introduce coupling is by considering the fact that countries are linked through trade.

The flow accounting descriptions of economies 1 and 2 are given by:

$$M_1(t + \vartheta_1 + \varepsilon_1) + Y_1(t + \vartheta_1 + \varepsilon_1)$$

$$\equiv C_1(t + \vartheta_1 + \varepsilon_1) + I_1(t + \vartheta_1 + \varepsilon_1) + X_1(t + \vartheta_1 + \varepsilon_1)$$

$$M_2(t + \vartheta_2 + \varepsilon_2) + Y_2(t + \vartheta_2 + \varepsilon_2)$$

$$\equiv C_2(t + \vartheta_2 + \varepsilon_2) + I_2(t + \vartheta_2 + \varepsilon_2) + X_2(t + \vartheta_2 + \varepsilon_2) \quad (12)$$

Following traditional lines, I shall assume that the demand for foreign goods is demand for final goods which is exposed to the same lag as consumption. Therefore:

$$M_1(t + \vartheta_1 + \varepsilon_1) = m_1 Y_1(t + \vartheta_1)$$
$$M_2(t + \vartheta_2 + \varepsilon_2) = m_2 Y_2(t + \vartheta_2) \quad (13)$$

Obviously the export of one country is the import of the other, so that:

$$X_1(t + \vartheta_1 + \varepsilon_1) = m_2 Y_2(t + \vartheta_1 + \varepsilon_1 - \varepsilon_2)$$
$$X_2(t + \vartheta_2 + \varepsilon_2) = m_1 Y_1(t + \vartheta_2 + \varepsilon_2 - \varepsilon_1) \quad (14)$$

In order to keep the model as simple as possible, I have kept the traditional assumptions of linearity and that of constant prices. Obviously these are highly simplifying assumptions and they could be relaxed. However, this would complicate the model and distract attention from the main theme, which is to analyse the rich dynamic behaviour emerging from a very simple model structure. Maintaining the model described by system (11), extended by (12) (13) and (14), and proceeding through a Taylor series expansion approximation we obtain:

$$\dot{Y}_1(t) = Z_1(t) \tag{15a}$$

$$\dot{Z}_1(t) = \omega\left(\Omega_1(t) + m_1\frac{(\varepsilon_1 - \varepsilon_2)}{\varepsilon_1}\Omega_2(t)\right) \tag{15b}$$

$$\dot{K}_1(t) = \varphi(v_1 Y_1(t) - K_1(t)) \tag{15c}$$

$$\dot{Y}_2(t) = Z_2(t) \tag{15d}$$

$$\dot{Z}_2(t) = \omega\left(\Omega_2(t) + m_2\frac{(\varepsilon_2 - \varepsilon_1)}{\varepsilon_2}\Omega_1(t)\right) \tag{15e}$$

$$\dot{K}_2(t) = \varphi(v_2 Y_2(t) - K_2(t)) \tag{15f}$$

where:

$$\Omega_1(t) = \frac{C_{01} - e_1 Y_1(t) - a_1 Z_1(t) + m_2(Y_2(t) + f_1 Z_2(t)) + \varphi_1(v_1 Y_1(t) - K_1(t))}{\vartheta_1 \varepsilon_1}$$

$$\Omega_2(t) = \frac{C_{02} - e_2 Y_2(t) - a_2 Z_2(t) + m_1(Y_1(t) + f_2 Z_1(t)) + \varphi_2(v_2 Y_2(t) - K_2(t))}{\vartheta_2 \varepsilon_2}$$

$$\omega = \frac{\varepsilon_1 \varepsilon_2}{\varepsilon_1 \varepsilon_2 + m_1 m_2(\varepsilon_1 - \varepsilon_2)};$$

$$f_1 = \vartheta_1 + (\varepsilon_1 - \varepsilon_2); \quad f_2 = \vartheta_2 + (\varepsilon_2 - \varepsilon_1);$$

$$e_1 = (1 + m_1 - c_1); \quad e_2 = (1 + m_2 - c_2)$$

The above six-dimensional dynamic system is composed of two coupled oscillators, where each oscillator can be seen as representing a country. A three-dimensional nonlinear dynamic system might be sufficient to generate chaotic behaviours. But, in particular, a two-dimensional oscillating system, exposed to an independent oscillating forcing term may be sufficient for generating chaos (Thompson and Stewart, 1986, pp. 84–131).

In the context of the analysis conducted here, it is not important to verify whether the variables will show chaotic behaviours, but whether the two economies could or would evolve synchronously. For certain sets of the parameters, the two economies will be highly synchronized, while for others highly a synchronized. A measure of synchronicity and a synchronicity may be derived by studying the Poincaré map (Thompson and Stewart, 1986). For a given set of parameters a trajectory is computed.

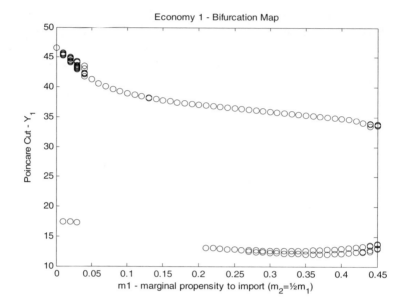

Figure 2. Equations 15. Economy 1.

Notes: The values of Y_1 for the Poincaré cut at $Z_1 = 0$ of the first country relative to the couple of parameter values (m_1, m_2), where $m_2 = 1/2^* \ m_1$ and the propensity to import assume values $m_1 \in [0, 0.45]$, $m_2 \in [0, 0.225]$. The remaining values for the parameters are reported in the appendix.

After a transient time, the trajectory converges towards a limiting set, which is either an equilibrium point, a limit cycle or a strange attractor. The Poincaré section (or cut) is represented by the points of the trajectory that go through an (hyper)-plane (see Figure 2). The invariant set of a Poincaré map is the set of points passed by the trajectory. For example, if the trajectory intersects the plane at constant intervals of time a sub-harmonic oscillation of order n would appear as a sequence of n dots repeated indefinitely in the same order (see Figures 3, 4 and 5). The dimension of the invariant Poincaré section is represented by the number of different points in the plane passed by the trajectory and a high dimension of the Poincaré invariant set reveals a remarkably complex structure. In the figures, to each couple (m_1, m_2) the dimension of the Poincaré invariant set for economy 1 and economy 2 is reported. The economy 1 seems to be, in general, least affected from the coupling with the second economy. The dimension of the Poincaré invariant set is, for large areas, equal to one. Nevertheless, there are still large areas in which the dimension of the Poincaré set is greater or equal to 4.

For each couple (m_1, m_2), the dimension of the associated Poincaré map is recorded in figure 6. White squares – dimension 1. Light grey squares – dimension 2. Dark grey squares – dimension 3. Black squares – dimension greater than 3.

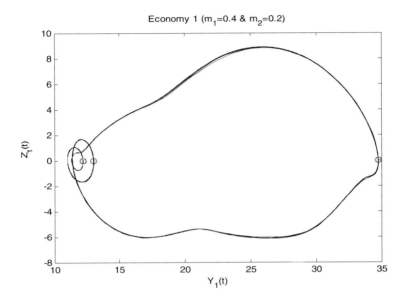

Figure 3. Equations 15. Economy 1. Example of an Attractor of System 15.

Notes: Example of an attractor of system 15. Dynamics of Y_1 and Z_1 with $m_1 = 0.4, m_2 = 0.2$. The remaining values for the parameters are reported in the appendix.

5. Mode locking, Devil's Staircases and Chaotic Dynamics

The coupling of the above two economic systems can account for a rich variety of behaviour, but which seem to be still classifiable as class 2 systems. As the strength of the coupling varies, one can observe interesting phenomena such as mode locking.[6] In the context of the above system of two coupled economies, the relative frequency of the oscillations may be constant also for large intervals in the domain of the parameters. In the example above, as the intensity of trade increases, the effects may not lead to a change of the cyclical behaviour and hence the two economies would be locked with each other. This is represented by the areas of Figure 6, where the ratio between the cardinality of the Poincaré cuts of the two economies do not vary. This is an interesting phenomenon which might have implications for the dynamics of the systems and for the possibility to control the system. Let us consider the case of a countercyclical economic policy. In that case, the policy may not exert the desired effects due to the strength of the locking. Although this enriches the dynamic behaviours of the models, the emergence of frequency locking implies the convergence of the system towards limit cycles; hence the system is generating class 2 dynamics.

The phase space representation of these limit cycles may generate or imply Poincaré cuts of high cardinality, but still of class 2. In order to move towards class 3, chaotic behaviours, the 'strength' of the locking has to be broken. In the case of the above system of two coupled oscillators, this is possible by introducing a 'forcing' and

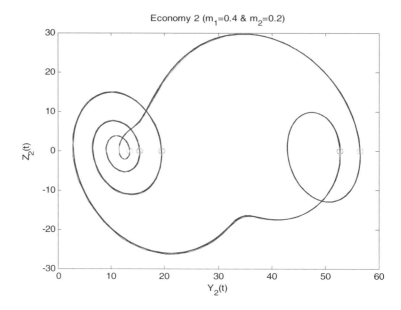

Figure 4. Equations 15. Economy 2.

Notes: Example of an attractor of system 15. Dynamics of Y_2 and Z_2 with $m_1 = 0.4, m_2 = 0.2$. The remaining values for the parameters are reported in the appendix.

independent oscillator, which would determine the breaking of the locking and which would permit that the system, for some parameter values, be classified as class 3, i.e. generating chaotic dynamics. Alternatively, the interaction of a high number of oscillators may give the same result.

The system of two countries captured by equations (15a–f) may be generalized to the case of n-countries. At time $(t + \vartheta + \varepsilon)$, the usual national income identity representation of this n-dimensional system is the following:

$$diag(\mathbf{e}'\mathbf{M})\mathbf{Y}(\mathbf{t} + \vartheta) + \mathbf{Y}(t + \vartheta + \varepsilon)$$

$$= \mathbf{C_0} + diag(\mathbf{c})\mathbf{Y}(t + \vartheta) + \varphi(\mathbf{v}'\mathbf{Y}(\mathbf{t}) - \mathbf{K}(\mathbf{t})) + \mathbf{MY}(t + \vartheta + \nabla\varepsilon) \qquad (16)$$

$$+ Forcing\,Term$$

Here $\mathbf{e}$ is the unit vector, $diag(\cdot)$ is n-dimensional diagonal matrix with diagonal elements those of the argument. $\mathbf{Y}(t)$, $\mathbf{Z}(t)$, $\mathbf{K}(t)$, $\mathbf{v}$, ϑ, ε, $\mathbf{C_0}$, c, are vectors and $\mathbf{M}$ is a matrix of marginal propensities to import (columns) and also of marginal propensities to export (rows). Here $diag(\mathbf{e}'\mathbf{M})\mathbf{Y}(\mathbf{t} + \vartheta)$ is the vector of imported quantities at times $(t + \vartheta + \varepsilon)$ and $\mathbf{MY}(t + \vartheta + \nabla\varepsilon)$ is the vector of exported quantities at time $(t + \vartheta + \nabla\varepsilon)$. The total exports of each individual country would be the sum of all the imports of all the other countries, but import decisions would be different in accordance to the specific lags. This is captured by $\nabla\varepsilon$.

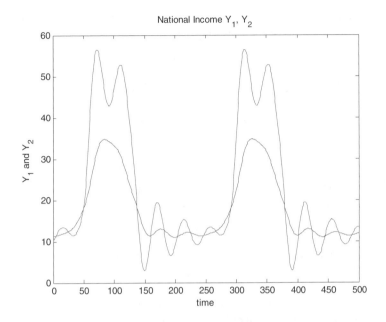

Figure 5. Equations 15.

Notes: Example of the dynamic evolution of Y_1 and Y_2 with $m_1 = 0.4$, $m_2 = 0.2$. The remaining values for the parameters are reported in the appendix.

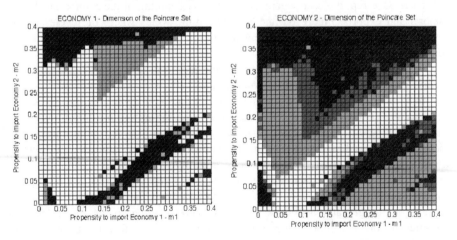

Figure 6. Equations 15. Economy 1, 2.

Notes: For each couple (m_1, m_2) the dimension of the invariant set of the Poincaré map is reported. *White squares*: The dimension of the Poncaré invariant set is 1. *Light grey squares*: The dimension of the Poincaré invariant set is 2. *Dark grey squares*: The dimension of the Poincaré invariant set is 3. *Black squares*: The dimension of the Poincaré invariant set is greater than 3.

A Taylor series expansion of the above national income identities, truncated after the linear terms, would give the following system:

$$\dot{\mathbf{Y}}(t) = \mathbf{Z}(t) \tag{17a}$$

$$\dot{\mathbf{Z}}(t) = [\mathbf{A}\text{diag}(\vartheta)]^{-1} \{\Omega + \mathbf{B}\mathbf{Y}(t) + (\mathbf{B}\text{diag}(\vartheta) - \mathbf{A})\mathbf{Z}(t)\} \tag{17b}$$

$$\dot{\mathbf{K}}(t) = \varphi\left(\mathbf{v}'\mathbf{Y}(t) - \mathbf{K}(t)\right) \tag{17c}$$

where:

$$\Omega = \mathbf{C_0} + \varphi\left(\mathbf{v}'\mathbf{Y}(t) - \mathbf{K}(t)\right) + \text{Forcing Term}$$

$\mathbf{A} = [diag(\varepsilon) - \mathbf{M}\nabla\varepsilon]$, where $\nabla\varepsilon$ is a vector encapsulating the difference in consumption lags (derived from the Taylor series approximation).

$$\mathbf{B} = [\mathbf{M} + diag(\mathbf{c}) - diag(\mathbf{e}'\mathbf{M}) - \mathbf{I}].$$

System 17 allows for very rich dynamic behaviour. It is a generalization of the Hicks–Goodwin flexible multiplier-accelerator model to the case of interacting open economies.

Figure 7a reports the projections of the limit cycle trajectories of six independent closed economies to the Y-K plane; Figure 7b reports the projections to the Y-Z plane and Figure 7c is the aggregate evolution of world output. The aggregate evolution is highly irregular, because the six independent closed economies are not coupled ($\mathbf{M}$ is an empty matrix).[7]

Figures 8a–c report a case where there is a mild coupling of the economies through imports and exports. Figure 8a and 8b show limit cycles where the cycles contain several ups and downs before it repeats itself. The evolution of world output is somewhat more regular.

Clearly, as the strength of the coupling increases the economies do tend to synchronize, but the synchronization would require a strong coupling. Figure 9 shows the same case as reported in Figures 8, but with a small cyclical forced exogenous perturbation. Figures 10 show the Poincaré set and the associated Devil's staircase[8] for which Figures 8 are just one instance. And Figures 11 show Poincaré set and the associated devil staircase for which Figure 9 is just one instance. But between a situation of no interdependence and one with high interdependence, there is a region of highly unsynchronized and seemingly erratic behaviour. This is well captured by Figure 10. Figure 10a reports the Poincaré cuts on the projections to the Y-K plane of the aggregated variables Y and K corresponding to the mean of Y. As the intensity of the coupling increases, one can identify different regions of 'regular' behaviours. That is, regions where the cardinality of the Poincaré cuts is low. Figure 11 is the average of the Devil's staircases. If now one considers that the data reported in Figures 10 and 11 are obtained with an invariant (but rescaled) $\mathbf{M}$ matrix, that is, with constant relative import and export ratios only, it becomes clear that in the case of an investigation considering all possible matrices $\mathbf{M}$, corridors of synchronicity have to be found inside a highly rugged n-dimensional space. That is, a space like that encapsulated for the two-dimensional case by Figures 6, but extended to the

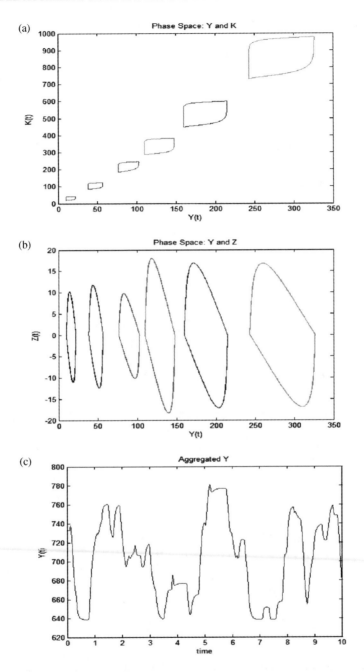

Figure 7. Uncoupled Economies. (a) Equations 17. **Y** and **K**: Phase Space: Example with 6 Economies. (b) Equations 17. **Y** and **Z**: Phase Space: Example with 6 Economies. (c) Equations 17. Aggregated Global Output.

Notes: Parameter values are reported in the appendix.

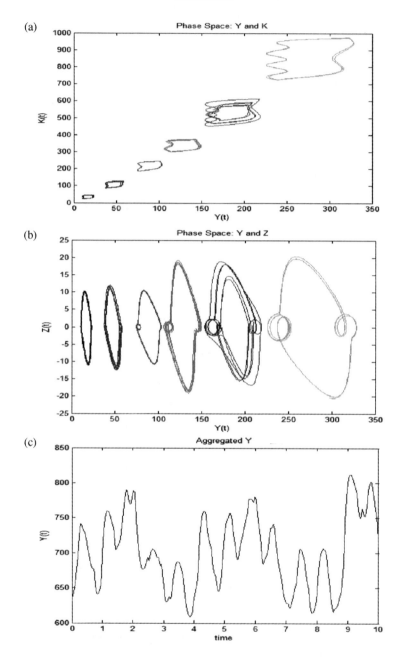

Figure 8. Coupled Economies without Forcing Term. (a) Equations 17. **Y** and **K**: Phase Space: Example with 6 Economies. (b) Equations 17. **Y** and **Z**: Phase Space: Example with 6 economies. (c) Equations 17. Aggregated Global Output.

Notes: Parameter values reported in the appendix.

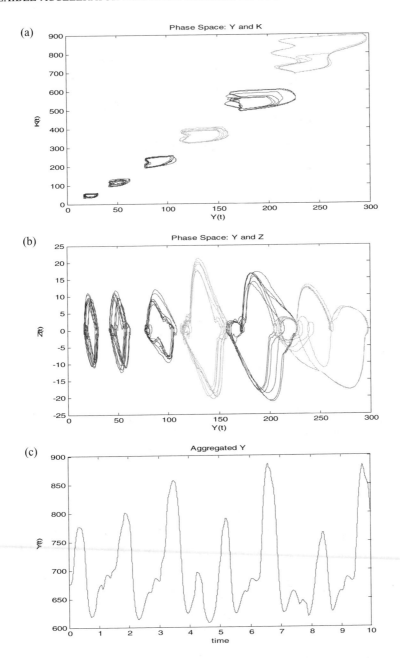

Figure 9. Coupled Economies with Small Forcing Term. (a) Equations 17. **Y** and **K**. Phase Space: Example with 6 Economies. (b) Equations 17. **Y** and **Z**. Phase Space: Example with 6 Economies. (c) Equations 17. Aggregated Global Output.

Notes: Parameter values reported in the appendix.

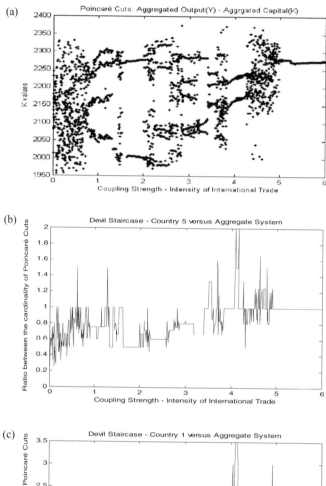

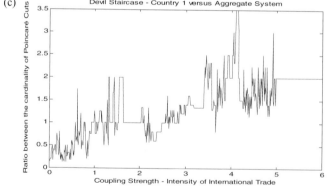

Figure 10. Coupled Economies without Forcing Term. (a) Equations 17. Poincaré Cuts. Aggregated Values of **K** Associated with Average (Equilibrium) Values of Aggregated Output **Y**. (b) Equations 17. Devil Staircase. Economy 5 Versus Aggregate Global System. (c) Equations 17. Devil Staircase. Economy 1 Versus Aggregate Global System.

Notes: Parameter values reported in the appendix.

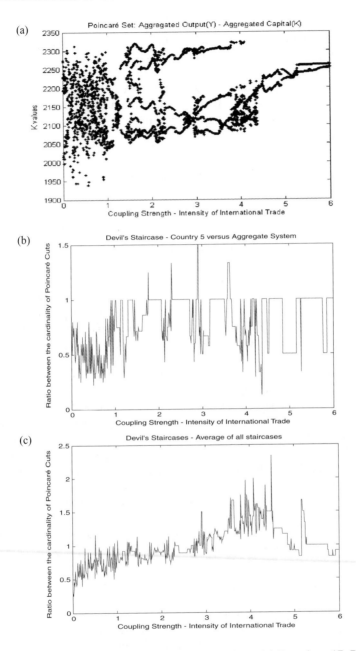

Figure 11. Coupled Economies with Small Forcing Term. (a) Equations 17. Poincaré Cuts. Aggregated Values of **K** Associated with Average (Equilibrium) Values of Aggregated output **Y**. (b) Equations 17. Devil Staircase. Economy 5 Versus Aggregate Global System. (c) Equations 17. Devil Staircase. Average of All Staircases.

Notes: Parameter values reported in the appendix.

n-dimensional space. Hence, it is probably appropriate to say that the identification of the corridors of synchronicity would require the acts of a Devil, which will be able to jump as the different propensities to imports and export change from one frequency locking condition to another.

Another way to put this would be that as the strength of the coupling increases, the path from a totally unsynchronized dynamics to a highly synchronized one is not smooth and the transition goes through highly irregular attractors, i.e. behaviours of the class 3 type.[9]

5.1 *Goodwin–Velupillai: One-Sided Oscillators and the Canard*

The above economic coupled systems are characterized by having two essential non-linearities captured by the flexible accelerator of equation (6). For completeness, it is interesting here to ask whether the existence of oscillators requires the existence of both nonlinearities. One nonlinearity might be enough to generate cyclical behaviour (see on this Velupillai, 2008b, pp. 336–340) and the type of nonlinearity is known as the Goodwin characteristic. In the context of the flexible accelerator model, as we have seen above, this implies that the existence of limits on the capacity to produce capital goods per unit of time or the full employment ceiling may alone be enough to generate cycles. These Canards would in general have shapes of the oscillations which would be different from those of the oscillators we have been studying in the previous sections, but could also be seen as particular cases of the two sided oscillators: cases in which one of the two nonlinearities in not binding. And this would obviously occur for a subset of the set of feasible parameters

Also, it has to be noted that, obviously, not all the uncoupled economic systems would behave in an oscillatory manner, but when coupled with an oscillatory economy, both would almost always end up oscillating. This does happen with the types of oscillators which we have been studying, but it is most likely not to be seen in general as a sufficient condition. If we substitute some of the representations of the economic systems with canards and non-oscillating systems coupled with some systems like the ones above, as the strength of the coupling increases even these systems would synchronize with the aggregated system at some point, but the true nature of the interdependencies that we are observing here would imply that the aggregated behaviour would be influenced by these effects as well.

5.2 *Digital and Analogue Computing*

The richness and the specific dynamic behaviour of coupled dynamical systems depend on several factors. The theoretical system (15) for two countries, which is generalized to the *n*-countries system (16) and (17) are Taylor series approximations of the original theoretical model. Moreover, in order to conduct digital computations the approximated systems (15), (16) and (17) are further approximated with difference equations. The different approximating algorithms (Euler, Runge–Kutta and so on) do generate different sets of difference equations that may generate themselves phantom type solutions: that is solutions that are far away from the actual dynamic theoretical system. We have seen above that the dynamic behaviour does depend crucially on the type of parameters. In particular, the strength of the coupling between different countries, the different flexible accelerators and the different national multipliers may determine quite different behaviour for autarkic systems compared to those in the presence of coupling.

One way to try to overcome some of these problems due to the different approximations is through the construction of analogue type computers.[10] It is extremely interesting to note that the Goodwin's nonlinear flexible accelerator, which is at the foundations of the system of coupled oscillators above, was already simulated with an analogue electrical system during the 1950s. This investigation has allowed some important findings: '*In addition to the limit cycles that correspond to Goodwin's, we found on the analog computer at least twenty-five other limit cycles that are also solutions to the same equation* ... (Strotz *et al.*, 1953, p. 398)'. Clearly, although it is true in theory, in practice what one can actually compute with a digital computer and an analogue one are not always the same.

In our case, whether the approximated systems (15), (16) and (17) shadow the original system of differential equations or not could be addressed with the aid of an analogue computer made of a system of coupled electrical oscillators. Clearly, with an analogue computer as well one may not be sure that the error does not grow exponentially, but one can check whether the two approximating systems – the analogue and the digital – do actually shadow each other. This check would not rigorously? guarantee that both systems do shadow the original one, but it could increase or decrease the beliefs of the researcher(s) on whether it does.

6. Back to Goodwin and the Fermi–Pasta–Ulam Problem

Clearly simulations alone are not always sufficient to reach a final conclusion about the behaviour of a dynamical system. On the other hand, simulations are often the only thing that one can do in order to shed light on the actual behaviour of a system. Ulam's famous statement '*Given an undecidable proposition there will be a preference as to whether one should assume it to be true or false* (Cooper, 1989, p. 312)' ... does in a way justify the role of symbolic or numerical simulations in order to strengthen the preferences or beliefs of the researcher-economist and/or policy maker.

In a more specific context, the importance of simulations have been emphasized in the famous Fermi–Pasta–Ulam (FPU) problem (Fermi *et al.*, 1955). In that case through simulation they studied the distribution of energy in a string where each small 'interval' of the string was 'coupled' with the neighbouring ones.[11] What they expected was a convergence towards a uniform distribution of energy which did not occur. Their surprising result was equivalent to a laboratory experiment and hence it gave among physicists an important status to the method of studying theoretical models and questions with the aid of simulations. In fact, this approach has lead to several investigations and to the discovery, among other things, of solutions. The Fermi–Pasta–Ulam problem remains an enigma, resisting a full understanding, despite varied 'attacks' to breach its 'defences'.

In similar situations where the simulations do not fit the *a priori* expected theoretical outcomes, most economists would modify their original assumptions and would change the individual local components (the equations describing the state of the intervals) and would derive a conclusion consistent with respect to their *a priori* views. There is a sort of dogma towards convergence and (saddle path) stability that confines the theories to models that allow dynamics of the class 1 type. But if the equations of the system are of the type (15), (16) and (17), transforming them so as to allow the convergence towards an equilibrium point and subsequently, introduce a pseudo-stochastic process into the modified system to account for 'irregularities' and for the maintenance of the cyclical behaviours is an absurd procedure. Prescott, in his Nobel Lecture, does clearly suggest such a Frisch-type procedure when he writes the sequence of steps that a real business cycle model builder has to follow. Prescott (2006, p. 217) writes, *Step 5: Make a linear-quadratic approximation* of the deterministic equations (higher moments equal to zero) and then study the equilibrium stochastic process.

But if the researcher thinks that an economic system is described with nonlinear equations, to work with a linearized system is most likely to be equivalent to confining the dynamic system to class 1 dynamic behaviour. And therefore it confines the dynamics far from the dynamics that the original (theoretical) model would have generated.

We have seen above that the coupling of a simple flexible-accelerator economic systems generate complicated dynamics. Goodwin (1947) did study the problem of dynamical coupling in the presence of production lags and in his pioneering work Goodwin did stress the importance of interdependence and of interconnectedness of economic units (in his case markets). Given the difficulties that arise due to dynamic interdependence, Goodwin (1947, p. 181) would seriously pose the question: *can we legitimately break down this monolithic problem in such a way as to get answers that are not seriously wrong.* His working proposal was to consider forced coupling for the case in which the effects of the single forced local unit to the global forcing unit was negligible. In this case '*The problem of coupling, or simultaneous dynamical equations, goes over into the much simpler one of forced motion, or inhomogeneity. Because of its essential asymmetry we might call it unilateral coupling. The quantitative importance of the return effect would fix the degree of error in making a partial analysis. Where it is large we are not justified in breaking up the problem into simpler ones* (Goodwin, 1947, p. 182)'. In a similar context, Goodwin (1946) had already shown that innovations and irregularities could be the results of the unilateral coupling of the single economic unit to an exogenous (non-stochastic) forcing term. This was quite a remarkable achievement because it did provide an alternative with respect to the Frisch's Rocking Horse metaphor. In a way, it was providing a formalism that would be more in line with the alternative approach of Goodwin's own teacher Schumpeter.[12]

But Goodwin was fully aware that the method of unilateral coupling could *get answers that are seriously wrong*. While computers were at their primitive state in the concluding section of his *Dynamical Coupling with Especial Reference to Markets Having Production Lags,* Goodwin (1947, 204) wrote that there are '. . . *complications arising with general dynamic interdependence. To go from two identical markets to n nonidentical ones will require the prolonged services of yet unborn calculating machines'*. The study of coupled systems were conducted a few years later by Fermi, Pasta and Ulam. Their computer was a slow primitive one that was slower than the first personal computers of the early 1980s. But their work did demonstrate the importance of simulations for the study of coupling in theoretical physics. But simulations are some form of computations. We know that most physicists know that there are things that can be computed and things that cannot. But they simply seem to accept this fact. Not many economists are aware of that, but maybe it time that they did.

7. Concluding Note

In this paper, some important aspects of the evolution of theoretical macro models with respect to their capacity to generate non-trivial dynamic behaviours has been studied. Partly for expository purposes and partly because the author believes it to be an important feature of modern capitalist economies, a chosen common element for these macro models has been the accelerator principle. Since the work of Mitchell (1913), the accelerator principle has had great historical importance for the history of thought both as a theoretical tool and for its explicatory capacity. The fact that it cannot be reconciled in any way with maximization principles is relevant here, in agreement with Samuelson's (1972, p. 256) Nobel Lecture.

Its importance is also due to the fact that some of the first linear mathematical models of the business cycles (Frisch, 1933; Samuelson, 1939; and partly also Metzler, 1941) and the first nonlinear ones (Hicks, 1950; Goodwin, 1951) had the accelerator principle at their core.

In this paper, we have discussed whether and under which conditions different versions of the accelerators, and/or different versions of the models in which they can be incorporated, fall in one of the four classes of Wolfram dynamic behaviours. It has been shown that when the economic systems are viewed as coupled oscillators, a rich variety of behaviours can be expected to occur. We go from a point attractor (class 1) to limit cycles (class 2) and chaotic attractors (class 3). A simple model composed of a few coupled-through-trade nonlinear systems is capable of highly irregular and at times highly unsynchronized behaviour. As the Devil's staircase graphs show, the systems may go through, as parameters change, different mode-locking regions. Hence higher trade integration – when point stability is not improperly imposed by the researcher – may be filled with irregularities like the Goodwin (1946) types: that is, irregular dynamics determined by the deterministic coupling between the economic systems and not by the presence of an exogenous stochastic forcing term.

There are several questions that are open and among them two somewhat related questions are particularly important. The first is to understand whether the systems like the above do generate class 4 dynamics.[13] I have not been able to give an answer to this question. The second is whether there exists, for any given couple system, a mechanical policy that allows to smooth out or remove the irregularities. This policy would be equivalent to choosing an initial condition that would converge towards a specific desirable attractor. Velupillai's (2007) answer to this problem is negative: there are problems that are simply undecidable and this could be one of them. This does not at all mean that there is nothing to do, but simply that there are no computable general mechanisms to evaluate a policy. However, this does not mean that policies cannot be implemented or do not exist, it simply means that for a given system policies have to be 'tried out'. A laboratory to try policies out, like in the Fermi–Pasta–Ulam problem, is by simulating them. And by doing so, one would reinforce or change his preferences. Paraphrasing Ulam: '*Given an undecidable policy one shall have preferences on whether to assume it to work or not*'.

Notes

1. On the first uses of the term macroeconomics see, for example, Velupillai (2008, p. 283).
2. This is clearly so by substituting $y(t)$ from the relation (1) into (2) and rearranging. Note that equation (3) is actually irrelevant for the solution and the dynamics of the system because there is no feedback between $z(t)$ and either $x(t)$ or $y(t)$. It is placed here so as to allow a comparison with the 'Macro-Dynamic System Giving Rise to Oscillations'.
3. A textual analysis would demonstrate that a nonlinear relation was already present in the works of Clark-Mitchell and Hansen. In relation to fluctuating magnitudes, Clark (1932, p. 693) wrote, *The actual contractions (and the more rapid expansions), if they do not arise as original movements produced by 'outside causes', can be explained as results of an intensifying mechanism whereby a fluctuation in the rate of growth may be converted into alternations of rapid expansion and absolute contraction. . . . the challenging problem is not why there are cyclical fluctuations but why there is any limit to the fluctuations short of zero, on the one side, or the full capacity of existing productive equipment, on the other. . . . The problem of defining limits of fluctuation on this assumption seems to be one to which the techniques of mathematical analysis are peculiarly adapted; and I sincerely hope that this discussion may stimulate some mathematical economists to produce a solution.* It was Hicks and Goodwin that did provide a mathematical solution – not Frisch.
4. To be precise, (1) would translates into $I(t) = F(C(t), \dot{C}(t)$- where $C(t)$ is aggregate consumption. This would be similar to the (linear) formulation chosen in Samuelson (1939).
5. The seminal works by Frisch (1933), Hicks (1950) and Goodwin (1951) contain a minor infelicity. The idea of the accelerator is the idea that investment is determined by the difference between the *desired* level of capital and the *actual* level of capital. The infelicity is given by the fact that a dynamic equation for $K(t)$ is not made explicit (although mentioned in the textual description) and is actually removed. Any attempt to reinsert will show that in all the three models while $Y(t)$ stays in between boundaries (like the constant in the computation of the primitive function of an integral) $K(t)$ will evolve without boundaries. Here, this is amended and the difference between desired capital, $vY(t)$, and actual capital, $K(t)$, are the determinants of investment decisions. This explains the formulation of the text.
6. Mode-locking occurs when, as parameter values change the frequency ratio of two oscillators does not change.
7. The numerical values for the generations of the figures are reported in the Appendix.

8. It is a *staircase*, in the sense that there are intervals of the parameters for which there is mode locking, and it is for the *Devil* to climb because the jumps between the different steps are an uncountable infinity (uncountable irrational numbers). In this paper, the Devil's staircase is to be understood in the broad sense of irregular jumps between the steps.

9. A way to check whether the attractor is chaotic is to compute the Lyapunov exponent. This has been done and positive Lyapunov's exponents have been found. This indicates a class 3 attractor.

10. The issue of the existence of a general purpose analogue computer for the solution of Goodwin-types economic models has been discussed in depth by Velupillai (2003) and the connection between the computation of trajectories by a Universal Turing Machine is sketched in Velupillai (1992, p.106) discussion of Goodwin's Rössler system (Goodwin, 1992) and is fully developed in Velupillai (2010, chapter 16). Clearly, if one endorses the *Church–Turing* thesis, both the general purpose analogue computer for the computations of the differential equations and digital computer for the computation of the difference equations approximating the original systems are both computable by a Universal Turing Machine, but this does not make the two systems isomorphic.

11. Note that the graphs reported in this paper are generated with coupling, i.e. exports and imports, occurring with neighbouring countries. See the Appendix where this is captured by the particular structure of the matrix **M**.

12. The last section of Frisch's (1933) *Propagation Problems and Impulse Problems* does present a discussion with Schumpeter in which a different metaphor with respect to the Rocking Horse metaphor is presented. This metaphor implied a nonlinear system of equations and the presence of a forcing element. Clearly, Schumpeter was more interested in an endogenous model of cycles and had very little interest on erratic stochastic sources. Goodwin (1946, 1947) provides foundations for a deterministic model of irregularities and interactions in which neither depend on stochastic drifts.

13. Probably, dynamical systems capable of generating class 4 (configurations poised at the borderline of strange attractors and limit cycles) dynamics are ones that are capable of computational universality (Velupillai, 2003). Our proposal for the construction of such a system is by applying to economics an analogue of the FPU problem and its methodology. An economic system capable of computational universality is here defined as a computing devise, whose scope is equivalent to that of finding the roots of a non-trivial system of Diophantine equations. Given the results by Matiyasevitch, one cannot in general know whether the system would stop 'computing' (would reach an equilibrium-attractor among the many) or would keep on 'searching' for a solution and hence would find itself in a condition of potentially perpetual out of equilibrium condition.

References

Clark, J.M. (1917) Business acceleration and the law of demand: a technical factor in economic Cycles. *Journal of Political Economy* 25(3): 217–235.

Clark, J.M. (1931) Capital production and consumer taking: a reply. *Journal of Political Economy* 39: 814–816.

Clark, J.M. (1932) Capital production and consumer taking: a further word. *Journal of Political Economy* 40: 691–693.

Cooper, N. (1989) *From Cardinals to Chaos: Reflections on the Life and Legacy of Stanislaw Ulam*. Cambridge, US: Cambridge University Press.

Fermi, E., Pasta, J., and Ulam, S. (1955) Studies in nonlinear problems. In E. Segré (ed.) (edited 1965), *Collected Papers of Enrico Fermi* (Vol. 2, Chapter 266, pp. 977–988). Chicago, IL: University of Chicago Press.

Frisch, R. (1931) The interrelation between capital production and consumer taking. *Journal of Political Economy* 39: 646–654.

Frisch, R. (1932a) Capital production and consumer taking: a rejoinder. *Journal of Political Economy* 40: 253–255.

Frisch, R. (1932b) Capital production and consumer taking: a final word. *Journal of Political Economy* 40: 694.

Frisch, R. (1933) *Propagation Problems and Impulse Problems in Dynamic Economics, in Essays in Honour of Gustav Cassel* (pp. 171–205). London, UK: Allen & Unwin.

Goodwin, R.M. (1946) Innovations and the irregularity of economic cycles. *Review of Economics and Statistics* 28(2): 95–104.

Goodwin, R.M. (1947) Dynamical coupling with especial reference to markets having production lags. *Econometrica* 15(3): 181–204.

Goodwin, R.M. (1951) The nonlinear accelerator and the persistence of business cycles. *Econometrica* 19(1): 1–17.

Goodwin, R.M. (1992) A chaotic reformulation of multiplier-accelerator models. In K. Velupillai (ed.) *Nonlinearities, Disequilibria and Simulation – Proceeding from the Arne Ryde Symposium on Quantitative Methods in the Stabilization of Macrodynamic Systems, Essays in Honour of Bjørn Thalberg* (pp. 87–101). London, UK: Macmillan.

Hicks, J. (1950) *A Contribution to the Theory of the Trade Cycle*. Oxford, UK: Oxford University Press, Clarendon Press.

Metzler, L.A. (1941) The nature and stability of inventory cycles. *Review of Economics and Statistics* 23(3): 113–129.

Mitchell, W. (1913) *Business Cycles*. Berkeley, CA: University of California Press.

Prescott, E.C. (2006) Nobel lecture: the transformation of macroeconomic policy and research. *Journal of Political Economy* 114(2): 203–235.

Samuelson, P.A. (1939) Interections between the multiplier analysis and the principle of acceleration. *Review of Economics and Statistics* 21: 75–78.

Samuelson, P.A. (1972) Maximum principles in analytical economics. *American Economic Review* 62(3): 249–272.

Strotz, R.H., McAnulty J.C. and Naines, J.B. (1953) Goodwin's nonlinear theory of the business cycle: an electro-analog solution. *Econometrica* 21(3): 390–411.

Thompson, J. and Stewart, B. (1986) *Nonlinear Dynamics and Chaos*. Chicester, Great Britain: John Wiley and Son.

Velupillai, K.V. (1992) Discussion of Goodwin (1992). In K.V. Velupillai (ed.), *Nonlinearities, Disequilibria and Simulation – Proceeding from the Arne Ryde Symposium on Quantitative Methods in the Stabilization of Macrodynamic Systems, Essays in Honour of Bjørn Thalberg* (pp. 105–106). London, UK: Macmillan.

Velupillai, K.V. (2003) Economics and the complexity vision: chemiral partners or Elysian adventures? Discussion Papers, Department of Economics, University of Trento.

Velupillai, K.V. (2007) The impossibility of an effective theory of policy in a complex economy. In M. Salzano and D. Colander (eds), *Complexity Hints for Economic Policy* (pp. 272–290). Milan, Italy: Springer-Verlag Italia.

Velupillai, K.V. (2008a) The mathematization of macroeconomics: a recursive revolution. *Economia Politica* XXV(2): 283–316.

Velupillai, K.V. (2008b) A perspective on a Hicksian non-linear theory of the trade cycle. In R. Scazzieri, A. Sen and S. Zamagni (eds), *Markets, Money and Capital: Hicksian Economics for the 21st Century* (pp. 328–345). Cambridge, UK: Cambridge University Press.

Velupillai, K.V. (2010) *Computable Foundations for Economics*. Oxon, UK: Routledge.
Zambelli, S. (1992) The wooden horse that wouldn't rock: reconsidering Frisch. In K. Velupillai (ed.), *Nonlinearities, Disequilibria and Simulation – Proceeding from the Arne Ryde Symposium on Quantitative Methods in the Stabilization of Macrodynamic Systems, Essays in Honour of Bjørn Thalberg* (pp. 27–54). London, UK: Macmillan.
Zambelli, S. (2007) A rocking horse that never rocked: Frisch's "propagation problems. *History of Political Economy* 31(1): 145–166.

Appendix

Here are reported the parameter levels associated with the generations of the different graphs.
Figures 2, 3, 4, 5, 6.

$$\vartheta_1 = 1, \quad \varepsilon_1 = 0.25, \quad C_{01} = 10, \quad c_1 = 0.6, \quad v_1 = 2.0, \quad k_1^* = -3, \quad k_1^{**} = 9,$$

$$\vartheta_2 = 0.5, \quad \varepsilon_2 = 0.25, \quad C_{02} = 2, \quad c_1 = 0.8, \quad v_2 = 1.4, \quad k_1^* = -2, \quad k_2^{**} = 4,$$

Figures 7, 8, 9 and 10 have been generated with the following values for the parameters.
Step size $h = \frac{2\pi}{90}$

	C_0	c	V	ε	ϑ	$\varphi_{\mathrm{inf}} = k^*$	$\varphi_{\mathrm{sup}} = k^{**}$
Economy 1	5	0.6	2	2/12	5/12	−1	4
Economy 2	15	0.65	2,2	3/12	5/12	−1.5	5
Economy 3	25	0.7	2.4	6/12	5/12	−2	6
Economy 4	30	0.75	2.6	4/12	4/12	−2.5	7
Economy 5	35	0.8	2.8	5/12	6/12	−3	8
Economy 6	40	0.85	3	6/12	8/12	−3.5	9

The trade matrix (marginal propensities to import, columns, and propensities to export, rows) is given by:

$$\mathbf{M} = \mu \begin{bmatrix} 0 & .1 & 0 & 0 & 0 & 0 \\ .1 & 0 & .1 & 0 & 0 & 0 \\ 0 & .1 & 0 & .1 & 0 & 0 \\ 0 & 0 & .1 & 0 & .1 & 0 \\ 0 & 0 & 0 & .1 & 0 & .1 \\ 0 & 0 & 0 & 0 & .1 & 0 \end{bmatrix}$$

where μ is the coupling strength.

The above is a simplified spatial matrix, where countries trade with 'neighbouring' ones. This is a highly simplified case. The entries of the matrix, in a highly globalized world should almost all be different than 0.

Figures 7 : $\mu = 0$

Figures 8 : $\mu = 0.1$

Figures 9 : $\mu = 1$

with *Forcing Term* $= 0.01 \dfrac{C_0}{1-c} \sin\left(\dfrac{t}{2\pi}\right)$

Figures 10 : $\mu = 0, 0.01, 0.02, \ldots, 6$

Figures 11 : $\mu = 0, 0.01, 0.02, \ldots, 6$

with *Forcing Term* $= 0.01 \dfrac{C_0}{1-c} \sin\left(\dfrac{t}{2\pi}\right)$

12

SHIFTING SANDS: NON-LINEARITY, COMPLEXITY AND RANDOMNESS IN ECONOMICS

Donald A.R. George

The CIFREM conference on non-linearity, complexity and randomness took place at the University of Trento, Italy, in October 2009, at the height of the financial crisis which was to lead most of the developed world into its most serious recession since the 1930s. A degree of soul-searching has taken place within Economics since then. With some honourable exceptions very few mainstream economists foresaw the crisis or, if they predicted its financial genesis, failed to predict the dire economic consequences which were to follow. Economists' reactions have ranged from suggesting minor modifications to mainstream theory to completely rejecting it, and abandoning the Nobel Prize in Economics as an embarrassment to the profession (see Taleb, 2007). The context of this discussion is different from the crisis of the 1930s in that there is now a much wider public debate about economic problems and policy, a debate which has placed the Economics profession under close public scrutiny. Immediately before the Trento conference there was a public meeting in Bologna titled 'Economists on Trial'. History does not relate whether they were found guilty. In fact the prosecution could have laid two separate but related charges, which are as follows:

- The failure of mainstream economics to predict the banking crisis or to correctly analyse its relationship with the resulting recession.
- The contribution of mainstream economics to the construction of exotic financial derivatives,[1] which were priced by mathematical models rather than by markets, and which played a central role in the failure of banks.

Some mainstream economists (the 'honourable exceptions' mentioned earlier) have expressed doubts about the direction much orthodox theory has taken and its increasing

Nonlinearity, Complexity and Randomness in Economics, First Edition.
Stefano Zambelli and Donald A.R. George.
© 2012 John Wiley & Sons. Published 2012 by John Wiley & Sons, Ltd.

irrelevance to the analysis of the real world. In his blog 'The unfortunate uselessness of most 'state of the art' academic monetary economics' Willem Buiter (2009) comments:

> If one were to hold one's nose and agree to play with the New Classical or New Keynesian complete markets toolkit, it would soon become clear that any potentially policy-relevant model would be highly non-linear, and that the interaction of these non-linearities and uncertainty makes for deep conceptual and technical problems. Macroeconomists are brave, but not that brave. So they took these non-linear stochastic dynamic general equilibrium models into the basement and beat them with a rubber hose until they behaved. This was achieved by completely stripping the model of its non-linearities and by achieving the transubstantiation of complex convolutions of random variables and non-linear mappings into well-behaved additive stochastic disturbances.

> Those of us who have marvelled at the non-linear feedback loops between asset prices in illiquid markets and the funding illiquidity of financial institutions exposed to these asset prices through mark-to-market accounting, margin requirements, calls for additional collateral, etc. will appreciate what is lost by this castration of the macroeconomic models. Threshold effects, critical mass, tipping points, non-linear accelerators – they are all out of the window. Those of us who worry about endogenous uncertainty arising from the interactions of boundedly rational market participants cannot but scratch our heads at the insistence of the mainline models that all uncertainty is exogenous and additive.

The first lesson to draw from the current crisis within Economics is clearly that our models must embrace non-linearity: linearized models with their saddlepoint dynamics and 'jump variables' no longer serve any useful purpose (see George and Oxley, 1999, 2008 for a detailed discussion of this point). Secondly, we need to revisit our analysis of randomness, uncertainty and rationality. The conference participants at Trento all addressed aspects of this agenda. They approached their topics from backgrounds in Economics, Physics, Computer Science and Philosophy, illustrating the *Journal's* founding principle, namely the need to escape the spurious specialisation of Economics and learn from other disciplines.

Discussion at the conference ranged from practical policy issues to methodological questions concerning the proper role for mathematical models in economics, and the appropriate type of mathematics upon which to base these models. Mainstream economists often justify their widespread use of mathematical modelling by appealing to the notion of intellectual 'rigour'. But this demand for rigour is not usually taken far: ask most economists if they subscribe to the Zemelo-Frankel axioms or the Axiom of Choice and you will usually get a puzzled response. However, these concerns were central for the Trento conference participants: much of the discussion concerned the possibility of an algorithmic basis for economics, particularly for non-linear dynamics, and the computability of economic models. A theme of the conference was that the foundations of economics need to be recast in algorithmic terms. Most mainstream economics rests on a relatively narrow range of (largely 19th century) mathematical techniques such as optimization and linear algebra. But the foundations of mathematics itself have long been the subject of intense scrutiny, although many mathematicians have thought it best to consign these discussions to the separate discipline of Logic. However, these ideas cannot be kept in their box, not least because Turing's ideas and theorems (among others) have led directly to the 20th and 21st century revolution in computing. Ideas of computability, algorithms and constructive mathematics are now much more familiar than they were even 30 years ago. There are distinct potential advantages to be derived from developing algorithmic foundations for economics. For example, it would bring economic theory closer to the data against which theories must be tested, and hence closer to applied and policy analysis, which must be numerical and computational.

The perspective outlined above has both micro- and macro-economic dimensions. At the micro level, the economist turns to bounded rationality and agent-based modelling. At the macro level, s/he focuses on the theory of non-linear dynamical systems and coupled markets, to which economists such as Goodwin (1947) made so many prescient contributions. From this type of macro-modelling one would hope to derive macro-policy prescriptions better adapted to dealing with global macroeconomic crises than the present, obviously inadequate, policy regime. At both micro and macro level, there lurks the ever-present methodological danger of 'reverse engineering'. By this I mean deciding on an interesting or desirable outcome of a model and simply making the right assumptions to guarantee that outcome. It may not be necessary to (in Buiter's words) 'beat them with a rubber hose until they behaved' but economic models are often forced into a Procrustean bed of highly implausible and misleading assumptions. This is a particular temptation in macroeconomics, where dynamical systems theory is employed. This theory puts the focus on the classification of attractors of dynamical systems. For example strange attractors, which generate chaotic motion have appealed to economists but, this approach presents the temptation to reverse-engineer one's model in such a way as to generate the desired attractor. Concerns with the methodological unsoundness of this practice provide another reason to search for algorithmic foundations for non-linearity, complexity and randomness.

This discussion leads naturally to a consideration of 'emergence'. Mainstream economics is characterized by a reductionist methodology. Macroeconomists are exhorted to provide 'microeconomic foundations' for their models, an approach will yields some well-known conundrums. For example the microeconomists' most general and 'rigorous' model, General Equilibrium, has no room for money or for the firm, something of an obvious weakness. Moreover, why stop at microeconomics? Fodor (1974) describes an 'immortal economist' who vainly tries to derive economic principles from a knowledge of physics and the distribution of physical qualities in space–time. The ideas of the British Emergentists (Mill, 1843; Broad, 1925; Alexander, 1920) have been given a new lease of life recently via the theory of non-linear dynamical systems. Discussion at the Trento conference focussed on the idea that emergent behaviour can be defined as behaviour which arises in the transition between the computable and the non-computable. It would be reasonable to conclude that macroeconomics should discard its reductionist methodology and focus on the relationship between non-linearity, complexity and emergence. It is distinctly possible that Goodwin would have approved such a programme. Velupillai ('Nonlinear Dynamics, Complexity and Randomness:

Algorithmic Foundations', this volume) asks how emergent behaviour can be generated from a dynamical system. His answer is that emergent behaviour should be defined as 'that exhibited by the behaviour of a dynamical system in its *transition* from one that is incapable of computation universality to one that is capable of such universal behaviour'.

Non-linearity, complexity and randomness are, for economists, inescapable. It has seemed to some that the present 'rigorous' mathematization of economics supplies a solid rock upon which to base their analysis and the policy prescriptions to which it leads. But 'rigour' is a slippery concept and the basis of most mainstream economics is less solid rock, more shifting sands. Participants at the Trento conference, although disagreeing on many things, would probably argue that there is a way ahead, which puts economics and probability theory on an algorithmic basis, replacing sterile formalism with fertile formalism, and tackling seriously some of the methodological problems which have bedevilled economics. Let us hope that this work proceeds at a smart pace, so that next time a major crisis looms, economists have the tools to respond to it in a rational and humane way.

Note

1. Warren Buffet's 'weapons of financial mass destruction'.

References

Alexander, S. (1920) *Space, Time, and Deity*. 2 vols. London: Macmillan.

Broad, C.D. (1925). *The Mind and Its Place in Nature*. London: Routledge & Kegan Paul

Buiter, W. (2009) The unfortunate uselessness of most 'state of the art' academic monetary economics. Available at http://www.voxeu.org/index.php?q=node/3210. Accessed April 18, 2011.

Fodor, J. (1974) Special sciences. *Synthese* 28: 97–115.

George, D.A.R. and Oxley, L.T. (1999) Robustness and local linearisation in economic models. *Journal of Economic Surveys* 13: 529–550.

George, D.A.R. and Oxley, L.T. (2008) Money and inflation in a nonlinear model, *Mathematics and Computers in Simulation* 78: 257–265.

Goodwin, R.M. (1947) Dynamical coupling with especial reference to markets having production lags. *Econometrica* 15: 181–204.

Mill, J.S. (1843). *System of Logic*. London: Longmans, Green, Reader, and Dyer.

Taleb, N. (2007) The pseudo-science hurting markets, *Financial Times*. Available at http://www.ft.com/cms/s/0/4eb6ae86-8166-11dc-a351-0000779fd2ac.html#axzz1 JaWxxHnK. Accessed April 18, 2011.

INDEX